BOTH HANDS TIED

JANE L. COLLINS AND VICTORIA MAYER

Both Hands Tied

WELFARE REFORM AND THE RACE TO THE
BOTTOM IN THE LOW-WAGE LABOR MARKET

THE UNIVERSITY OF CHICAGO PRESS / CHICAGO AND LONDON

JANE L. COLLINS is the Evjue Bascom Professor of Community and
Environmental Sociology and Gender and Women's Studies at the
University of Wisconsin–Madison and the author of *Threads: Gender,
Labor & Power in the Global Apparel Industry*, among other titles.
VICTORIA MAYER is assistant professor of sociology at Colby College.

The University of Chicago Press, Chicago 60637
The University of Chicago Press, Ltd., London
© 2010 by The University of Chicago
All rights reserved. Published 2010
Printed in the United States of America

18 17 16 15 14 13 12 11   2 3 4 5

ISBN-13: 978-0-226-11405-7 (cloth)
ISBN-10: 0-226-11405-8 (cloth)
ISBN-13: 978-0-226-11406-4 (paper)
ISBN-10: 0-226-11406-6 (paper)

Library of Congress Cataloging-in-Publication Data

Collins, Jane Lou, 1954–
     Both hands tied : welfare reform and the race to the bottom in the
  low-wage labor market / Jane L. Collins and Victoria Mayer.
       p.   cm.
     Includes bibliographical references and index.
     ISBN-13: 978-0-226-11405-7 (cloth : alk. paper)
     ISBN-10: 0-226-11405-8 (cloth : alk. paper)
     ISBN-13: 978-0-226-11406-4 (pbk. : alk. paper)
     ISBN-10: 0-226-11406-6 (pbk. : alk. paper)
     1. Working poor—United States. 2. Poor—Employment—
  United States. 3. Poor women—Employment—United States.
  4. Public welfare—United States.   I. Mayer, Victoria.   II. Title.
  HD8072.5.C656 2010
  331.5'4—dc22
                                                        2009030879

CONTENTS

ILLUSTRATIONS

A gallery of photos follows page 82.

ACKNOWLEDGMENTS

We conducted the initial research for this book, a study entitled "Mother's Family Networks and Livelihood Strategies," with the support of the Child Support Demonstration Evaluation, Phase III, administered by Professors Maria Cancian and Daniel Meyer at the University of Wisconsin's Institute for Research on Poverty and funded by the Wisconsin Department of Workforce Development. We thank Maria and Dan for their support and guidance and Maria especially for her continuing interest in and engagement with the project as it grew beyond its initial goals and scope. Victoria Mayer received additional research support through a grant from the Office of the Assistant Secretary for Planning and Evaluation, U.S. Department of Health and Human Services, administered by Thomas Kaplan, associate director of Programs and Management and senior scientist at the Institute for Research on Poverty. The Women's Studies Research Center and the Graduate School at the University of Wisconsin provided resources for Jane Collins in the later phases of the research.

Many individuals at the Institute for Research on Poverty provided invaluable assistance in the day-to-day management of the project. We are grateful to Pat Brown and Steve Cook for their help with sample selection and access to quantitative data, Emma Caspar for her project management skills, Bill Wambach for budget administration, Allison Hales Espeseth and Margaret Darby Townsend for their oversight of human subjects research protocols, and Robin Snell for many kinds of help. Thomas Kaplan provided essential introductions to the network of Temporary Assistance to Needy Families (TANF) agencies in Milwaukee and valuable insight into the history of welfare reform in Wisconsin. David Pate Jr., then a postdoctoral researcher at the Institute for Research on Poverty and now assistant professor of social work at the University of Wisconsin–Milwaukee, helped us design our methods, from the initial letter we sent to potential interview subjects to the interview experience itself. His moral support and intellectual feedback enriched the project immensely.

Two superbly dedicated and gifted research assistants helped with the interviews: Nicole Breazeale, a doctoral student in sociology, and Angela Cunningham, a student in the master of social work program, both at UW–Madison. Nicole and Angela participated in the time-consuming work of scheduling interviews and later transcribing them; they also conducted or participated in many of the interviews, proving themselves to be deeply engaged, empathetic listeners who offered women optimal conditions for the telling of their stories.

A number of researchers and activists talked with us about this work as it developed, including Andrea Robles, Pamela Fendt, Laura Dresser, and Marcus White. Heidi Herschede provided an excellent "sociological orientation" to Milwaukee. Micaela di Leonardo, Maria Cancian, Jeff Maskovsky, William Jones, Chad Goldberg, Myra Marx Ferree, and an anonymous University of Chicago Press reviewer provided insightful and engaged critique of various versions of the manuscript. Micaela, in particular, pushed us to make the book accessible to a broader audience and provided brilliant advice and editing as we did so. Members of local TANF agencies took time from demanding schedules to discuss their work and graciously accepted our presence while they interacted with program participants.

The women at the heart of our study (the names reported here are all pseudonyms) were bold, thoughtful, witty, generous, and kind. They believed in the importance of having their stories heard and sought to tell them as clearly and comprehensively as possible. They inspired us in so many ways.

Victoria thanks her husband, Todd Miller, and her son, Isaiah Miller, for the joy they brought that sustained her through this work. And she thanks her parents, Joan and Paul Mayer, and her friends from Madison, who, though too numerous to name, were vital in helping her balance the needs of family and work while conducting this research. Jane thanks her son, Robert Painter, for his support and good humor and her sister Bonnie Landry and friends Nancy Kaiser, Aimee Dechter, Patricia Hodson, Alda Blanco, Michaeline Crichlow, Timothy Moermond, and Thomas Schweigert for their many acts of kindness.

PREFACE

In February 2009, the *New York Times* published two articles charting trends in U.S. employment and income security. On February 6, it announced that women, holding more than 49 percent of the nation's jobs, were poised to surpass men in the labor force for the first time in American history. The article reported that men's loss of good manufacturing jobs and women's greater employment in areas less sensitive to downturn left more women serving as breadwinners for their families. "Women may be safer in their jobs," the author noted, "but tend to find it harder to support a family. . . . The jobs women have—and are supporting their families with—are not necessarily as good."[1] On February 2, the paper reported that despite soaring unemployment and the worst economic crisis in decades, eighteen states had cut their welfare rolls in 2008. Indeed, the number of people receiving cash assistance in the nation was at the lowest level in more than forty years.[2] Seemingly unrelated, these news stories reference trends that are integrally connected in the lives of poor working families, contributing to the increasing difficulty women face in combining work and family responsibilities at the low end of the labor market. Their dilemma is the subject of this book.

Americans tend to think of work and welfare as opposites, as the poles of a spectrum of diligence or virtue. At one end is the industrious wage earner, the epitome of citizenship since the 1840s. At the other are imagined to be slothful and shiftless "welfare queens" and others who refuse to work. This overwrought distinction obscures several facts. The first is that "welfare" programs, writ broadly, benefit a wide swath of the population. Imagine life without, for example, social security, workers' compensation, unemployment insurance, tax deductions for interest on homes, or federally insured mortgages and student loans. Second, welfare writ small—those means-tested assistance programs directed toward the poor—has always been a safety net designed to mitigate labor market and family failures. Since welfare "reform" in 1996, however, the federal government has introduced new rules and structured revenue streams to encourage states to reduce their caseloads, and the net has become drastically skimpier. No longer an entitlement, public assistance is subject to the discretion of state bureaucracies, covers far fewer families, and is time-limited and tied to work. Nationally, states cut caseloads from 11.5 million recipients in 1996 to fewer than 4 million in 2008, while instituting behavioral requirements—such as thirty to forty hours per week of work outside the home—for the receipt of benefits.

At the same time, conditions in the low-wage labor market became harsher. Real wages stagnated or declined, jobs became less secure, fewer carried benefits, sick days became a rare luxury. Under these circumstances, means-tested welfare programs such as cash assistance under Temporary Assistance to Needy Families, food stamps, medical assistance, the Women, Infants, and Children (WIC) nutrition program, and subsidies for child care and housing became crucial to the survival of the working poor, and particularly poor single mothers. We have all read the news stories about Wal-Mart and other low-wage employers sending their workers to sign up for Medicaid and food stamps. These programs increasingly subsidize the wages and benefits of the working poor, but as this book shows, poor women also rely on them as a substitute for the unemployment insurance, workers' compensation, and maternity leave not offered by their jobs, and for federal disability insurance, which has become more difficult to access in recent years.

This book reports on the intersection of welfare and work in the lives of thirty-three women in Milwaukee and Racine, Wisconsin, where welfare reform was launched in its earliest and starkest form and where deindustrialization and the growth of the service economy present paradigmatic challenges for low-wage workers. Using a work history approach, we asked these women to talk about the kinds of jobs they had held and how they moved through them, what crises at work or at home led them to turn to welfare, how they used its programs, and what impact welfare subsequently had on their work lives. Our story delves deeply into women's daily lives, presenting their narratives and analyzing their trajectories. But we also connect their particular journeys to several profound shifts in our nation's politics and economy. In many cases, the women themselves perceived these shifts and articulated their own critique of them. In others, we have connected the dots in order to offer an interpretation of how—to paraphrase sociologist C. Wright Mills—biography and history are linked.

The changes we consider here precede the economic crisis that began in 2008. Economic shifts include the massive movement of women into work since the 1970s and the increasing role they play in supporting their families, as documented in the above-mentioned *New York Times* article. It is significant that most of the jobs women have found are in the low-wage service sector. Many of these jobs—in areas such as child care, certified nursing assistance and home health care, food service and restaurant work—actually substitute for labor formerly performed at home. This commodification of women's domestic labor, with its unique racial legacies, not only has fostered the growth of the low-wage service sector but has shaped its work conditions and wage levels. In combination with the unusual productivity challenges that result from the labor-intensive and place-bound character of this work, the drive to increase profits has led to a "race to the bottom" in low-wage service jobs, which we chart in the pages that follow.

Political paradigms of market fundamentalism, emerging in the 1970s, also shaped the opportunities and constraints these women faced. The emphasis on market rationality in many spheres of life led to government and corporate assaults on unions (seen as antimarket forces) that undermined their ability to struggle for improved wages and working conditions. This was accompanied by the systematic dismantling of social programs—in the name of market efficiency and individual responsibility—which culminated in the welfare reform of 1996.

The overarching logic within which these two shifts took place was a change in societal consensus about the proper responsibilities of the government, employers, and individuals for providing the support working families need. The consensus that dominated American thinking from the mid-nineteenth to the mid-twentieth century—the so-called "family wage"—stipulated that employers pay (relatively privileged) white male workers enough to support themselves and their families. Most benefits and health insurance were tied to jobs. This ostensible agreement has broken down on all fronts, as family structure has changed and employers have off-loaded responsibilities. It is our contention that no comparable social compact has emerged to replace it. Or, to put it more starkly, that during an era of market fundamentalism, the lack of such an agreement about how families would be supported *was* the agreement. Representative Newt Gingrich's famous Dickensian suggestion, in 1994, that poor children be placed in orphanages marked this change.[3]

In the fall of 2008, as we were finishing this book, the United States entered both the greatest economic crisis since the Great Depression and a period of political realignment and national reflection. In this context, Americans started a national conversation about how health care should be provided and what role government should play in regulating the economy. We began to consider, in other words, how a new division of labor among government, employers, and families might work. In the spring of 2009, the U.S. Congress passed a recovery bill that funded a variety of job-creation initiatives and provided short-term funding to bolster unemployment insurance, food stamps, and the Women, Infants, and Children nutrition program. It increased federal support for Medicaid and for Temporary Assistance for Needy Families and, in a reversal of previous policy, provided incentives for states to increase caseloads. And it provided incentives for states to modernize their unemployment insurance programs in ways that would benefit working women, most importantly by enabling workers who leave a job for compelling family reasons to qualify. In Wisconsin, after Democrats gained a majority in both houses of the legislature in 2008, some of the onerous welfare rules described in the pages that follow were revised. The governor's budget loosened restrictions on education and training, and lifted two-year state limits on specific cash assistance programs in favor of the federal five-year lifetime limit. While these patchwork efforts to undo the damage wrought by the punitive reforms of 1996 were welcome, they fell far short of a comprehensive response to the needs of poor working families. Cash payments remained at 1996 levels: $628 and $673 a month. And faced with declining revenues and a full-blown budget crisis, the state continued to encourage its service providers to cut the welfare rolls, thus denying most families access to crucial forms of support. In 2007, even before the worst of the recession, child poverty in Milwaukee had already soared past 25 percent.[4]

We wrote this book in the hope of inspiring discussion of how we, as a society, provide for the work of "social reproduction"—the labor of caring for children, the elderly, the disabled, and the ill, of managing the affairs of the household, of feeding and cleaning and providing clothing. Over the past four decades, the gendered family arrangements that had sustained such care gave way to a more commodified system. Welfare reform, with its new work requirements, extended the logic of commodification to our nation's poorest families—confronting single mothers with frequently untenable choices between degraded jobs and family well-being. Taking as our focal point the lives of poor women in two deeply segregated, deindustrialized Midwestern cities, we trace the dilemmas that our current labor markets and social policy regimes have created for struggling families, in the faith that through a sustained national conversation about revisions to our social programs—about child care subsidies, expanded unemployment insurance, the attachment of more benefits to part-time work, paid sick days, family/medical leave, and universal health insurance—we can find a way to do better.

Our title, *Both Hands Tied*, refers to these dilemmas—to the ways that a failure on the part of both the state and employers to address the new realities of family care prevents women, on the one hand, from parenting as they feel they should and, on the other, from performing as ideal workers. In a nation where social benefits have long been tied to work and where work has been a hallmark of citizenship, this has left poor women with families working but unable to defend their interests as workers and to exercise their rights as citizens. Until they can do both, the race to the bottom in the low-wage service sector will work hand in hand with the punitive structure of post-1996 welfare to perpetuate gender- and race-marked forms of inequality that are neither just nor necessary.

CHAPTER ONE

INTRODUCTION

THE CONNECTION BETWEEN WELFARE AND WORK

Low-wage work apparently must be mandated, just as a draft has sometimes been necessary to staff the military.
LAWRENCE MEAD, *BEYOND ENTITLEMENT*[1]

If I were President . . . I'd start paying women a living wage for doing the work we are already doing—child raising and housekeeping. And the welfare crisis would be over. Just like that.
JOHNNIE TILLMON, NATIONAL WELFARE RIGHTS ORGANIZATION[2]

PUTTING WELFARE REFORM IN ITS CONTEXT

Walking from Walnut Street to Capitol Avenue on Milwaukee's near north side on a weekday afternoon, one is struck by the absence of adults in the neighborhood. Teenage boys work on cars and talk on cell phones, and teenage girls walk their little brothers and sisters home from school. An occasional grandmother supervises kids at yard work. But there are no working-age adults in sight. Brightly painted day care centers tucked between grocery shops and storefront churches provide a clue to their whereabouts. "First and second shift," the signs announce. "Six a.m. to midnight. Four weeks to 12 years. Free transportation available." With names like Pristine Child Care, the Early Childhood Academy, and Imagination Station, the centers offer upbeat slogans: "Where young minds possess a bright future" or "Where faith and learning come together to build strong families." They also speak to the end of welfare and the widespread movement of the neighborhood's mothers into work.

The year 1996 marked a sea change in our nation's system of welfare provision.[3] In that year, the U.S. Congress passed the Personal Responsibility and Work Opportunity Reconciliation Act (PRWORA)—a law that ended the statutory entitlement to welfare for people in need and tied benefits, for those who continued to rely on them, to work. A year later, state officials in Wisconsin implemented their own vehicle for the new policies, known as Wisconsin Works, or W-2. Many who promoted these reforms held them to be a step toward fiscal responsibility; others considered them morally necessary to restore self-reliance and personal accountability, values that they perceived to have eroded among the poor.[4] But welfare reform was intimately connected to gendered changes in labor force participation and to profound underlying shifts in the responsibilities of family, firms, and the state. The reforms were tied to the movement of women out of the home and into the workforce in unprecedented numbers, the growth of a racially and gender-segregated service sector that depended heavily on women's labor, and the withdrawal of corporations and government from the business of providing a safety net for workers. These trends have generated new forms of economic insecurity that are felt by most wage-dependent American households. This book documents how welfare reform has intersected with such changes for poor, single-parent families, eroding their social rights in ways that affect their ability to care for their members and undermining their civil rights and labor protections.

The chapters that follow recount the experiences of a number of women living and working in Milwaukee and Racine, Wisconsin, in 2004. These women had all relied on welfare at some point in 2003, but most had also worked a great deal over the past few years. All were mothers of young children. Our book tells the story of their struggle to balance child care and wage-earning in poorly paid jobs with inflexible schedules, and the moments when these jobs failed them and they turned to the state for aid. We write about these experiences not just to provide a window into the harsh reality of conditions at the low end of the labor market. There are numerous books by journalists and social scientists that document these conditions eloquently and effectively.[5] Rather, we place these women's accounts in the context of two profound institutional shifts: first, the growth of the low-wage service sector and its particular productivity and profitability challenges, and second, the erosion of the bargains between workers and employers, on one hand, and citizens and government, on the other, that led to the end of the "family wage system" that stabilized working-class life in the twentieth century. We show how new political rationalities based on free market principles enabled these shifts. Perhaps most importantly, we document how changes in the institutions of welfare and work came together to produce patterned challenges for the women we interviewed.

Even a casual conversation with women working in low-wage jobs reveals how tightly work and welfare are interwoven. As forty-three-year-old Ebony Walker told us:

> My very first job—I was sixteen. And I worked for Burger King. I can sing the Burger King song—that's what got me hired. After that it was school bus, modeling, factory . . . not counting factory, I'd say I've had about twenty-five different jobs over the years.

Between many of Ebony's jobs were episodes on welfare, occasioned by illness, injury, and childbirth. As we shall see, the kinds of jobs in which she worked did not provide workers' compensation, maternity leave, or even sick leave, and welfare was the lifeline that allowed her to feed herself and her family as she recovered and regrouped. For women like Ebony, it was a source of support that, while punitive and insufficient, allowed them to deal with the inadequacies of jobs in the low-wage labor market and the absence of other, less stigmatized forms of assistance.

Consider the case of Natasha Castinelli, a twenty-three-year-old mother of two from Racine. She had turned to welfare twice between 1999 and 2004, once while recovering from a back injury sustained in her nursing home job and again at the time of our interview, just after the birth of her youngest child. Because she was not covered by a workers' compensation program when she injured her back, Natasha applied for welfare. After three months of physical therapy, her doctor said that she could return to work and her welfare case manager assigned her to a workfare job sorting clothing at Goodwill Industries. When a job opened up with her former employer, she returned to work as a certified nursing assistant. Natasha turned to welfare a second time two years later, receiving twelve weeks of caretaker-of-newborn benefits after the birth of her second child. The "absent actor" in both of Natasha's episodes on welfare was her employer, which relied on her work cleaning and feeding patients in its Alzheimer's unit, but did not give her steady enough employment to be covered by workers' compensation and did not offer maternity or sick leave. Without savings or a partner who could support her, when Natasha faced a health crisis or childbirth, she turned to welfare. As she struggled to summarize her experience at the end of her interview, she articulated what was wrong with this situation:

> So how are you supposed to get ahead? You're gonna stay in one spot 'cause you get to a certain spot and you fall right back on your face, you

drop right back down. As soon as an emergency pops up, you're gonna be right back in the system again. And they're not giving you what you need.

In America, we tend to think of welfare as the opposite of work and to associate it with idleness and lack of moral fiber. In our national conception of civic virtue, we set those who receive welfare at one end of a continuum and "hard-working taxpayers" at the other. Yet history tells us that welfare and work often intertwine. Welfare rolls have expanded and contracted in inverse relation to employment—swelling in times when jobs were scarce and dwindling when they were readily available. And policymakers have often shaped welfare programs to serve the needs of employers. When Congress passed legislation authorizing Aid to Dependent Children in 1935, it allowed states to establish "employable mothers" clauses, insuring that localities could cut off mothers' payments during months when southern planters needed hands. Federal law allowed states to set benefit levels that would not undercut the local labor market—insuring that work would always be more lucrative than welfare, even for women raising children alone in very low-wage regions of the country (a principle known as "less eligibility"). But today, the connections between welfare and work may be tighter than ever before. Since Congress enacted the latest round of reform in 1996, welfare has literally *become* workfare. Its new rules compel all who are able to work to do so as a condition of receiving aid. Under these circumstances, welfare programs bump up against the lowest tiers of the labor market with mutually constitutive effects.

The crafters of the twentieth-century welfare state in the United States and Europe saw themselves as producing institutions that would compensate for the failure of labor markets. During the 1930s and 1940s, when many U.S. social programs were developed, Keynesianism—the concept that government should play a strong role in stabilizing employment and managing demand—offered a powerful vision of how the state and the economy could work together. Roosevelt's famous "Four Freedoms" provided a rationale for the redistribution of some national wealth. Acting in response to the Great Depression and following these principles, lawmakers developed pensions and compensation for the injured and unemployed. Provision of welfare kept domestic markets functioning even as it responded to unrest among the unemployed.[6] This welfare regime was linked to institutionalized compromises between capital and labor predicated on rising profitability, labor productivity, and real incomes. These compromises were premised on the notion that productivity gains should be shared between employers' profits and workers' wages and on assumptions of relatively full employment, monopoly regulation, and the family wage. And it was assumed that the state could and should provide for those who could not participate in the workforce.

By the 1970s, however, the economy faced new challenges, which led some policymakers and legislators to rethink welfare state commitments. Beginning in 1973, for a variety of reasons, productivity gains fell short of what was required to finance the arrangements that had been worked out among capital, labor, and the state, and a series of economic shocks ensued. Oil price increases led to inflation, compounding the dilemma. In the face of these crises, employers began to look for ways to roll back their commitments to workers. Once Ronald Reagan took office in 1980, the state led the way by weakening the National Labor Relations Board and using the Taft-Hartley Act to fire striking air traffic controllers, setting an example that inspired employers to challenge labor in new ways that struck fear into the heart of workers. Meanwhile, capital flowed outward from the United States in search of new, more profitable investment opportunities. In transferring their capital, firms also escaped many of the regulatory arrangements that had been established at the level of the national state. By the 1980s proponents of a new brand of free market orthodoxy, promoting ever-expanding deregulatory projects and antiunionism, had gained the upper hand. Under the influence of these new ideas, state actors began to construct and construe their own projects in market terms.[7] New market rationalities became an increasingly important part of welfare policy as the reform project progressed from the passage of the Family Support Act in 1988 to its culmination in 1996.

One of the most serious attempts to specify how welfare intersects with labor markets in this new context is found in the work of geographer Jamie Peck. Peck argues that welfare is a "boundary institution of the labor market," meaning that it helps to regulate the flow of workers in and out of work as well as to prepare them for the kinds of jobs that are available. He says that welfare reform's workfare programs—which made benefits contingent on the performance of mandatory work assignments—represented the state's response to late-twentieth-century labor market dilemmas.

Peck argues that free market policies, applied to the sphere of welfare, shape the low-wage labor market in two ways. They serve "to numerically adjust the flows of workers into and out of wage labor, but also to remake the workers themselves, their attitudes toward work and wages, their expectations about employment continuity and promotion prospects, economic identities."[8] With regard to the first of these effects, welfare systems have historically established a floor below which wages could not fall, and have provided a temporary or permanent alternative to labor market participation for those who were willing to subsist at this level. Their specific rules and practices determined who could and could not have access to support outside the market. Eliminating an "escape" option for those at the bottom of the labor market drives workers, even those who might have been considered unemployable in other periods due to disabilities or family responsibilities, into whatever jobs they can find. This makes life difficult for the workers who are directly affected by having state provision withdrawn, but its effects also reverberate throughout the labor market. Frances Fox Piven puts it bluntly: "As hundreds of thousands of women lose welfare benefits . . . they will stream into the labor market to compete with other women (and men) for less skilled and low-paying jobs."[9]

The second way that welfare can reshape the low-wage labor market, according to Peck, is by remaking expectations about hours and wages, stability of employment, the responsibilities of employers, and other aspects of work. Workfare programs, he argues, "define and enforce norms of labor market participation in ways that are inscribed into the very identities of contingent workers."[10] They are a training ground for contingency, low wages, the loss of protective rules, and the absence of opportunity. Like the removal of a wage floor, this training reverberates beyond the lives of the workers directly involved. It demonstrates to others that these conditions are possible, dramatizing, and ultimately normalizing, workplace practices that had been unthinkable since the early twentieth century.[11] Peck's account generates provocative questions for our analysis, as we explore the ways in which welfare reform has reshaped the institutions and practices of the low-wage labor market, changing networks of support and accountability and altering women's work histories.

In the pages that follow, we suggest that the effects of welfare reform cannot be understood apart from the forces constituting demand for labor at the bottom of the labor market. The primary development in this domain is the growth of the service sector. Low-wage retail and service sector jobs—jobs serving burgers at McDonald's and TGI Fridays, emptying bedpans and bathing patients in nursing homes, and stocking the shelves at Walmart and Target—accounted for 70 percent of all new job growth between 1989 and 2000.[12] And the majority of these new jobs were filled by women.

What was paradoxical about this period was the fact that the growing demand for workers in low-end service jobs coincided with stagnant or declining wages. The entry of vast numbers of women into the labor market, and the increase in the number of hours they worked, was both a cause of the paradox and its consequence. Women's entry into the labor market created more competition for jobs at the bottom and thus played a role in keeping wage rates down. These low wages, in combination with a broader decline in working-class men's wages over the same period, reduced family incomes and made it necessary for more women to work.[13] This was the context in which welfare reform took place, and yet it rarely enters national discussions.

It was not completely absent, however. It was there in the congressional testimony that preceded passage of the Family Support Act in 1988, when then-senator Russell Long noted that "in practically every city in America there are jobs available as waitresses and dishwashers."[14] It was there when a committee of influential "experts" who came together to offer recommendations on welfare reform wrote: "Among other kinds of work for which such mothers can be trained . . . are child care and pre-school education. In most cities . . . hotels and service establishments have many needs for entry-level employees."[15] It was there when Lawrence Mead, one of the intellectual fathers of welfare reform, wrote in *Beyond Entitlement*, "low-wage work apparently must be mandated, just as a draft has sometimes been necessary to staff the military."[16] But broader public discussions have rarely recognized that the need for labor in the expansion of the low-wage service sector has formed the context for welfare reform, focusing instead on welfare "dependency," "babies having babies," or the need for fiscal conservatism.

The term "service sector" covers a broad range of jobs, from the performance of sophisticated computer operations to mopping floors. While many ways of mapping the complexity of the sector have been suggested, Appelbaum and Albin have offered one of the most incisive. They suggest making a distinction between "knowledge and information intensive" and "labor intensive" subsectors.[17] Despite media hype suggesting otherwise, growth in labor-intensive service sector jobs has been far greater than that in knowledge-intensive positions. As Katz points out, projections of the need for skilled service workers have confused numbers with percentages: "Employment in computer science and engineering will grow by 100 percent compared to 11 percent in food service. But food services is a vastly larger industry than computer science, which means that the smaller percentage yields a great many more jobs."[18] The fact that most new job growth has been in the labor-intensive branch of the service sector is key to our story.

The women in our study changed bedding and bedpans in nursing homes, pushed the elderly in wheelchairs, fed them, and changed their clothes. They supervised the daily activities of disabled persons in sheltered workshops and in group homes. They cared for infants and toddlers in day care centers, fed children in school cafeterias, and cleaned empty apartments, schools, government offices, and hotel rooms. They sorted clothing to be resold in thrift stores and packaged items distributed by food pantries. They worked in fast food: burger joints, pizza parlors, chicken shacks, and taco stands. They counted items in warehouses and grocery stores, stocked shelves, and processed returns. They drove school buses, assembled cookbooks in printing warehouses, and made telemarketing calls. They were receptionists, clerks, and waitresses. They processed parking tickets and worked as security guards. Sometimes repetitious and boring, often physically strenuous, usually face-to-face with customers or individuals needing care, their jobs kept key sectors of the economies of Milwaukee and Racine running.

In the pages that follow, we will argue that U.S. welfare reform intersected with the growth of the low-wage service sector in a variety of ways. In the tight labor markets of the late 1990s, when reform was enacted in a stepwise process, it provided new workers for the growing number of low-wage service jobs. Nationally, between 1994 and 2004, the number of individuals receiving welfare fell by twelve million.[19] In Wisconsin, where reforms began earlier, caseloads declined by 270,000 recipients between 1986 and 2000.[20] Not all of these individuals went directly to work, but studies show that more than half did so.[21] By any standard, this represented a large infusion of workers into the labor market.[22]

Those women who remained on welfare after 1996, or turned to the system after the reforms were implemented, were confronted with strict work requirements. The reforms that were passed did not allow much room for training, and the few training opportunities that were provided were primarily for child care workers and certified nursing assistants—the kinds of jobs for which demand was high in the low-wage service sector. More often, however, the programs placed women directly in low-wage service jobs, where they worked in return for benefits. Peck's argument that workfare serves to remake workers' "attitudes toward work and wages, their expectations about employment continuity and promotion prospects, their economic identities," was not far from the stated goals of welfare reform's framers, who argued that "one purpose of social policy can be to discipline the poor."[23]

THE SOLITARY WAGE BARGAIN AND DILEMMAS OF SOCIAL REPRODUCTION

The free market advocates who designed welfare reform proposed programs grounded in a new vision of work and of workers. Their views stood in stark contrast to the union and civil service models of employment that had structured working arrangements for much of the twentieth century, both of which promised stable work, a living wage, and benefits.[24] Instead, they imagined a labor market in which each worker was "free" to pursue his or her best interest, and was on his or her own in doing so. They imagined this individual to be unencumbered by family responsibilities or disabilities. While conservative political thinkers did not give a name to this new paradigm, we have chosen to call it the "solitary wage bargain" to distinguish it from the "family wage bargain" that had been the goal and achievement of labor struggles over the past century and a half.

The family wage concept emerged during the 1820s and 1830s. As households became more separated from the livelihood supports of farms, trade unionists began to press the idea that employers should pay male workers enough to fully support both themselves and their families. By the turn of the twentieth century, this concept extended far beyond union rhetoric, as historian Martha May argues, to become a key standard that Progressive Era reformers used to assess poverty and standards of living.[25] Government support became an important part of the equation. New programs carved out a role for the state and employers in insuring the male breadwinner against injury through workers' compensation and offered pensions to widows caring for children. With the advent of the New Deal in the 1930s, the federal government protected workers against loss of work through unemployment insurance. Through Social Security the government also bolstered the male worker's ability to care for his family after his death or when he became too old to work. And it offered limited and means-tested aid to women who, due to family failures, did not have access to a male wage through Aid to Dependent Children. This arrangement was not a feminist's dream, but it acknowledged that society had an interest in the reproduction of its members and that the state, employers, and families all had a role in insuring it. While only a privileged _oup of mostly white, unionized workers ever received a family wage, the arrangement provided an ideal vision of how responsibilities for the well-being of citizens should be divided among social actors.

This complex set of relationships structured what we might call a system of social reproduction. The concept of social reproduction has its roots in Marxist social science, where it refers to the renewal of classes and class relationships over time. Feminist scholars have reworked the term, using it to refer to the labor necessary to keep households and communities functioning and to allow them to send productive members out into the world to work. In this sense, it entails the activities involved in reproducing and supporting family members from day to day, as well as from generation to generation. While we often gloss social reproduction as child care, it also includes care for the ill and the elderly, the work of consumption, cooking, cleaning, paying bills, talking to teachers and doctors, taking children to activities, organizing transportation, and dealing with landlords, utility companies, and banks. In the words of Claudia von Werlhof, it is "the healing-all-wounds ... the putting everything again in order ... the helping out in all matters . . . the pulling the cart out of the mud."[26] Or as Delia Carter, one of the women in our study, put it:

> It's all the stresses in the world. You know what I'm saying? You have to do all these things and then you have to worry about child care, making it home in time to feed them, put them in the tub, clean up the house. . . . You're trying to do all this on your own, with no help. What's the word for it? I don't even know the word for it.

Accomplishing the work of social reproduction requires a societal division of labor. Political sociologist Claus Offe has written that there is no past or present society where, at any one time, more than half the members participate in the labor market. In his view, a society that does not permit children to be socialized and educated, the elderly to retire, the ill and infirm to refrain from work, and some individuals to care for others "would soon bring the institution of the labor market to an end. The reproduction of the capacity for work would be prevented."[27] The concept of social reproduction underscores the fact that care is central to the continuing ability to labor—to society's productivity over the long term—and suggests that the responsibilities for that care should be socially distributed. It is a concept that reminds us of something we are prone to forget.

Feminist theorists have exposed the sleight of hand through which, historically, we have come to construe the labor of care as separate from the world of wage work. Joan Tronto argues that this blindness has very deep roots. She traces it to the Aristotelian model of the citizen as an individual who participates in public life but whose public activity presupposes a separate realm of existence in which economic chores and the work of care take place. "The Aristotelian citizen," she says, "floats his citizenship on previously accomplished work that is beneath the observance of political institutions, but nonetheless is essential for his life." While we see the citizen as someone who contributes to society through waged work, the reproduction of citizens depends on the existence of family labor that can convert the wage into the care that humans need to survive. We thus need to redefine our conception of citizenship, Tronto argues, "and with it the boundaries between public and private life, to include caring." "Let us think of citizens as engaged in a citizenship act when they are engaged in processes of care."[28]

Enlightenment-era paradigms that give pride of place to the individual contribute to the invisibility of social-reproductive labor. In *The Autonomy Myth*, legal theorist Martha Fineman writes about our national obsession with concepts of autonomy, independence, and self-sufficiency. The ways we use these terms, she argues, reveal the value we place on not being influenced by or reliant on others, on providing for our own needs without external assistance. But this disconnectedness is a myth, a myth built on unwaged labor. As children we all require protection and care, as we do when we are ill, disabled, and elderly. Historically, the long working days and relentless schedule of industrial work were enabled by the presence of someone in the home whose efforts restored the laborer on a daily basis. We have long understood the family as a separate, private space where these tasks are performed without pay. Given this arrangement, caring for others creates what Fineman calls a "derivative dependency." Because caregivers forego waged work to perform unwaged care, they become dependent on others for their sustenance and support.[29]

In their powerful treatise on the concept of dependency, Nancy Fraser and Linda Gordon argue, like Fineman and Tronto, that independence in the public sphere relies on care provided in private to restore and reproduce citizens and workers. They remind us that in earlier eras, people considered *wage earners* dependent because they did not own property and relied on their employers for their livelihood. By the mid-nineteenth century, however, workers had begun to forge new claims of independence based on their adherence to values of hard work. Fraser and Gordon point out that as workers transformed the meaning of independence, our understanding of dependence shifted also. As wage labor became the norm, those excluded from it came to personify dependence; in particular, this stigma fell upon the pauper, the slave, and the housewife.[30] In the twentieth century, despite the fact that male wage earners depended on their employers, on government insurance programs such as Social Security and workers' compensation, on union-negotiated benefits like sick leave and pensions, and on the unpaid labor of their wives, the public construed them as "free laborers" and focused on poor single mothers who received state support as the emblem of dependency. By the 1960s and 1970s, it was common for racialized discourse—at odds with the actual demographics of those receiving support—to demonize and belittle African American mothers receiving welfare in ways that gave little attention to the social reproductive work they were performing.

As Fraser and Gordon point out, critics of welfare have frequently made their case by reviling poor, single mothers in the language of dependency, shifting the meaning of the term from a description of a relationship to a characterization of a personality flaw. From Daniel Patrick Moynihan's 1973 proclamation that "the issue of welfare is the issue of dependency. It is different from poverty,"[31] critics of welfare have argued that it stunts citizenship by preventing individuals from developing self-reliance. "For such persons," the drafters of the 1987 *New Consensus on Family and Welfare* proclaimed, "low income is in a sense the least of their problems; a failure to take responsibility for themselves and for their actions is at the core."[32] The point here is not that welfare critics misapprehend the reality of mothers on welfare—although that is undoubtedly true. The point is that, by translating their critique of dependency into policy, welfare reformers created the situations that women described in our interviews. They crafted a set of policies that in radical, and perhaps historically unprecedented ways, have cut poor women off from societal support.

Welfare reform put into place a relationship among working families, employers, and government that was intrinsically different from the family wage system. Despite the fact that its policies were applied for the most part to single mothers of young children, the reform highlighted the individual as an actor in the labor market and as a responsible citizen. It envisioned a worker who was able to respond flexibly to the needs of employers, without requiring training, benefits, or even sick leave, in order to gain a foothold in the labor market. It emphasized a citizen who would not rely on government programs and therefore could enjoy autonomy and self-respect, while ignoring the labor she provided to care for those who depended on her. It is this new set of arrangements, in which both government and private employers have rolled back their contributions to social reproduction, that constitutes the solitary wage bargain. As mothers of young children, the women in our study were not only required to work but were cut off from earlier forms of support for their family responsibilities. This is the first hand tied behind the back of women who turn to welfare.

CONTRACTUAL CITIZENSHIP AND THE EROSION
OF CIVIL AND LABOR RIGHTS IN WORKFARE JOBS

As a "boundary institution," welfare abuts the labor market, but the relationships it manages and structures are between individuals and the state. Thus, changes in the meaning and structure of welfare imply changes in the meaning and structure of citizenship. Citizenship is a complex concept that can refer narrowly to *membership* in a polity—that is, to "nationality and the legal recognition that a person is a member of a state."[33] But it can also refer to various forms of inclusion in the polity, what political scientist Suzanne Mettler has called "incorporation" and "participation."[34] Laws govern each of these forms of citizenship, but so do public policies and institutions. As we shall see, welfare institutions mediate between individuals and the state in ways that powerfully shape the manner and extent of incorporation into political community.

The first evidence that citizenship was going to be a terrain of struggle in welfare reform came from the elaboration, in the 1980s, of theories of "welfare contractualism," or "new paternalism." These theories drew on long-standing and widely held notions that citizenship involved both rights and responsibilities, and reformulated them to argue that rights should be *contingent* on the performance of responsibilities. As political philosopher Stuart White has argued, there is a general presumption in most Western societies against restrictions on individual freedom—unless the individual can be shown to lack the capacity to govern him- or herself.[35] Many of those involved in the 1996 U.S. welfare reform premised their advocacy of welfare contractualism on exactly this argument. Lawrence Mead, in *Beyond Entitlement*, offered the clearest and most influential articulation of this approach to welfare. "One of the things a government must do to improve social order," he wrote, "is to use these programs to require better functioning of recipients who have difficulty coping."[36] He saw this "difficulty coping," in the post–Civil Rights era, as the main barrier to acceptance and success for the poor. Thus,

the role of public authority is precisely to make *obligatory* the norms that people commonly affirm but do not reliably obey, a gap that is

especially wide for the underclass. . . . Such standards require government to decide, not only who is needy, but who is able to function and
who is not.[37]

Legal theorist Patricia Williams, in "On Being the Object of Property," provides an alternative vocabulary for discussing the premises of contractual citizenship. She uses the term *will* to refer to the capacities that Western political
theory has traditionally held to be required for citizenship; she labels their
absence *anti-will*. Williams demonstrates how these concepts grew out of the
history of slaveholding—slave owners claimed their charges were incapable of
rationality or willful decision making. She shows how notions of will continue
to inform legal judgments about such issues as the involuntary sterilization of
poor women, who are presumed not to know their own interests. These same
arguments underlie reformed welfare's behavioral requirements and curtail-
ment of rights.

Williams points to another strategy by which rights may be constrained:
when individuals are asked to enter into contracts in which they surrender
basic liberties in return for something else. She raises the question of whether
there are valuable items or rights that lie outside the marketplace that contracts regulate, thus rendering agreements to trade them "spurious" or "il-
lusory": "Traditionally, the Mona Lisa and human life have been the sorts of
subjects removed from the fungibility of commodification, as priceless. Thus,
when black people were bought or sold as slaves, they were placed beyond the
bounds of humanity."[38] As we shall see in the chapters that follow, new theories
of welfare contractualism are premised on the trading of civil rights for aid.
By accepting assistance from the state, poor women are asked to relinquish a
range of rights and liberties, from the freedom to decide whether to stay home
with their children and to maintain ties to the fathers of their children, to the
right to choose when and where to work and at what kind of job, to basic labor
rights and protections while working at that job.

Welfare contractualism did not arrive on the political scene fully formed
in the 1980s. Its historical antecedents emerged in debates over the shape and
scope of welfare in the New Deal and post–World War II eras. This was the
period when the British sociologist T. H. Marshall published his renowned
essay "Citizenship and Social Class," in which he distinguished three types of
citizenship—civil, political, and social—which he argued had emerged succes-
sively as Western society progressed. Marshall argued that civil rights, such as
freedom of speech, association, and self-determination, were achieved in the

eighteenth century and political rights (voting and political participation) in the nineteenth. He portrayed social rights as the crowning achievement of the twentieth century. The premise of these new social rights, according to Marshall, was that the state should insure the minimum levels of economic security needed "to share to the full in the social heritage and to live the life of a civilized being according to the standards prevailing in society."[39]

As Stuart White points out, Marshall's essay celebrated the new commitment of Western states to full employment and to protection during unemployment, ill health, and old age. It described these accomplishments within a narrative that White calls "a social democratic teleology"—that is, as the seemingly inevitable product of a progressive expansion and elaboration of rights that had been at work for centuries.[40] But, as White argues, this was not to be the case. At the very moment of the articulation of new social rights, there were forces afoot that would struggle against their expansion. These forces gained traction beginning in the 1970s and by the 1990s, they could be said to have definitively reversed the tide.[41]

The elements of a critique of social rights arose alongside new institutions of social provision even as they were being built during the New Deal era. Defenders of free market ideologies argued that regulation and state assistance to the poor stifled capitalism and infringed on human freedom (particularly the freedom not to be burdened by the cost of the resource claims of others). Friedrich Hayek took this view in *The Road to Serfdom*, published in 1944, touting the superiority of the free market to the forms of collective planning emerging in the Soviet Union and Eastern Europe. Beginning in the 1950s, Milton Friedman became a key spokesperson for a society built around market principles. In *Capitalism and Freedom* and other works, he emphasized the need for free individuals to pursue their preferences and to produce wealth.[42] With the economic dislocations of the 1970s, these perspectives gained a broader set of adherents among economists and policymakers, who began to argue that attaining economic stability and productivity growth would require rolling back many elements of the New Deal, including the favorable environment that had been created for labor unions and many social programs and entitlements.[43] Welfare was a key target for such rollback.

Conservatives began laying the groundwork for welfare reform in the 1960s, in direct response to the expanded social programs of Lyndon Johnson's War on Poverty, but their views attained greatest prominence during the Reagan administration in the 1980s. George Gilder, whose 1981 book *Wealth and Poverty* was one of the key texts opposing the expansion of the welfare state, argued that power, privilege, and property should be distributed according to morally meaningful criteria. Capitalism, he argued, requires disciplined and creative actors and should evoke and reward these characteristics. But racial integration disrupted the transmission of cultural traits required for success by denying white families the freedom to choose the moral influences that would surround their children. With reference to welfare, he drew on a rhetoric of "moral perversity," which suggested that aid harms the poor, writing that redistributive social programs break the link between reward and effort, and thus exclude the poor from the path to success. (He also suggested that such programs harm the middle class because the taxes required to fund them reduce income and thus push mothers into paid employment.)[44] Three years later, in *Losing Ground*, Charles Murray espoused many similar themes, casting black Americans as cultural outsiders who flouted moral principles by avoiding work and having children out of wedlock, and argued that transfer programs such as welfare should be eliminated because they fostered poor moral choices and forced middle-class Americans to "subsidize a lifestyle" that deviated from their own.[45]

While Gilder advocated reducing aid to the poor, and Murray suggested abolishing it, Michael Novak was the first to suggest that welfare programs could be used to instill the self-reliance that he too believed was essential to a well-functioning capitalist society:

It is a problem of human potential. . . . Many of the poor, especially among the young, need help in learning skills and attitudes: how to read, how to apply for and hold a job, how to govern themselves and conduct themselves. Self-reliance is a virtue of many parts . . . and it can be taught.[46]

This was an early articulation of welfare as a program of behavioral change—enforced through a contract with a paternalist state.

The notion that welfare could become a tutelary institution designed to instill proper values about work and family reached its fullest expression in the writing of Lawrence Mead. As we have seen, Mead's paternalist theory of welfare contractualism held that the state was responsible for disciplining poor parents and that, by conditioning benefits on proper behavior, it could make them self-reliant citizens. In *Beyond Entitlement*, published in 1986, he referred to the need for an "authoritative" social policy that would "enforce social obligations, at least for the dependent," by setting standards for their behavior and persuading them to "blame themselves" for their failures.[47] Most dictionaries, we might note, define the word *authoritative* to mean "of acknowledged accuracy." Mead here appears to be substituting it for *authoritarian*—"favoring obedience or subjection to authority"—which is closer to the sense of his argument. His sensitivity to potential negative reaction to his endorsement of authoritarian social policy emerges in the text:

> The idea of programs inculcating values may nevertheless seem foreign to American political mores. It conjures up a brutal, Hobbesian image of government deciding what is good for people and then imposing it on them by force. For policy to involve itself in the personal competences of individuals is inherently sensitive.[48]

But he resolves this dilemma by arguing that the competences in question are prerequisite to freedom and citizenship: "American political culture gives pride of place to the value of freedom. But a 'free' society is possible only when the conditions for order have been substantially realized."[49] Welfare recipients, then, are not entitled to equal citizenship until they acquire these values:

> For how can the dependent be equal, except in the most metaphysical sense, with those who support them? . . . Those who *only* make claims can never be equal, in the nature of things, with those on whom the claims are made.[50]

Mead later came to call his vision of government's tutelary function "paternalism," defining it as a situation in which the state makes demands on welfare recipients and "supervises them closely to make sure that they fulfill those expectations."[51] Reading Mead makes it clear that when critics of welfare reform argue that its measures treat participants as less than full citizens and deny them equality, they are not observing a set of unintended consequences. Indeed, these were the basic premises on which the new program's reforms were constructed. Both in the nation as a whole and in the state of Wisconsin, reforms embodied Mead's paternalist ethic, rewarding both marketlike work and efforts at family formation. This shift to welfare contractualism represented, in the view of many, "a fundamental reorientation of the welfare state away from broadly emancipatory purposes" and its reinvention "as an institution for the maintenance of social order in the context of a highly unequal society."[52]

Principles of contractual citizenship were the foundation for workfare programs like those the state of Wisconsin implemented. These programs tied cash assistance to mandatory work assignments for all who were able to perform them. Policymakers, based on the erroneous premise that welfare participants had never worked, designed these programs to socialize women to the norms of the workforce. The assignments were meant to emulate the real world of employment but, in fact, they placed women in a never-never land of uncertainty. Quoting anthropologist Victor Turner, Chad Goldberg has written:

> Because workfare participants are perceived to be in a process of transition, they are "neither here nor there; they are betwixt and between the positions assigned and arrayed by law, custom, convention and ceremonial." . . . [They] are *anomalous* figures who seem to be situated on both sides of the worker/relief distinction. At the same time [they] are *liminal* figures who seem to be situated on neither side.[53]

Workfare programs put women to work while labeling the wages they receive as aid. When a woman holds this type of job, she is considered to be receiving welfare. The "time clock" that limits her lifetime benefits under PRWORA is ticking. Agents of the state monitor her work attendance and dock her pay if she misses hours. This ambiguous status, eerily reminiscent of workhouses in the nineteenth century, denies women both the respect and many of the protections and prerogatives associated with wage earning since the Jacksonian period.

In Milwaukee and Racine, women who participate in workfare plant flowers and water shrubs on the islands of highways, and cut brush along the shoulders of roads. They clean public housing and the offices of private agencies administering welfare programs. They sort clothing for Goodwill and work alongside the disabled in sheltered workshops. These community service job placements—the centerpiece of Wisconsin's welfare program—send women to work for both public and private employers. These jobs pay only $673 a month, and they count toward what is now a lifetime limit of sixty months of state assistance. But the worst thing, many participants say, is the lack of freedom to choose when, where, and under what conditions to work. As one woman put it, "You can't decide where you want to go. You have no opinion on any of this. It's like you're a child and your parents are running your life for you, because you don't have no choice."[54] This loss of freedom of contract and ambiguous status in relation to labor laws is the second hand tied behind the back of the women in our study.

Here is an example from Milwaukee. In 2003 Aurelia Knotts showed up at a welfare office there in a dejected state. When her caseworker asked her what was wrong, she said she was working on her brother's funeral arrangements. He had been in a nursing home for the past three years, and she had power of attorney over his affairs. Moreover, she was destitute. She had broken up with her partner, who had been her main source of income. She had an eviction notice in her pocket. With all of this going on, she had started drinking again. The caseworker took all this in and methodically started working through the kinds of help that were available. She quickly established that Aurelia had a range of problems that made her eligible for the state's W-2 Transitions program, which provided aid to poor individuals who were unable to work due to illness or disability. She was suffering from depression, which had troubled her since her daughter was murdered twelve years earlier; she also had problems with the circulation in her legs, chronic obstructive pulmonary disorder, diabetes, and alcohol addiction. But there was a catch—Aurelia already had used up her twenty-four months of eligibility for Transitions. She had applied for federal Supplemental Security Income but was denied, and she had not known that she could appeal. Because the caseworker elected not to offer her an extension on her W-2 Transitions eligibility, all that was left was a community service job—that is, a workfare assignment.

Aurelia said she understood. "I like to take care of old people," she suggested, "or working in a group home." She and the caseworker quickly determined, however, that because of a prior conviction for assault, she was not eligible for nursing assistant positions. "I like cooking," Aurelia offered, "but I can't take standing for long hours." The caseworker told Aurelia she would assign her to a sewing position, which she would have to attend from 8 to 4 five days a week. "I'm not a seamstress, I'm a cook," Aurelia protested. "You've been here three years," she said, referring to the caseworker's own situation. "You like what you're doing." "We have food service, but you would have to stand," the caseworker replied. "I might as well live in Uncle Tom's cabin," Aurelia replied, "but I'm going to do what I got to do." Aurelia's reference to slavery reflects her understanding that a constitutional right to freely contract one's labor—to choose when and where to work—is at stake in such assignments.

The solitary wage bargain and contractual citizenship were key concepts structuring welfare reform. In the pages that follow, we will demonstrate how each, in distinct ways, impaired the functioning of women raising families in poverty. The solitary wage bargain rolled back social rights that had previously supported families, while contractual citizenship eroded the civil and employment rights of women who labored within the workfare programs that welfare reform established. Each of these losses represented a significant blow to poor women, but as we will demonstrate, there is also a powerful connection between them. In a nutshell, the predicament is this: the ever-present and unmet need for time to care for families while engaged in low-wage work throws women back into a punitive and stigmatized welfare system again and again, while the loss of civil and labor rights in the context of workfare impedes their ability to defend their interests as workers and to gain the kinds of jobs and benefits that would allow them to weather these crises. Our title, *Both Hands Tied*, refers to this double dilemma. Without a new model of how social reproduction is to be accomplished—and without jobs that adequately support women in their dual roles as workers and mothers—this dynamic will solidify a caste of low-wage workers with attenuated rights at the bottom of the labor market, and punish them for attending to their families.

STUDYING WELFARE AND WORK IN PLACE: NOTES ON RESEARCH METHODS

Isaac Martin has observed that evaluations of welfare programs too often "limit their attention to the effects of the provisions on individuals rather than their effects on American society."[55] Even studies that focus on individual behavior, Martha Fineman notes, often deal with abstractions, recognizing neither "an individual's relevant history nor [his or her] location in the context of the greater society."[56] In many cases they have imagined participants in the welfare system as abstract actors who will respond correctly to the right mix of incentives. In designing our research, we sought to replace abstract individuals with real ones and to place them in the larger context of their local labor market and the economy as a whole.

Our study reconstructs the work and family histories of thirty-three women who relied on social programs, showing how participation in the post-1996 welfare system affected their trajectories of work, their arrangements for their children, and their ideas about what to expect from employment. It traces the ups and downs of the labor markets of Milwaukee and Racine, Wisconsin, showing how these women's struggles to make a living intersected with that region's difficult transition from manufacturing to services; its deep-seated racial segregation and, thus, racially segmented workforce; and its gendered histories of craft unionism and service work. And it tracks the national, state, and local policies that shaped the availability of aid and jobs. In the spirit of Michael Burawoy's "extended case method," we have worked to draw links between micro and macro domains, constituting each social situation "in terms of the particular external forces that shape it."[57]

We began by randomly selecting from the administrative database names of women receiving benefits in Milwaukee and Racine in December 2003, using a sampling frame that insured proportional coverage of differences in race and other important factors. Nearly 70 percent of the women we contacted agreed to be interviewed, and we met with these women in the summer of 2004. Thus, we feel confident in saying that what we report is representative of the situation for southeastern Wisconsin in 2004.[58]

Two points about this representativeness need to be highlighted. The first is the racial composition of our sample, which was 58 percent African American, 22 percent white, and 20 percent Latina.[59] The disproportionate number of African American women on welfare (African Americans make up 37 percent of the population of Milwaukee and 20 percent of the population of Racine) reflects trends in participation that have arisen since the implementation of reform in 1996. Despite widespread perceptions that welfare served mainly African Americans, this was not the case prior to PRWORA. Nationally, in 1994, just over 37 percent of families on welfare were non-Latino white, around 36 percent were African American, and 20 percent were Latino.[60] While even these numbers may suggest a disproportionate participation rate among women of color, they are, as Mink has noted, commensurate with the racial distribution of poverty.[61] That is, the percentage of women of different ethnic groups who are on welfare closely tracks their percentage among those in poverty. In Wisconsin, a series of welfare experiments that began in the late 1980s, and culminated in the W-2 program in 1996, pushed many women out of welfare. As Cancian and her coauthors have suggested, women with the most education and skills and the fewest barriers to work (such as illness, sick children, or addiction) left first.[62] Because education, skills, and illness have all been shown to be linked to poverty, and to race, African American women were more likely to remain on welfare or to return to the rolls. This accounts for their higher participation rates in southeastern Wisconsin in 2003 and consequently their share of the interviews in our study.

A second issue of representativeness has to do with family size. There is a common stereotype that women who turn to welfare have more children than the average. Yet nationally, nearly three-quarters of welfare participants in 1994 had two children or fewer (the average was 1.8).[63] (Since the welfare benefits of Aid to Families with Dependent Children, and later Temporary Assistance to Needy Families, were available only to parents, this figure is not directly comparable to the mean for all families, which includes many childless households.) Among the women in our study, 62 percent had two children or fewer, and only 3 percent had four or more.[64]

Many studies have looked at women who left welfare and have asked how they fared afterward.[65] Most have concluded that moving off the rolls did not much improve their circumstances. Around half of the women found work, but only a few worked steadily enough, at high enough wages, to rise above the poverty line. Policymakers have not been able to account for a substantial proportion of former welfare participants, who show up neither in unemployment insurance data nor on social service rosters. In any case, scholars conducted the majority of these "leavers" studies in the early days of welfare reform (1996–2000), when the economy was undergoing a spurt of unprecedented growth and unemployment was relatively low.

In this study, we look at a different group of women and ask somewhat different questions. We examine the work histories and social program use of a group of women who either entered, remained on, or returned to the rolls in 2003—after seven years of policies designed to discourage them from doing so. And we ask somewhat different questions than have most investigators: Who are the women turning to welfare, well into a policy regime meant to move them off the rolls? What are their reasons for seeking assistance from a program that is, by design, punitive and stigmatized? What made it difficult for them to work? How did their use of state programs affect their subsequent path through the labor market? Building on the accounts of the women we interviewed, we explore the ways in which Wisconsin's reformed welfare practices both adjusted the flow of workers in and out of the labor market and remade workers.

Arguably, the most memorable insights into how society functions have come, not from detailed quantitative hypothesis testing, but from case studies, street-level ethnographic investigations like St. Clair Drake and Horace Clayton's *Black Metropolis* or Hortense Powdermaker's *After Freedom.* These works provide incisive glimpses into social process—moments in which we come to understand, to quote C. Wright Mills, "how an individual's troubles relate to the larger issues of the age." It is their particularity that creates the value of case studies, the detailed empirical evidence they provide about how things happen in a given time and place.

Case studies of welfare reform allow us to explore the complex intersections of local labor market dynamics with particular state policy regimes and to investigate the effects of both on participants' lives. These results are never fully generalizable to other labor markets and policy environments, and they do not allow us to speak about how something we have observed is distributed across space and time. In fact, it is more accurate to speak of "transferring" insights from a case to other instances that share key characteristics. But if we understand what is special about our case, and where it sits in relation to others, we can establish which insights are relevant to understanding particular other contexts.

Wisconsin is a policy environment of special interest because its reformed welfare programs are the most work-focused in the nation.[66] As Cancian and her coauthors have noted:

> Since 1997, *no cash assistance* has been available to families unless they participate in work or work-like activities, or unless they have a child less than 13 weeks old. Moreover, cash benefits are only available after a period of program participation, to mirror the world of work. Wisconsin began work-based welfare reform in the 1980s, well ahead of the rest of the nation.[67]

Moreover, these authors argue, other states have looked to Wisconsin as a model in crafting their own reforms, particularly to the state's many and diverse "welfare experiments" in the ten years prior to the federal reform bill. As Republican congressional leader Newt Gingrich is reported to have said in response to welfare reform's early skeptics, "we're not talking theory here. . . . Go visit Wisconsin."[68] Thus, Wisconsin is not a typical or "average" policy environment; it does not provide an accurate picture of welfare reform in every other state. Rather, it reveals what workfare looks like in its starkest form, and it is important because it serves, and has served, as a model for reforms across the nation.

In some respects, the labor market in southeastern Wisconsin resembles that in other deindustrialized regions struggling with problems of economic transition. The area lost many good manufacturing jobs in the 1970s and 1980s. Many service jobs have since emerged, but few offer comparable wages and benefits, and most are in the suburbs surrounding Milwaukee and Racine, not the urban core. But one feature is unusual: the 2000 census found Milwaukee to be one of the most segregated urban areas in the country, and this feature has deeply distorted the opportunities for poor black and Latina women to find jobs.

The timing of our study is also specific. As we have seen, the early days of welfare reform coincided with an unprecedented period of economic growth.

All analysts agree that this made it easier for women leaving the rolls to find work and that it kept wages in the lower ranks of the service sector from dropping dramatically in response to the influx of new workers. But the recession that began in March 2001 and ended in September 2003, and the "jobless recovery" that followed, changed the economic landscape for low-wage workers. Wages stagnated or declined during this period, and even the least desirable low-wage jobs became scarce, particularly in inner-city areas of Milwaukee and Racine. The situation had only begun to improve when the major economic downturn that began in 2008 pulled the rug out again, both nationally and in southeastern Wisconsin.

In addition to our interviews with welfare participants, our account is based on fifty-four interviews with welfare policymakers, "front-line" caseworkers, and local activists, and on participation in open meetings with welfare policymakers, Department of Workforce Development administrators, and officials in agencies contracted to implement reformed welfare. Victoria Mayer observed 109 appointments in welfare and child support offices and sat in on four job-preparation training programs. We reviewed local newspapers and scoured data collected by local think tanks and research institutions to help build our understanding of the labor market context, and combed the local business press to track employers' responses to labor market changes and welfare reform. Each of these sources helped us identify the forces and contradictions in the low-wage labor market and in state policy that the women in our study confronted.

Moving back and forth between the worlds of policymakers and workers was sometimes disorienting. Advocates of reform had argued, for example, that welfare recipients must be taught the value of work. But with few exceptions, the women with whom we spoke had been working since their early teenage years. They had lengthy and diverse work histories punctuated with episodes of unemployment. They told vivid stories about work: quitting a job cleaning hotel rooms after encountering one too many vomit-spattered bathrooms, arguing with bosses who insisted they lift forty-pound bags of water softener salt, getting their own desk for the first time. They grasped the essentials of the new programs but had their own opinions as to what worked and what didn't. They were often eager to tell their stories. "The reason I met with you," Darla Tanner told us, "is because it's gonna take people like me to do these interviews, to make suggestions, and to participate in things in order to make a difference." Delia Carter echoed this motivation. "Going through all of this is the baddest feeling," she said, "but being able to talk about it, to speak up for people who might not be able to speak up for themselves, is good enough for me."

At the time we interviewed these women, society had spoken, and it had said "only work shall pay."[69] Pundits on the left and right lauded the returns in income, independence, and self-respect that welfare reform was bringing poor women. To hear many of those who advocated welfare reform talk, the new policies had successfully initiated poor women into the pride, satisfaction, security, and self-esteem that come from rendering a day's work for a day's pay. The women we spoke with had something to say in response. What they had to say was not just about hard times and struggles, although they documented those. It was an analysis of how the programs were out of sync with what was needed to prepare them to work productively in the new economy. But beyond that, it hinted at a larger betrayal. These women understood that they were being asked to do something that has never been the norm in the labor market—to be the sole breadwinners and the sole caregivers for their families, on wages that even the designers of welfare reform had acknowledged were insufficient, and in some of the least flexible and most punitively structured jobs the economy has to offer. They also knew that, by entering (or reentering) the low-wage labor market through the boundary institution of the welfare system, they were losing rights that American workers had always cherished. They were being asked to trade basic aspects of their citizenship for the meager help they received.

CHAPTER TWO

WELFARE REFORM'S CONTEXT

THE GROWTH OF THE LOW-WAGE SERVICE SECTOR

> In the first half of the [twentieth] century, racial-ethnic women were
> employed as servants. . . . [Now, they] are disproportionately employed
> as service workers in institutional settings.
>
> **EVELYN GLENN, "FROM SERVITUDE TO SERVICE WORK"[1]**

LOCAL LABOR MARKETS:
WHERE WORK HISTORIES ARE LIVED

In a former industrial district of southwest Milwaukee, a vine-covered factory building dating to the turn of the last century houses the welfare office.
The structure used to be home to the Allis-Chalmers Corporation, a firm that
manufactured tractors and other machinery from 1840 to 1999 and that pioneered in hiring African American workers in the mid-twentieth century. Today, the occupants of the five-story, block-long building include the welfare
office, Kmart, a Walgreens drug store, a Big Lots outlet, and an Office Depot.
This single block of urban landscape tells a story about the loss of good jobs
in manufacturing, the rise of employment in services, and a change in social
policy that sends single mothers with small children out to work.

Local labor markets are complex entities. If we look beyond the abstract
idea of the market, we see employers large and small, corporate megaliths and
corner stores. We see a population of workers with a range of ages, educational
attainments, and skills, and a particular spatial distribution. And joining the
two, we find a set of institutions, rules, practices, and ideas: temporary staffing
agencies, labor unions, and employer associations; federal labor law, state welfare policy, and local minimum wage ordinances; recruitment networks for
undocumented workers and patterns of residential racial segregation; and
notions about who should work outside the home and who within it, or what
constitutes a "good worker" and a "fair wage." Geographer Jamie Peck has de-

scribed a local labor market as "a socially constructed and politically mediated structure of conflict and accommodation," one that is shaped by the intersection of global, national, and local trends, as "flows of capital accumulation collide with the structures of community."[2]

What exactly does it mean—this collision of capital and community structures? In the case of Serena Clark, it means that she lives on the south side of Milwaukee in a neat but dilapidated, hundred-year-old row house. Her neighborhood, once home to working-class Polish immigrant families, is today predominantly Latino, although with many families of southeast Asian origin as well. Most of the Polish families have moved to the suburbs; the central-city factories in which they worked—making leather goods and apparel, appliances and automobile parts—closed down in the 1970s as companies shifted production contracts overseas. It's a tough place to find work. The ratio of job seekers to full-time entry-level jobs in Serena's neighborhood was about ten to one in 2005. During the height of the recession that began in 2001, it was closer to thirty to one.[3] The opportunities available within a reasonable bus ride are mostly in fast food franchises, hotels, and restaurants. These are the jobs that Serena's caseworker at the welfare office is encouraging her to take.

Serena sees another kind of opportunity in the prevalence of addictive disorders in her community. It makes sense to her that these people need services and that she, as a recovering drug user with ten years of sobriety, could be in a special position to provide them. If the government were spending more on rehabilitation, or if state welfare programs supported a broader range of training, then she might have a better chance to move into such a career. But at the time we spoke to her, neighborhood segregation, deindustrialization, central-city unemployment, and the low level and punitive design of federal and state social service spending—along with dilemmas of child care, housing, and transportation—combined to thwart her plans. These forces held her in a position of constant readiness—to paraphrase Peck and Theodore—for low-wage service sector work.[4] We will learn more, in a later chapter, about the ways that Serena experienced her local labor market, and the strategies she eventually used to move outside its well-etched paths.

Telling the story of a particular labor market thus involves moving back and forth between the big picture—global and national economic trends—and its local instantiations. It requires mapping the ways that opportunities and workers are distributed across the landscape. And it entails disaggregating the news about opportunities or their absence by race, gender, and skill in order to determine which streams of workers can actually fill which jobs

what labor market participation is like for different groups. We concentrate here on the kinds of jobs most likely to be available to poor, urban Wisconsin women—those that require no more than a high school education or
a relatively short-term training program. These jobs generally pay less than
$20,000 a year for full-time work.

It is impossible to tell the story of how workers and opportunities "are distributed across the landscape" in places like Racine and Milwaukee without
talking about race. Milwaukee, by many measures, is the most segregated city
in the United States, and Racine is not far behind.[5] The employment picture for
the Milwaukee and Racine metropolitan areas (the cities plus their suburbs) is
vastly different than that for the central city of either town, leading University
of Wisconsin–Milwaukee economists to talk about the "two Milwaukees"—
one, the prosperous suburban ring and the other the decaying Inner Core.[6] Most
of the women who relied on Aid to Families with Dependent Children prior
to 1996, or who receive Temporary Assistance to Needy Families under welfare
reform now, live in the racially segregated neighborhoods of the central city.

It is not just the geographical distribution of jobs that creates a racially segmented labor market, however, but also the ways in which employers draw on
historical understandings of race and gender as they make contemporary employment decisions. Firms draw on long-standing concepts about who should
perform particular types of work, deeply affecting the gender and racial composition of the workforce, not just in factories, but in hospitals and nursing
homes, day care centers, and retail sales outlets. Clearly, the disappearance of
factory jobs in Milwaukee and Racine disproportionately affected male workers, and the growth of the service sector has benefited women entering the
labor market. Yet educated women have been far more likely to enter "good"
service sector jobs (those that pay a living wage and offer benefits), while poor,
less-educated women, who are disproportionately women of color in these
cities, have found lower-paid positions that mirror work performed in domestic
service in earlier decades (child and elder care, cleaning, food preparation and
sales). In this chapter, we track these changing opportunities and how they
shape the livelihood chances of households and communities.

THRIVING FACTORIES, DIVIDED WORKERS:
MID-TWENTIETH CENTURY

The labor markets of the cities of Milwaukee and Racine, which sit twenty-
five miles apart on the shore of Lake Michigan, have historically been quite
similar. While the two cities differ in size—at the time of the 2000 census,

Milwaukee had just under six hundred thousand inhabitants and Racine just over eighty thousand—their economies are remarkably alike. Both were originally fur-trading posts, so tanneries were the earliest "industry." In the nineteenth century, both were ports in the Great Lakes grain trade—though Milwaukee was larger and vied with Chicago for dominance until the latter city's connections to the railroad gave it an edge.[7] Both were wholesaling centers and homes to lumberyards, flour mills, slaughterhouses, and meat packers. To this mix Milwaukee added a number of small and large breweries. Each city was a haven for Old World immigrants, first British and Irish, then German and Polish. Beginning around World War I, both cities took off as industrial centers, specializing in tool and die making and manufacturing. Milwaukee became known as the home of Harley Davidson motorcycles, Johnson Controls, Evinrude outboard motors, and Briggs & Stratton lawn mower engines. Racine grew famous for Johnson's Wax, InSinkErator garbage disposals, and Golden Books. From 1940 to 1970, one in three jobs in these southeastern Wisconsin cities was in manufacturing, and workers with high school diplomas could buy houses and live well.[8]

The *Wall Street Journal*, in a 2005 article probing the fate of former industrial cities, offered the case of Milwaukee's Wayne Hall as typical of the "escalator ride to the middle class" that characterized the region in the mid-twentieth century. In 1957, when he was twenty-four, "Hall responded to a help-wanted shingle outside Badger Die Casting on the city's south side. He started work the next day, and over the years, rose from machinery operator to machinery inspector to chief inspector. He helped organize a union, got regular raises, enjoyed generous pension and health benefits and, eventually, five weeks of vacation."[9]

As Hall's story suggests, Milwaukee was historically a center of labor organizing. The Knights of Labor counted sixteen thousand members there as early as 1880, and several workers were killed in the city's Bay View Massacre as they struck for the eight-hour day in 1886 (the same week as the Haymarket Riots in Chicago). Milwaukee unionism was dominated by the immigrant craft guilds of the American Federation of Labor from the formation of the Milwaukee Federated Trade Council in 1887 until the 1930s, but the influence of the Congress of Industrial Organizations grew from 1936 onward. Racine's labor militancy was so strong that radio commentators dubbed it "little Moscow" in the 1930s.[10] It sustained one of the nation's most vibrant labor newspapers—*Racine Labor*—from 1941 to 2001, with a circulation of over twenty-five thousand during its peak years.[11] The unions of Milwaukee and Racine waged hundreds of strikes in the 1930s but were shaken badly by the purging of Communists and their supporters from the labor community in the late 1940s.[12]

But not all Milwaukee and Racine workers shared Wayne Hall's experience of upward mobility. African American migrants in the early twentieth century found work in the industrial sector, but factory owners typically hired them for low-skilled, "sweat and muscle" jobs.[13] In his history of Milwaukee's earliest black workers, Joe Trotter Jr. shows that the majority of black men found work in four settings: foundries, meatpacking, tanneries, and construction. Employers assigned them jobs at the lowest rungs in each of these industries. For example, in packinghouses most blacks worked as muckers and slaughterers. They labored in hip boots in the lime pits in tanneries and fed the blast furnaces in the rolling mills that made rails for locomotives. Partly due to lack of seniority, partly to discrimination by employers, and partly to the hostility of American Federation of Labor unions, which denied them membership, they clustered in the hardest, dirtiest jobs. Trotter quotes one worker as saying blacks "only did the dirty work . . . jobs that even Poles didn't want."[14]

Because of this discriminatory environment, few blacks traveled to southeastern Wisconsin during the migrations from the South that began in the early 1900s, nor were many migrants drawn by job opportunities during World War I. Some black families did, however, respond to the lure of northern industry during World War II when cotton belt mechanization was destroying their livelihoods in the South. Even so, as recently as 1945, Milwaukee's population was less than 2 percent black. Unlike Detroit's auto industry or the stockyards and meatpacking plants of Chicago, the region's employers were reluctant to hire black workers. Despite Milwaukee's tradition of radical governance—it had three socialist mayors whose terms spanned thirty-eight years of the twentieth century—racial equality was not part of the civic equation. It took Franklin Roosevelt's Fair Employment Practices Committee, established in 1941 to prohibit racial discrimination in defense industries, as well as a shortage of labor brought on by the wartime manufacturing boom and a determined push by the Milwaukee Urban League, to begin to pry open factory doors. Slowly, over the 1940s and 1950s, some of the region's largest manufacturers began to hire black men, and even to recruit African American workers from southern locales.[15] Not until the 1970s, however, did African Americans come to constitute a significant share of the local population, rising to 16 percent in 1970, 30 percent in 1990, and 37 percent in 2000.[16] While the racism of many industrialists and labor unions barred blacks from the "escalator ride to the middle class," most of those who arrived and gained a foothold in industry were able to move out of poverty and to grasp at least the lower rungs of working-class life. By the 1970s, over 55 percent of Milwaukee's black male workers held manufacturing jobs, compared to 42 percent of white men, and black workers in Wisconsin earned median wages above those of their national counterparts.[17]

Local historians suggest that the "late migration" of black workers to Milwaukee and Racine meant that they had to bridge a formidable cultural chasm in moving from agricultural labor to factory work. A poll taken by local businessmen in the early 1960s found that over 80 percent of African American migrants came from southern states, though some had worked in domestic service or craft occupations in southern cities before moving north.[18] While the existence or impact of a gap in educational background and industrial culture is not clear, what is incontrovertible is that black workers had a very short period to gain a foothold in Wisconsin's factories before the shock wave of deindustrialization hit in the 1970s.[19] Their late labor market entry meant that few black workers had the chance to build significant seniority. This was exacerbated by the fact that turnover rates for jobs in lime pits and feeding blast furnaces were high, since most workers could not tolerate such harsh conditions for extended periods without a rest. As a result, when deindustrialization struck the region, Milwaukee and Racine's working-age black men were the first to get the axe.

Before recruiting African American workers in the 1940s, many Milwaukee and Racine tanneries and foundries had brought Mexican and Puerto Rican men to the region to work in their enterprises. In 1924, for example, the managers of Pfister and Vogel Tannery brought two hundred men from Michoacan, Mexico, to break a strike being waged by European immigrant workers. The first Mexican workers were men who traveled alone and were housed in warehouse dormitories, but subsequent cohorts brought their families. Nearly half of these families were repatriated during the Great Depression, but they returned to Wisconsin once economic conditions had improved. Similarly, tanneries and foundries recruited Puerto Rican workers in the 1940s, drawing them mainly from sugarcane plantations. By 1950 there were approximately 12,500 Latinos (10,000 Mexicans and 2,500 Puerto Ricans) living in formerly Polish working-class neighborhoods on Milwaukee's near south side, and by 1970 over 30,000 were living there and in near north side communities.[20] Racine was the second largest destination for Mexican and Puerto Rican families who came to Wisconsin.

Segregation was a fact of life for black and Latino working-class families at mid-twentieth century. In Milwaukee, most lived in the Inner Core or on the near south side. One report from the 1950s noted, "These zones are substandard compared to the norms or averages which prevail for the city generally. . . . In comparable areas, Negroes are paying higher rents than whites for . . . similar or inferior accommodations." The author added, "The free choice of residence in the open housing market . . . is not operative in the case of Negroes. . . . The Negro middle and upper classes, regardless of their education, skills, or professional accomplishments—if their skin is dark—must reside in the slum."[21]

White Wisconsinites' uneasy acceptance of labor migrants of other races was reflected in the opinion surveys collected by Milwaukee's Inter-collegiate Council and in a campaign ploy that gained national attention. During the 1956 mayoral election, opponents of incumbent socialist mayor Frank Zeidler spread rumors that he had used city funds to erect billboards all over the South inviting blacks to Milwaukee. The Milwaukee Federated Trades Council wrote to southern labor organizations asking if they were aware of such "recruiting," but none were. This episode was reported in *Time* magazine's April 2, 1956, cover story, entitled "The Shame of Milwaukee."[22]

Despite segregation and discrimination, mid-twentieth-century Milwaukee and Racine boasted vibrant African American and Latino neighborhoods and commercial areas. For Milwaukee, the most notable was Bronzeville, a predominantly black business and cultural district clustered around Walnut Street in the central city. Walnut Street's jazz and blues clubs competed with those of Chicago, attracting many of the same performers. Adjacent Third Street was the neighborhood's shopping district—more than a hundred small businesses flourished there.

As in many urban settings, the economic backbone of this inner-city neighborhood was broken by "urban renewal" and highway construction in the 1950s and 1960s. In Milwaukee, a group of local business representatives known as the Greater Milwaukee Committee, formed in the aftermath of World War II, oversaw the channeling of tax dollars into housing, highways, and buildings.[23] In 1954 the *Milwaukee Journal* published a series of articles entitled "The Blight within Us," calling for urban renewal in the 98 percent black Hillside area adjacent to Walnut Street. Despite vigorous protests by community members, a Hillside Redevelopment Project was approved by the city council. According to one account:

> Walnut Street was devastated by urban renewal. Better housing was built, but there were fewer places to live, forcing many black homeowners to move. The racist practices of local real estate dealers and the surge of
> il neighborhood associations around the city with restrictive cove-

nants made relocation a nearly impossible task. Ultimately, the housing shortages scattered the black population, its talent and capital.[24]

Still, the neighborhood struggled on,

> until another symbol of post-war progress—the interstate highway— dealt it a mortal blow. . . . Despite public complaints . . . that freeway con- struction was progressing without any plan for the displaced, ground was broken in 1952 for the construction of Milwaukee's segments of the interstate freeway system. By 1959, construction of the north-south free- way began.
>
> This segment ran directly through the heart of the black commercial district, through West Walnut Street. . . . Construction lasted until the 1970s, but it did not take that long for the freeway—which later became known as interstate 43—to destroy Bronzeville.[25]

Lost were 426 businesses, including 57 taverns, 34 grocery stores, 28 furniture stores, 26 automobile shops, 16 restaurants, 106 service retailers, 22 small man- ufacturers, and 9 wholesale firms. The city demolished more than 11,000 hous- ing units in the Inner Core and rebuilt only 7,700, leading to greater crowding in black neighborhoods.[26] Developers also destroyed Borchart Field, home to the Milwaukee Brown Brewers, an African American semiprofessional baseball team, as well as parks, playgrounds, and music clubs.[27] These assaults on black neighborhoods and businesses undermined African American efforts to build assets and to participate in the city's postwar prosperity.

The racial exclusion that structured southeastern Wisconsin's industrial landscape at mid-twentieth century intersected with gender. Black and La- tino women found few jobs in factories and worked predominantly in do- mestic service for most of the twentieth century. Even during World War II, when factory owners hired white women in large numbers as replacements for drafted male workers, they passed over black women. African American women seeking work filed appeals with the federal Fair Employment Practices Committee and, when that failed, wrote to first lady Eleanor Roosevelt.[28] This discrimination led to unusual alignments of interest. In 1943 white women members of United Steelworkers Local 1527 who worked for the Chain Belt Company balked at the firm's demand that they work a ten-hour day and a six-day week to meet wartime production demands. They suggested, instead, that the company hire black women to meet its need for extra labor.[29] As in the rest of the country, industrial managers laid off most women, black and white, at war's end. Those who could not afford to withdraw from the labor market altogether returned to low-end service jobs as domestics or in personal care. Ironically, the gender bias that confined them to the service sector left women better positioned to keep their jobs when deindustrialization hit the cities in the 1970s and 1980s.

By the 1960s in Milwaukee and Racine, as in the rest of the nation, social movements protesting structures of segregation and discrimination grew rapidly. In 1962 NAACP attorney Lloyd Barbee began a series of boycotts of segregated inner-city schools and in 1965 filed a lawsuit against the city of Milwaukee. He argued that the school board drew boundaries based on segregated housing patterns, citing as evidence that most schools outside Milwaukee's Inner Core had less than 10 percent African American students. More than a decade later, a federal judge ruled in favor of the plaintiffs and required the school board to take immediate remedial action, but the board appealed to the Supreme Court, which ordered a new trial. The case was settled out of court in 1979 when the city agreed to implement a five-year desegregation plan.[30]

Activists tackled housing discrimination as well. Vel Phillips—the first woman and first African American elected to Milwaukee's Common Council—first introduced open housing legislation to the council in 1962 and continued to submit it every year until 1968. In 1967 Father James Groppi led a series of fair housing marches in the face of rock-throwing crowds, and the NAACP Youth Council marched to Kosciusko Park to protest the council's refusal to pass an open housing ordinance. Finally, in 1968, the passage of federal open housing law forced the city to adopt measures of its own.[31]

At mid-twentieth century, Milwaukee and Racine were rapidly growing and industrializing cities. The relative prosperity of this period, the growth of the freeway system, and the easy availability of housing loans under the GI Bill, led an increasing number of white families to move to the outskirts of the city and beyond. Lured by cheap land and lower tax rates, businesses followed. A pattern of suburbanization that would continue unabated into the twenty-first century had been born. This pattern deepened the segregation of the city as black families, veterans included, found their opportunities to buy suburban homes circumscribed by mortgage and insurance redlining.[32] City and county spending favored development of new suburban sites, leading to urban decay. In the words of city historian John Gurda, "As the urban fringe, both city and suburban, looked newer and newer, the heart of Milwaukee looked more and more decrepit."[33] The neglect of central-city infrastructure and the exodus of business left the families who remained there separated from jobs.

The deteriorating conditions fed a downward spiral, fueling "white flight," as families with more resources left for areas with better services and schools. Unlike many other cities, there was very little concomitant suburbanization of the black population, as redlining and discrimination continued well into the 1990s.[34] The confluence of city-suburban disparities and racial segregation had devastating consequences for the labor market prospects of central-city families. According to economist Marc Levine, during this period Milwaukee began to evolve into two highly segmented labor markets, one in job-rich suburbia, which was almost exclusively white, the other in the job-poor central city, which was predominantly black.[35]

Segregation in housing and education, and discrimination in labor markets, not only affected the people of color they were designed to exclude or contain. They shaped the fates of all families who could not afford to move outside the central city and who shared in the poor city services, dilapidated housing stock, and substandard schools of the Inner Core. When certain occupations became associated with blacks or immigrants—for example, work in tanneries, foundries, or domestic service—working conditions and wages declined for all who held those jobs. The fate of the very poor in Milwaukee and Racine—whether black, white, or Latino—was thus shaped by forces of racial exclusion.

LOST FACTORY JOBS, NEW JOBS IN THE SERVICE SECTOR, AND THE ASSAULT ON UNIONS: 1970–2000

In the 1970s southeastern Wisconsin, like most other northern industrial regions, found itself struggling to hold onto its employment base. Manufacturing firms, faced with rising oil prices and a sharp decline in profits, searched for new investment opportunities abroad and sought to lower labor costs through outsourcing production. Emerging technologies and organizational strategies offered previously unimagined possibilities for integrating and managing spatially dispersed global enterprises, while new trade rules and financial practices, as well as protections for Western intellectual property and technology, made it easier for firms to abandon their U.S. production facilities for more lucrative arrangements elsewhere.

This "spatial fix"[36] for struggling firms devastated Milwaukee and Racine. Between 1979 and 1995 the Milwaukee-Racine metropolitan area lost more than 35 percent of its manufacturing jobs.[37] The story for inner-city Milwaukee was even more dramatic: between 1970 and 2000, 80 percent of manufacturing jobs disappeared.[38] Firms with a deep history in the region—Johnson Controls, Miller Brewing, Briggs & Stratton, Johnson's Wax, Delco Electronics, and many others—fell into debt and closed or laid off workers. In the 1960s American Motors and General Motors had provided UAW jobs, Heil made truck bodies, and A. O. Smith welded undercarriages for nearly every American-made passenger car. The Allis-Chalmers Corporation made electric generators in a "cluster of cathedral-sized factories."[39] Similarly, Racine was home to S. C. Johnson and Sons, which produced household wax and other chemicals in a sprawling facility whose corporate offices were designed by Frank Lloyd Wright. Other Racine employers included J. I. Case, a heavy equipment manufacturer; Hamilton Beach, which produced small electrical appliances; and Bombardier Motors. One by one, these long-established industries began to lay off workers and shut their doors. No longer could workers expect a lifelong career in manufacturing at union wages, with pensions, health benefits, and vacation. Any job at all became the goal, particularly since new information sector jobs paying comparable wages required far more education and specialized training.

The *Wall Street Journal* told the story of Ron Larson—Wayne Hall's stepson—to illustrate the new situation in which southeastern Wisconsin workers found themselves. In 1971 Larson went to work as a welder in a fabrication shop. "By 1981 he was earning roughly as much as his step-father. But the shop closed that year. Mr. Larson has held many jobs since—tour boat operator, trucker, air-conditioning repairman. Except for one year, he has yet to earn as much as he did at the welding job. Today he works as a computer support technician, but the contract job runs just six weeks and he doesn't know if he'll still be working after that."[40]

As with the growth of job opportunities in manufacturing, their decline did not affect black and white men and women in the same way. Because black men had not attained significant seniority, their job loss in the 1970s and 1980s was devastating—twice as severe as that experienced by the nation as a whole during the Depression. The *Milwaukee Journal Sentinel* noted:

> In little more than a generation, Milwaukee has morphed from an El Dorado of unrivaled opportunity for African Americans—and a beacon for their middle-class aspirations—to a locus of downward mobility without equal among other big U.S. cities.....In 1970, the black poverty rate in Milwaukee was 22 percent lower than the U.S. national figure.... By 2000 ... [it] it was 34 percent higher.[41]

While chronicling manufacturing decline and its effects on workers, these media reports spent little time exploring a contemporaneous pattern of service sector growth, tied to a reconfiguration of the norms of social reproduction. Stable, lifelong blue-collar jobs *were* disappearing, but new jobs were being created. For many reasons, including the declining wages of working-class men, women's work hours outside the home rose by 40 percent between 1973 and 1996, creating a new demand for services to replace their household labor.[42] Families began to purchase more restaurant meals and take-out dinners, and more care for children and the elderly. Those who could afford it took more clothing to laundries and hired cleaning and gardening services. In a self-reinforcing cycle, the new consumption patterns associated with women's work created new demands for services.

At the same time, the health care sector expanded dramatically. Aurora Health Care—a corporation that owns hospitals, clinics, and nursing homes and in 2003 was southeastern Wisconsin's largest employer—took over the Heil truck factory.[43] Public services grew as well—jobs cleaning streets and parks, processing parking tickets, and serving school lunches. Temporary work proliferated. Manpower Inc., which started its operations in Milwaukee in 1948, emerged in the 1990s as the nation's largest temporary services firm (and for a while, its largest employer) with over $5 billion in annual revenues. Milwaukee topped a list of U.S. cities in *low-wage* job growth between 1970 and 1990. In both Milwaukee and Racine, services surpassed the number of manufacturing jobs in 1981 and low-wage service sector employment accounted for virtually all new jobs in the 1980s.[44]

Three service industries alone accounted for half of U.S. employment growth between 1992 and 2005: retail trade, health services, and business services.[45] A review of the top ten firms in the Milwaukee area in 1970 and in 2004 reflects these national trends (see appendix D). All of Milwaukee's top employers in 1970 were manufacturers or brewers. In contrast, in 2004 the top ten all provided services; four were in health services and two in retail. These firms offered mostly low-end, labor-intensive service sector jobs—positions that were far more likely to be filled by women. Nationally, over 80 percent of women hold jobs in service industries, compared to 55 percent of men, and this trend holds for Milwaukee and Racine as well.[46] As southeastern Wisconsin shifted from an industrial to a service sector base, labor market opportunities for men—and particularly less-educated men—saw a steep decline, while those for women increased. The median wages for these low-end service sector jobs hover close to the poverty line, if not below it, even for full-time work, et at least a third of retail jobs and a quarter of other low-wage service sector jobs are part-time.[47]

Across the nation, the low-wage service sector employs not only a dispro-portionate number of women, but a disproportionate number of women of color. As Evelyn Nakano Glenn has shown, the segmentation of this part of the labor market is closely tied to the racial histories of particular regions, fol-lowing what she calls the "racial-ethnic caste lines" that structured the growth of their economies. In *Unequal Freedom*, Glenn recounts the evolution of labor market segmentation in three parts of the United States, tracing labor rela-tions between blacks and whites in the U.S. South, Mexicans and Anglos in the Southwest, and Japanese and other immigrants in Hawaii. She shows how historic labor market boundaries, bolstered by notions of inherent traits that suited women of color to domestic work, structured these women's entry into low-wage service sector jobs once domestic employment was commodified and moved outside homes. As more-educated women moved into high-end service sector jobs, or midlevel positions in schools, offices, and hospitals, the firms producing the services that replaced their labor in the home disproportion-ately hired women of color.[48] In her analysis of data from the Bureau of Labor Statistics, sociologist Susan Thistle also documents this trend: "Though their employment in private household work has dropped sharply, black women are over-represented among teaching assistants in preschools, maids in hotels, cleaners in office buildings and cooks and cashiers in fast food outlets and they make up one-quarter of those in poorly paid health service occupations."[49]

Moreover, conditions in these jobs often mimicked the lack of regulation in domestic employment. As Jason DeParle has written:

> Nursing aides do difficult, dangerous work. They get hurt twice as often as coal miners and earn less than half the pay. They traffic in infectious fluids, in blood, urine, vomit and poop. They handle corpses. They get attacked by patients. Above all, they lift. They lift people from beds and wheelchairs; they lift them from toilets and showers. They lift at awkward angles and times, and the people they lift can slip and resist. Nearly one in six nursing aides gets injured each year, and nearly half the incidents involve back injuries, where the risk of recurring problems is great. Coal mines and steel mills have grown safer with the years. Nurs-ing homes have grown more dangerous.[50]

Legacies of discrimination and racial hierarchies likewise structured employ-ers' attitudes toward African American men. New jobs in the information-intensive branches of the service sector required high levels of education, placing them out of reach for laid-off factory workers, but black men also had special difficulty finding jobs in the *low-wage* service sector. Several national studies help clarify why this was the case. Philip Moss and Chris Tilly have studied employers' gender- and race-coded ideas about postindustrial skills.[51] They note that most low-wage services and retail sector jobs involve communication with customers. They require interpersonal skills and a friendly and personable demeanor—abilities that, along with enthusiasm, a "positive work attitude," and dependability, are often referred to as "soft skills." Based on surveys at fifty-six firms in four industries in Detroit and Los Angeles, Moss and Tilly found that the vast majority of employers harbored negative views of black men's interactional skills and motivation.

Other studies confirmed these findings with different methods. Using an experimental audit approach, in which testers of different races but with identical qualifications apply for jobs, Pager, Western, and Bonikowsky showed a powerful employer bias against black men—and especially young black men—for service sector jobs. In their experiment, 31 percent of white testers applying for jobs received callbacks, compared to 15 percent of blacks. White testers were frequently encouraged to apply for better positions that involved more public contact (for example, an interviewer would encourage a person who applied to be a dishwasher to try for a wait staff position), but no black testers received such encouragement. Conversely, employers "channeled down" many black testers (offering, for example, a position as a stocker when they had applied for a job in sales), but in only one instance did this happen to a white tester.[52] By the year 2000, in part as a result of these biases, for every ten African American women who held a job in Milwaukee, only seven black men had work.[53] This reduced the overall income of black families and shifted the burden of their support to black women.

The 1970s and 1980s saw not only the loss of manufacturing jobs but also a shift in the relative power of employers and workers. During this period, firms, financial institutions, state government, and federal agencies began to adopt newly ascendant free market principles that supported the free movement of capital and sought to roll back many forms of regulation and social programs. They mounted a number of initiatives that undermined the rights of workers and the labor contracts they had forged in previous decades of struggle and negotiation. In 1981 Ronald Reagan signaled this new era when he used the Taft-Hartley Act to fire striking air traffic controllers and break their union. Equally important, although perhaps less noticed, were two regulatory decisions taken during Reagan's presidency. In 1985 the Federal Trade Commission ruled that firms could hire workers from temporary service agencies to replace strikers. And in 1986 the National Labor Relations Board allowed companies to legally replace their permanent workers with temporary workers during an employee lockout.[54] These actions signaled a new era of government support for employer-led retrenchment on labor rights. At the height of McCarthyism in the 1950s, the number of U.S. workers fired each year for trying to organize a union was in the hundreds, but by the 1990s more than twenty thousand workers per year claimed discrimination for engaging in union activities.[55]

Organized labor in southeastern Wisconsin felt these legal and regulatory shifts. In 1977, in response to a strike by Milwaukee police, the Wisconsin state legislature passed a law that prefigured Reagan's use of Taft-Hartley; it required binding arbitration of public employee strikes, virtually ending such job actions in the public sector.[56] A failed strike at the Briggs & Stratton plant in Milwaukee in 1983 gave managers new leverage to demand concessions from workers. It was widely suspected that managers, encouraged by the new legal and regulatory environment under the Reagan administration, provoked the strike in order to gain these concessions.[57] In the late 1980s, during a twenty-seven-month strike at the Patrick Cudahy meatpacking plant in Milwaukee County, managers used minority workers as strikebreakers to undermine the United Food and Commercial Workers union. When the strike ended, workers saw both their wages and their benefits reduced. These actions, and others like them, created a situation in which all workers were less willing to stand up for themselves and more likely to yield ground.

The growth of the service sector in Milwaukee had presented new opportunities for unions. In the late 1970s, 1199—a national union of hospital and health care workers—organized locals in a number of Milwaukee and Racine hospitals and nursing homes. The Service Employees International Union (SEIU) also organized in this sector and the American Foundation of State, County and Municipal Employees (AFSCME) represented a significant proportion of public sector workers. Multiracial groups of women led many of these locals. Members publicized their activities in mimeographed newsletters and in the pages of *Racine Labor*.[58]

Reviewing the stories in *Racine Labor*, we can trace shifts in the power of employers and workers in the service sector during this period. In May 1985 the employees of SEIU local 150 in Racine celebrated a victory in a long-running conflict with their employer, Saint Luke's Hospital. The economy was still reeling from the recession of the early 1980s, and the hospital was demanding wage concessions of 10–15 percent, but the new contract signed by both parties provided wage increases, improved insurance benefits, and continued protections against subcontracting of jobs. Local 150 represented 186 workers in dietary, laundry, housekeeping, nursing assistant, maintenance, and skilled trade classifications. Most of its members were African American and Latina women. These women were aware that their wages were far lower than those of southeastern Wisconsin's industrial workers. "Hospital workers have long been second class members of our economy," one bargaining committee member told the newspaper. "Our wages are typically lower than those found in manufacturing, but due to the fact that we care for human lives, we feel our wages should be closer together."[59]

At that point in the 1980s, unions representing health care workers were enjoying the gains of growth in the sector. Locals not only protected their members' interests but launched community programs and engaged in charitable work. For example, in March 1985 local 150 had joined five other community organizations to raise funds for famine victims in Ethiopia.[60] But, in the increasingly antiunion climate of that decade, employers were emboldened to challenge labor in new ways. The first in a series of ultimately fatal assaults on local 150 came a mere two months after members had successfully negotiated their contract. In June, Saint Luke's Hospital called all of its nursing assistants to a meeting, handed them a letter saying that their jobs were permanently eliminated, and escorted them off the premises. The hospital claimed the new contract did not offer recourse if an entire job classification was dropped.[61] The nursing assistants who were fired had earned a living wage and received benefits through their jobs. Over the ensuing years, employers throughout the nation succeeded in rolling back wages and benefits in these positions. By 2004 nursing assistants who were demographically and economically identical to the women who had bargained with Saint Luke's in the 1980s depended on the state for food stamps and medical assistance. Many of the women we interviewed had held these newly devalued and insecure nursing assistant jobs.

The growth of such poorly paid positions in the service sector could not compensate for the loss of so many good manufacturing jobs, and by the 1990s southeastern Wisconsin's economy was in crisis. The city's business elite, represented by the Greater Milwaukee Committee, began working with city officials to use strategic public investments to attract "high-end" knowledge and information sector employers. Milwaukee spent more than a billion dollars on tourism promotion and downtown sports, cultural, and enter-tainment facilities.[62] Heavily influenced by Richard Florida's notions of the "creative class" as a linchpin of urban development, the local Chamber of Commerce sponsored organizations of "young professionals" and roundtables to mentor small business executives.[63] Racine invested, albeit on a smaller scale, in a downtown revitalization project, turning its decaying warehouses into a harbor complex to attract tourism and convention activity, and drawing new retailers and office space rentals to the central city.

While modestly successful in their pursuit of urban redevelopment, the cities' attempts to capture high-end services worsened income disparities within the region. As Sassen has noted, the shift from manufacturing to services in urban centers is a process in which "polarization tendencies embedded in the organization of service industries come to the fore."[64] While in 1979 the wealthiest 10 percent of Milwaukee's households earned six times as much as the bottom tenth, in 1999 they earned fifteen times as much. Like former disparities in industrial employment, this polarization did not affect black and white families equally. In 1991 the *New York Times* published a scathing indictment of the way that Milwaukee's downtown renovation and transition from a manufacturing to a service-based economy left black residents behind:

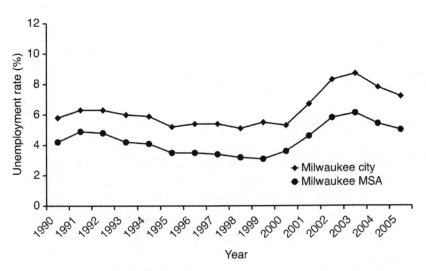

FIGURE 2.1. Average annual unemployment rates in city of Milwaukee and in Milwaukee Metropolitan Statistical Area. *Source:* U.S. Bureau of Labor Statistics, Local Area Unemployment Statistics, http://stats.bls.gov/lau/#tables.

Milwaukee pulled itself out of a serious slump . . . and staved off the current recession. . . . But that strategy has had an unintended but equally profound secondary effect. It has devastated the city's poor black neighborhoods, whose residents thrived in the high-wage union jobs of the city's manufacturing heyday and are now adrift on a rising tide of unemployment, crime and despair.[65]

Despite downtown redevelopment, the flight of business from central-city Milwaukee to suburban sites accelerated in the 1990s.[66] All net job growth in the region after 1995 was suburban, leading economists to talk about a "structural spatial mismatch" between pockets of high unemployment and the locations of new jobs.[67] The city of Milwaukee gained just over 1,000 jobs between 1991 and 2000, while its surrounding suburbs gained more than 107,000.[68] In 2000, 92 percent of the Milwaukee metropolitan area's black labor force lived in the city, compared to only 21 percent of its white labor force. Figures 2.1 and 2.2 show the difference in unemployment rates between the cities of Milwaukee and Racine and the metropolitan areas that encompassed their suburbs as well. Unemployment rates were regularly two to six points higher in the city of Racine and one to three points higher in the city of Milwaukee than in the larger metro areas. Despite hefty investments in urban renewal, both

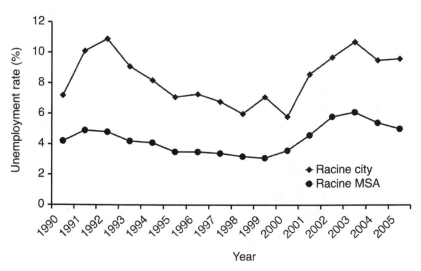

FIGURE 2.2. Average annual unemployment rates in city of Racine and in Racine Metropolitan Statistical Area. *Source:* U.S. Bureau of Labor Statistics, Local Area Unemployment Statistics, http://stats.bls.gov/lau/#tables.

Milwaukee and Racine lost population between 1970 and 2005. Milwaukee's population dropped from a high of 740,000 in 1960 to under 580,000 in 2005. Racine's high point of 95,000 came in 1970, dropping to under 80,000 by 2005.

THE POSTINDUSTRIAL LABOR MARKET: 2000–PRESENT

As white families and jobs moved to the suburbs, the inner-city areas of Milwaukee and Racine became both poorer and more segregated. Social scientists using 1990 census data classified both Milwaukee and Racine as hypersegregated—characterized by profound racial inequality.[69] Based on data for the year 2000, the Census Bureau labeled Milwaukee the most segregated city in the nation.[70] Racine was not populous enough to be considered in the latter analysis, which focused only on the largest U.S. cities, but other data reveal significant segregation there as well. In a national study that compared black and white income inequality across metropolitan areas, the only two cities outside the South on a list of the ten most unequal places were Milwaukee (ranked fifth) and Racine (tenth).[71] Over 80 percent of the Racine metro area's "minority" population resided within the city boundaries in 2000.[72] Such segregation made it easier for conservative politicians and pundits to frame southeastern Wisconsin's economic problems as issues of race. Unemployment and welfare caseloads were presented as evidence of the moral failures of the inner-city poor, rather than of business decisions and trends in government investment. It made it easier for conservatives to apply denigrating discourses to inner city residents, and to argue that new doctrines of contractual citizenship were needed to "solve" their problems.

Between 2000 and 2002 the bottom fell out of the southeastern Wisconsin labor market as the region experienced first its version of the nationwide recession and then a "jobless recovery." While the recession was in itself relatively mild, the labor market downturn was severe and the recovery extraordinarily slow. The lack of job creation in the years that followed was unprecedented, with unemployment in 2004 higher than it had been at the recession's start.[73] Federal Reserve chair Ben Bernanke noted, in observing these trends, that the resulting weak labor market "imposed hardship on millions of American workers, their families and communities."[74] In metropolitan Milwaukee, economist Marc Levine noted that the black unemployment rate was more than four times the white rate in 2001.[75]

As many social scientists have argued, the unemployment rate itself downplays the problem of joblessness. Official measures of unemployment consider only the number of civilians actively seeking work who cannot find it. They do not include working-age people who do not have jobs but are not "in the labor force" in the sense of seeking employment. This group can include students, homemakers, and the voluntarily self-employed but also "discouraged" workers (who have given up looking for a job), the formerly incarcerated, and the disabled. For this reason, some analysts prefer to use a measure of "joblessness," which counts unemployment among the entire working-age population.[76] Applying this measure, the University of Wisconsin–Milwaukee's Center for Economic Development found that in 2002 nearly 60 percent of working-age black men in Milwaukee were jobless, by far the highest rate of any city surveyed by the Bureau of Labor Statistics.[77] In some inner-city neighborhoods, where black men had official unemployment rates of more than 20 percent, joblessness rates ran as high as 64 percent. In all, Milwaukee had sixty-two census tracts in which the majority of black men were jobless. The disparity in white and black unemployment in the city was higher than in any other major cities except Washington, D.C., and Baltimore.[78] This lack of employment for black men challenged African American families and households, shifting the burden of household support to the shoulders of black women. As primary caregivers and as sole wage earners for their families, they found themselves drawn into the new terms of the solitary wage bargain.

Patterns of deindustrialization and employers' racial attitudes explain, in part, the large number of African American men who Levine found to be "outside" the workforce in 2002. But social policy in other areas also played a role. The "war on drugs" that began in the 1980s and the tough incarceration policies that followed took their toll in Milwaukee and Racine, even more dramatically than in most cities. While new drug laws led to disproportionate rates of imprisonment of African American men across the nation, the imbalance in Wisconsin was particularly striking. The state's ratio of black to white incarceration rates at the end of the 1990s was 20:1—the third highest in the nation. During that decade, the black:white ratio of new prison sentences for *drug* offenses had risen from 22:1 (in 1990) to 67:1 (in 1999), with nearly half of those new sentences for the ambiguous crime of "intent to deliver." Researchers have attributed much of this disparity to "back end" criminal justice processing, such as sentencing decisions, but also to law enforcement practices such as "sweeps," where police clear out "high-crime" neighborhoods by arresting everyone they can on any plausible charge.[79]

A history of drug convictions has a strong impact on men's subsequent labor market prospects. Using experimental audits with trained testers in the city of Milwaukee, sociologist Devah Pager found that 34 percent of white applicants who did not report criminal records received callbacks compared to 17 percent of those who did; among black applicants, 14 percent of those without criminal records received callbacks, versus 5 percent of those with records. The bottom line for black men—who even without records received less favorable treatment than whites with records—was that their already slim chances of gaining employment were reduced significantly once they had a felony conviction.[80]

A profile of one Milwaukee zip code in 2007 revealed the severity of this problem and the way it intersected with welfare reform and a jobless recovery to devastate poor households and communities. The area with zip code 53206 roughly corresponds to the inner-city neighborhoods of North Division, Borchest Field, and Arlington Heights. This is one of the poorest parts of the city, and it has been called a "bellwether for poverty changes in Milwaukee" and the nation.[81] It also historically has had the highest number of welfare recipients in the city. As a result of welfare reform, this number dropped from 4,779 in 1994 to 663 in 2000 (though by June 2001, as the region felt the recession, it rose to 744).[82]

The neighborhoods of zip code 53206 look like a movie set for a film about the early twentieth century. Most of the housing stock was built around the time of World War I. The frame and tar-paper two-flats and bungalows show the wear of the dozens of families who have rented them since that time. Corner grocery stores of the same vintage abound, as do hairdressers, storefront houses of worship with names like Church of the True Faithful, Sweet Communion Baptist, and Higher Love Ministry, and, increasingly, day care centers offering "first and second shifts" for children four weeks to twelve years.

The resident population of zip code 53206 is 97 percent black. In 2001 Department of Corrections data showed that nearly two-thirds of men aged thirty to thirty-four—more than twenty-five hundred individuals—were, or had been, incarcerated. The number of adults released from prison into the community had risen 336 percent since 1993, and the number of residents doing time for "drug offenses only" had increased fivefold during that period. As a result of these trends, the demographic profile of the neighborhood was deeply skewed. While the numbers of African American men and women living in the zip code were equal for those under fifteen years of age, for the twenty- to twenty-four-year age group there were seventy-four males for every hundred females. For thirty- to thirty-four-year-olds, the situation was even more dramatic, with only sixty-four men present for every hundred women. The entirety of this disparity was due to incarceration of men in state and local correctional facilities.[83]

The economic effects of male incarceration on central-city neighborhoods were profound. Released prisoners faced severe barriers to employment but also found their access to social services and educational programs limited. Many were barred from subsidized housing and from receiving federal grants in support of education. Those with drug convictions were ineligible for food stamps. Child support obligations—enforced by the state when a man's partner received social services—added a debt burden that complicated attempts to gain financial stability.[84] Based on similar data for inner-city Chicago, Peck and Theodore have argued that the prison system contributes to the hyper-segmentation of the labor market along lines of race, to the social production of systematic unemployability among black men, and to the economic and social decline of communities to which men return from prison.[85]

As Pager's study suggests, families suffered from the loss of men's income not only during the time they were incarcerated but afterward. As one woman in our study explained:

> You've got everybody's daddy, brother, and uncle locked up in the Wisconsin prison system. These men come home after ten and twelve years, and they still can't get a job to provide for their kids . . . which makes them become repeat offenders. Because they're gonna sell dope or they're gonna steal something . . . to get shoes for their kids. How can you live your life if you've done your time, but you can't go get a job? Even McDonald's won't hire convicted felons.

Another woman echoed these concerns:

> Get these men jobs. Give them a chance to work. Give them a chance to go to school. Give them a chance to get their foot in the door of a good company where they can provide for their kids. Then you can sweat them about child support, because then they'll have the money to pay it. . . . My brother, he went to jail on purpose once because he got back out here after two years and nobody would give him a job.

The absence of so many working-age men from the labor force, and the difficulties encountered by those who had done time in finding work, had a tremendous impact on the earnings and stability of central-city families.[86] In zip code 53206, the percentage of family income-tax filers who were single parents rose from 80 percent in 1993 to 91 percent in 2005. Over half of these families, almost all headed by women, had income below the poverty line, and more than a third reported earnings below $10,000.[87]

The quantitative evidence from this inner-city neighborhood suggests that single mothers began entering the labor market in large numbers in the early to mid-1990s—a period that saw both strong economic growth and shifts in welfare policy that made enrollment more difficult.[88] Their labor market presence continued to grow through 2000 and beyond. Over time, however, as welfare reform tightened rules and encouraged diversion of applicants, those entering the workforce included more women with greater obstacles to full-time employment: health problems, or family members with health problems, or a profound lack of job skills. Researchers at the University of Wisconsin compared cohorts of women who left welfare for work in 1995, 1997, and 1999. They found that the vast majority (81–84 percent) worked in the year after exiting welfare programs but that earnings were lower for each successive cohort. While mean earnings for those leaving in 1995 were $9,600 a year, the figure dropped to $8,100 for those leaving in 1997 and $7,300 for those leaving in 1999. This decline, they argued, is consistent with the hypothesis that the increasingly stringent work-first welfare program was "perhaps pushing people with fewer skills and more barriers to working into the labor market where they accept lower paying jobs or work fewer hours."[89]

These women shouldered the burden of raising families on their own in communities where working-age men were disproportionately absent. They entered a labor market where deindustrialization had eradicated the decent, unionized, working-class jobs of earlier decades and where the growth of the service sector created far more employment in nursing homes, fast food chains, and big-box retailers than in financial services or office work. Many found jobs cleaning and caring for children or preparing and selling food. These positions—continuous with women's earlier work in domestic service—provided neither a living wage nor supportive benefits. Such were the new terms of the solitary wage bargain. But it was not only employers who had abrogated their responsibilities. The state had eliminated welfare entitlements and restructured programs in ways that made them less sufficient and more punitive. The reforms limited recipients' lifetime eligibility for benefits and imposed strict work rules and other behavioral requirements. Welfare thus became a resource to be used strategically to compensate for the uncertainties and inadequacies of the low end of the labor market—a tattered, threadbare safety net to support their families.

BAD JOBS IN A STAGNANT ECONOMY: EMPLOYMENT AMONG THE WOMEN IN OUR STUDY

The stories of how the women in our study ended up on welfare had a great deal to do with the kinds of jobs they found in the cities' postindustrial labor markets. Contrary to the presuppositions built into TANF, the women we interviewed all had extensive work experience. Nearly three-quarters of them had held onto jobs for a year or more, and some had histories of promotions and responsible managerial positions. As we sat with each woman and mapped out her employment history, a complex picture of the low-wage economy emerged: Popeye's and Walmart, grocery stores and pharmacies, temp work and stints cleaning hotel rooms.

These women's work histories reflected the region's transition from a manufacturing to a service economy. All knew that the era of good manufacturing jobs was over. Many (nearly 40 percent) had worked in factories at some point in the past but as temporary employees supplied by the region's booming temp-staffing firms and franchises: Manpower Inc., Adecco, P. A. Staffing, Kelly Services, and others. As one woman said, "Factories—you can't do that—because the factories are picking up and moving overseas." Another woman who had tried for years to get a job at S. C. Johnson in Racine said, "After you work there for eighteen months [as a temp], they have you fill out an application and go on the waiting list, and the waiting list is like two years long." A woman who was making $8 an hour in a bookbinding factory was keenly aware of how lucky she was: "There's not a lot of jobs at this time, you know. It's not like you say, 'Oh, I'm going to quit this job and I'm going to find another tomorrow.' I don't think that's gonna happen because of the problems in the economy. So it's better you stay in the job you have."

In their last jobs prior to receiving welfare, nearly a quarter of women in our study had worked in retail sales or telemarketing, around a fifth in fast food or food service, 15 percent as nursing assistants, and 12 percent as clericals. Only 9 percent had worked in manufacturing. Two women had held positions in day care, one as a security guard, one as a janitor, and one as an exotic dancer (see figure 2.3). This distribution of jobs was consistent with that reported by the

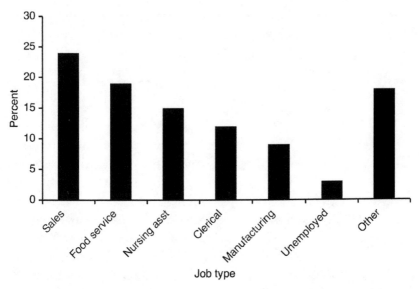

FIGURE 2.3. Distribution of women in the study by type of job last held. *Source:* Interview data.

state of Wisconsin's Legislative Audit Bureau: the top three job categories for women transitioning from welfare were nursing assistance, food service, and retail.[90] A third of the women we interviewed had obtained their current or last job through a temporary staffing agency. The state audit found that an even greater proportion—42 percent—had obtained jobs through this channel.

These women received hourly wages that ranged from $5.57 to $13.75 an hour, with an average of $8.63. Their mean annual earnings in these jobs were far below the poverty level, which was $14,494 for a single parent with two children in 2003. We had access to state data on the women's earnings from 1998 to 2004, which peaked at $5,617 in 2002 and dropped to $1,950 in 2003 (see figure 2.4).[91] Because we selected our sample from women receiving cash assistance in December 2003, we would expect their earnings to have dropped in that year, as a result of the crisis or loss of earnings that had led them to turn to welfare. Only four study participants had earnings above the poverty line in 2002. In comparison, the legislative audit found that the average annual income of all Wisconsin workfare participants who entered the workforce in 2003 was $9,291, with less than 22 percent earning above the poverty level.[92] The writers of the state report cautioned, however, that their figure was an overestimate because it was based on tax returns and employer reported wages and excluded several thousand women who left workfare but could not find jobs and reported no earnings. This explains the higher average earnings they report.

Consistent with other studies of individuals receiving welfare, we found that women supplemented their low wages with a variety of other forms of income, which nonetheless yielded incomes that were well below the poverty threshold (see figure 2.5). Figure 2.4 shows the array of sources on which women relied. The category "social support" includes W-2 cash payments and food stamps as reported in the state data base. We were not able to include the value of housing subsidies (received by one-third of the women), or of WIC or child care subsidies (received by nearly all). We did include child support in our calculations: about half (45 percent) of the women to whom we spoke had received more than $1,000 of child support from their children's fathers over the past six years. In addition, five women were receiving Supplemental Security Income for a disabled child or because of their own disability.

About two-thirds of the women shared living expenses with, or received fairly substantial support from, a partner or other family members. We did not attempt to quantify this aid, given that it was informal and intermittent, often not in cash, and given that there were complex reciprocities involved.

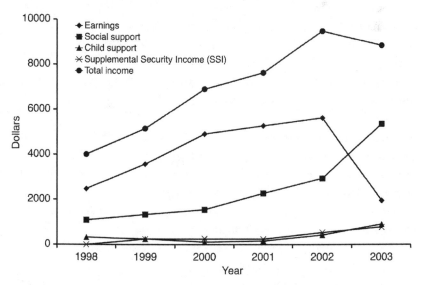

FIGURE 2.4. Mean annual income of women in the study by source. *Source:* Authors' calculations using data from the state of Wisconsin's unemployment insurance and social program use databases. See note 93.

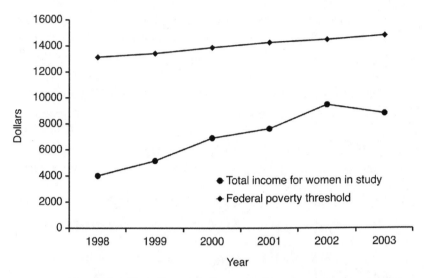

FIGURE 2.5. Mean income (from all sources) of women in the study compared to poverty threshold. *Source:* Authors' income calculations (see note 93); U.S. Census Bureau, Housing and Household Economic Statistics Division, Poverty Thresholds 2003, http://www.census .gov/hhes/www/poverty/threshld/thresh03/html.

But the existence of such support helps to explain how women survived on incomes that were only 30 to 65 percent of the poverty threshold. In addition, 70 percent of women had "informal" earnings. Nearly half had done baby-sitting, more than a quarter had done hair or nails, and about 15 percent of women had cleaned houses or other buildings for off-the-books cash payment. Two sold plasma to blood banks, and one cooked and sold hot lunches to city workers.

Even entry-level low-wage service sector jobs were hard to come by in the years leading up to our study. In the summer of 2003 the economies of Milwau-kee and Racine were in recession. That year, the cities' unemployment rates reached 9.5 percent and 11.8 percent, respectively, and these numbers stayed high through 2004. By October 2005 some analysts were saying guardedly that the region had turned a corner, as metro-area jobs showed some growth—up 0.6 percent over the previous year. Nevertheless six of ten major industries were still recording employment declines (trade, transport, and utilities; finance; other services; information services; government; and manufactur-ing). Only construction, leisure and hospitality, health services, and business services posted modest gains. Production and earnings indicators were still declining, with both average weekly and average hourly wages down. Home sales and new construction contracts were lower than a year before, while the local consumer price index was rising.[93] Observing these trends, the Center on Wisconsin Strategy concluded, "Wisconsin has done better the past few years than much of the depressed Midwest region, but that's cold comfort when you consider these broader trends. . . . The working class in Wisconsin is getting hammered."[94]

One woman, who had been hired at Walmart just prior to our interview, described the difficulty she had experienced finding work in this environment:

> These past two years, I was just working for temporary agencies—just one day here and another day there. Then, a whole week without nothing. Some of them lasted a week or two weeks, some of them a month. I couldn't find a job! It was just crazy. I applied everywhere. And they didn't call me. I called them. I didn't know what was wrong with me.

Another woman made the same point more succinctly: "Jobs right now are an endangered species!"

Most women recognized that even low-wage entry-level jobs required more skill and educational qualifications than they had. One explained:

> I know I need my GED, and with the Lord's help and time I'm gonna get that. As you can see on that paper [her work history timeline] I'm not scared of work. I'm a hard-working person. But right now all I need is a chance. I ain't been working in a long time. You know the hardest thing is to get a job in Milwaukee and I don't understand why.

Aside from the difficulty of finding employment, women were aware of the inadequacy of the jobs that were available, especially when compared to those of the past. One summarized the situation: "A lot of businesses are closing and people are losing their jobs. . . . There's so many people here that look for jobs every day and all you can find is fast food restaurants, and that's not gonna pay the bills." A mother of three echoed this sentiment: "You know, working at McDonald's is not going to take care of three or four kids. I just went to a whole job fair where none of the employers were offering jobs that pay over $6 an hour."

While 2001–2003 were years of downturn, from a longer-term perspective the service sector jobs these women held had proliferated from the 1970s onward, at least in part as a replacement for the labor of women in the home. In food service and waitressing jobs, in nursing homes and home health care, in day care and cleaning, poor women plugged gaps in other women's strategies for combining work and family, while generating care dilemmas of their own. In the 1990s, as the number of manufacturing jobs declined, positions of this ilk multiplied in Milwaukee and Racine, leading local business executives to worry about rising wages and the availability of labor in the sector. Meanwhile, in Washington, advocates of welfare reform touted the widespread availability of these jobs as evidence that women cut from the welfare rolls would be able to find work.

By the early days of the twenty-first century, however, it was clear that labor markets were not functioning as they had for most of the twentieth. In a frenzied search for "flexibility," employers had ditched a long list of responsibilities for their workers: a commitment to job security if the employee performed well, benefits after a probationary period, provisions for sick leave, predictable hours. From 1970 through 2008, they had held wages to 1970s levels, despite vast increases in productivity.[95] These trends diminished temporarily during the late 1990s, but by 2001 they were back in force. Working under these conditions was difficult for anyone but nearly impossible for people with significant family responsibilities. And yet women—among them single mothers—increasingly worked in these jobs.

This was the labor market context faced by the women in our study. While jobs in the low-wage service sector had proliferated from 1970 to 2003, their working conditions were shaped by the racialized and gendered legacies of domestic labor. These conditions worsened as employers were emboldened to confront unions and roll back wages and benefits during the Reagan years. Men's employment was undercut by deindustrialization; black men found their subsequent entry into jobs in the low-wage service sector barred by discrimination. The racially skewed enforcement policies of the war on drugs also took a toll on their ability to find and keep a job. As low-wage women took on greater and greater responsibility for the support of their families, suburbanization and the racial segregation of labor markets limited their access to decent jobs in good times, and left them bereft of employment opportunities during periods of economic downturn. As a boundary institution of the labor market, welfare was the safety net on which women relied in periods when they could not work or could not find jobs. We now turn to the changing structure of that institution.

CHAPTER THREE

WELFARE REFORM'S CONTENT

BUILDING CONNECTIONS BETWEEN
WORK AND WELFARE

I think there's two ways to look at the W-2 program. One is as an economic program designed to allow participants to become more part of the economic fabric of the community. The second—maybe just as motivating—is to get a low-cost workforce into the economy so that employers don't have to pay ever-increasing wages.

**DIRECTOR OF CASE MANAGEMENT SERVICES,
MAXIMUS, INC., W-2 CONTRACT AGENCY**

THE NEXUS OF WORK AND WELFARE

Sitting in an office in inner-city Milwaukee, well into our lengthy interview, a manager in one of Wisconsin's contracted welfare agencies grew more reflective. "I have a belief that W-2 was formulated when it was for a number of reasons," she said.

It was a work-first program because the labor market demanded that there be a work-first program. When you need workers—we've seen over and over that this country, the business people, will do whatever is necessary to find workers, whether that means NAFTA, illegals—it doesn't really matter—prisoners. So, that was a driving force in W-2.

She continued:

At the time W-2 started, poor people, the unemployed, had higher value than they had ever had in many, many, many years—and maybe never before—because of the demand of the labor market. So there was a high value given to that group of people. Their value's not quite so high right now. The economy has been struggling. Everyone is saying they are seeing an upswing, but I think we are probably headed for a jobless recovery. . . . So I have always seen it as an economic development issue. I see it as a supply and demand issue. However, I'm willing to parlay that into something that's a good thing for people, you know, so I'm not cynical about that at all.

This manager was not the only one to suggest that Wisconsin's version of PRWORA—called Wisconsin Works, or W-2—was deeply intertwined with the state's labor market dynamics, and especially those of the southeastern cities of Milwaukee and Racine. When state officials first unveiled the proposal for the new program at public hearings in 1995, representatives of the Restaurant Association and other Milwaukee employers spoke in its favor, connecting the need for welfare reform to issues of labor scarcity and what they perceived to be high wages in the local retail and service sectors. From its inception, when business interests played a strong role in designing the program, through its early days, when a robust economy and tight labor market helped many women who left welfare find jobs, to the recession and jobless recovery that began in 2001, when it became impossible to place many of the women required to work by the program, labor market dynamics shaped the implementation of reform, and reform altered the shape of the local labor market.

Simply revoking the entitlement to cash assistance and sending those who had benefited from it to work was not enough to stabilize the new nexus between local employers and poor communities of mothers and fathers in Milwaukee and Racine. Rather, welfare reform entailed the building of a new "boundary institution" between households and the labor market: a framework to socialize mothers to the norms of the new moral economy of low-wage, contingent work and to regulate their entrance, participation, and exit from employment. Wisconsin officials and local agencies constructed new institutions, rules, practices, and concepts to replace Aid to Families with Dependent Children (AFDC) and to regulate participation in the new low-wage labor market. Before we can understand the ways that women's experiences with welfare shaped their ability to care for their families and marked their own work histories, we need to explore the new institutional framework the state devised to replace earlier systems of social provision.

DESIGNING A NEW REGULATORY REGIME

Historically, Wisconsin was a generous state when it came to welfare. In 1960 it ranked sixth among states in aid per welfare recipient, and its rank in welfare payments has consistently exceeded its rank in per capita income since that time.[1] Beginning in the 1970s, however, the local press and some politicians began to claim that the state's benefits were too generous: critics claimed they were drawing migrants from across the state's southern border—most notably from Chicago. Conservative legislators heatedly proclaimed that Wisconsin's benefits had made the state a "welfare magnet" and therefore required reform, despite uncertainty over whether the data on migration supported such a claim.[2] In 1986 then–state assembly minority leader Tommy Thompson seized on this issue as a central component of his gubernatorial campaign, in which he soundly defeated Democratic incumbent Tony Earl. Later that year, the state enacted the first of many welfare demonstration projects, the Work Experience and Job Training Program. Once inaugurated in 1987, Thompson used the governor's line-item veto to begin to reconfigure welfare. He reduced the state's need standard and its benefit payment, disqualifying numerous families from claiming assistance and generating funds for subsequent reform experiments.[3]

Thompson's platform was in step with the agenda of the national Republican Party and with conservative thought more generally in the 1980s. *Losing Ground*, Charles Murray's critique of welfare, appeared in 1982, and Lawrence Mead's *Beyond Entitlement* was published in 1986. Mead brought his ideas about welfare reform to the state during a term as scholar-in-residence at the University of Wisconsin's LaFollette Institute.[4] In 1986 Ronald Reagan had established a Low-Income Opportunity Working Group that recommended "giving states the broadest possible latitude to design and implement experiments in welfare policy," and in 1988 Congress passed the Family Support Act (FSA), which established a Job Opportunities and Basic Skills Training Program (JOBS) that imposed new work requirements on mothers with young children while providing some additional resources for training and child care.[5] Thompson and the state's conservative lawmakers were poised to take advantage of these trends.

That corporate employers felt they had a stake in welfare reform was evidenced by their participation in congressional hearings on the Family Support Act. Nancy Naples has analyzed the testimony and quotes as exemplary this assessment by William Kolberg of the National Alliance of Business:

> We have a window of opportunity in the next few years. The demographics make it possible for us to do something. There are two-fifths less young people coming into the labor force over the next ten years....
> We have the smallest growth in our labor force that we have had since

the Thirties. If our job creation can continue on even a moderate path over the next ten years, we have a chance to find jobs, entry-level jobs, for people that are trained, willing, and able to work.[6]

Pierce Quinlan, executive vice president of the National Alliance of Business, drove home the point: "In sum, the training of welfare recipients to fill vacancies in the private sector is not only good social policy; it is good economic policy."[7]

Having won office on promises of welfare reform, Governor Thompson served up a dizzying array of experimental programs designed to foster work and "responsibility" among welfare recipients. To do so, he took advantage of the federal waivers of AFDC rules that Reagan's Low-Income Opportunity Working Group had made more easily available. These experiments included Learnfare—new rules that required all teens in households receiving aid to attend school regularly. Despite Learnfare's extremely high cost and its rocky start—in its first year the state Legislative Audit Bureau found that 84 percent of sanctions for failure to attend school were imposed in error due to faulty records and processing—the program remained a part of Wisconsin's welfare statutes until 2009.[8] As Thomas Corbett points out, Learnfare broke new ground in giving legitimacy to "efforts that conditioned welfare benefits on client behavior."[9] It was, in other words, one of the first instances of welfare contractualism in practice.

Thompson's experiments were premised on the idea that Wisconsin's welfare participants needed to be taught the value of work. While Milwaukee had only about 38 percent of the state's caseload at the time,[10] and only a portion of that city's participants were black, the programs he crafted spoke to stereotypes of black "welfare mothers." His experiments included a "two-tier" payment system that limited the checks of new Wisconsin residents to the amount they would have received in their former home states for six months, reductions in payments for additional children conceived while on welfare, a twenty-hour-per-week work requirement for mothers with children over the age of one, "work incentives" allowing recipients to keep modest amounts of earned income without having their checks reduced, and a "Bridefare" plan (the Parental and Family Responsibility Initiative), announced with much fanfare in the White House Rose Garden, which allowed women to continue to receive aid after marriage if they participated in work programs and received training and counseling.[11] By 1994 the governor had earned a reputation as a pioneer of welfare reform, and Wisconsin's program had achieved fame as "the most aggressive of current efforts 'to end welfare as we know it.'"[12] Thompson had also provided a template for "an innovative style of programming that not only makes greater demands on its recipients [but] supervises them closely to make sure that they fulfill those expectations."[13]

Many analysts have pointed out that, despite their popularity, Thompson's early initiatives lacked cohesiveness. "The initiatives that resulted do not appear to have been planned carefully or developed in context of a coherent welfare reform strategy," Michael Wiseman has noted. Even one of their staunchest advocates, Lawrence Mead, called them "casual policy-making."[14] The Wisconsin legislature generally supported Thompson's ideas but worried about their systemic impacts. In 1993 Thompson submitted a waiver request to the federal government for a new "Work Not Welfare" program, featuring an array of new requirements and incentives. It required participants to "earn" benefits through work activities up to forty hours a week, imposed a "family cap" on children born to women after they entered the rolls, and incorporated a two-year time limit. When Thompson brought the program to the legislature in 1994, lawmakers voiced concern over the administration's piecemeal approach to reform. They passed the legislation but called on the state's Department of Health and Social Services to submit a proposal for comprehensive welfare reform by January 1995. In so doing, they opened an opportunity to systematize Thompson's disparate projects and bring them into a coherent ideological framework.[15]

That "coherent framework" had been brewing for several years in the nation's conservative think tanks. Thompson accepted an offer from the Hudson Institute to assist in designing the reforms. The institute promptly set up an office in Madison and established a task force called the "99 Group." Milwaukee's Bradley Foundation, created by the founders of the Allen-Bradley Corporation, a manufacturer of rheostats that opened its doors in 1903 and was purchased by Rockwell Automation for nearly two billion dollars in 1985, put up $175,000 in support of the project.[16] As one of the largest conservative grant-making foundations in the country, Bradley funds numerous projects opposing the influence of organized labor, including campaigns against living wage movements and in favor of right-to-work laws. It had previously provided grants to Charles Murray while he was writing *Losing Ground* and to the Working Seminar on Family and American Welfare, which drafted the *New Consensus on Family and Welfare*, a publication that prefigured many aspects of the Family Support Act of 1988.[17] But just as Democrats and Republicans came together at the federal level to support welfare reform, it was not only conservatives who played a role in funding Wisconsin's welfare reform plan. The moderately liberal Annie E. Casey and Charles Stewart Mott Foundations provided support to Hudson as well.[18]

With assistance from the Hudson Institute, the Thompson administration unveiled another series of ambitious welfare reform demonstration initiatives. Self-Sufficiency First experimented with diversions: requiring applicants who met means tests for welfare eligibility to search for work before being placed on the rolls. Pay for Performance toughened the sanctions imposed on families when the welfare participant did not perform all of her work activities. Formerly, only the adult caregiver's portion of the check had been withheld, but under Pay for Performance, the entire family's aid bundle was reduced by the equivalent of the minimum wage for every hour missed; if a participant did not show up for 75 percent of her hours, the grant was ended.[19] Thompson's experiments led to a dramatic caseload decline long before the national-level reforms of 1996. The state's caseload had peaked at just over one hundred thousand families in 1986. By the time of the implementation of W-2 in September 1997, it was just over thirty-one thousand.[20] This success came at a price. Despite reduced caseloads, Thompson's experiments cost a great deal. While welfare administrative costs grew 5 percent nationwide between 1988 and 1994, in Wisconsin they doubled. And for all the talk of efficiency, the programs built bureaucracy. They also drew new actors from the private and not-for-profit sector into the government's service delivery system.[21]

As a result of Hudson's planning and Wisconsin's experimental initiatives, when President Bill Clinton signed PRWORA on July 31, 1996, Wisconsin had its own bill—broadly consistent with the federal legislation—poised and ready to go. It was completed in the early spring of 1995, and the state legislature passed the enabling legislation, with bipartisan support, in March 1996. As the new federal law required, its programs embodied a rigorous "work-first" philosophy that held that any job is better than aid. That philosophy was communicated through features such as diversionary tactics that made it difficult to enroll; eligibility criteria that were not limited to financial need and thus gave agency caseworkers broad discretion; requirements for forty hours a week of work or worklike activities, coupled with financial sanctions for hours missed; and extremely limited opportunities for job training or vocational education.[22] To underline the program's mantra, "Only work should pay," the legislature housed the new program, not in the Department of Health and Social Services, where AFDC had been located, but in the new Department of Workforce Development. This move institutionalized the legal and programmatic ambiguity of welfare participants—their status as both (or neither) workers and aid recipients.

BUILDING INSTITUTIONS AND
IMPLEMENTING NEW PRACTICES

Participation in W-2 shifted the ground on which individuals approached the state. They were no longer claiming a statutory right as citizens but rather entering into a contract with the state Department of Workforce Development in order to receive aid. These contracts required participation in a set of work or work-related tasks and made cash benefits conditional on completion of these activities. They also imposed other behavioral conditions, such as cooperating with the state in collecting child support from noncustodial parents and, for mothers under the age of eighteen, residing with (eligible) parents or marrying.

Caseworkers who drafted and enforced the contracts were called "financial employment planners" (FEPs), emphasizing their role in moving welfare recipients into jobs. Working for agencies contracted by the state to administer its W-2 program, they determined eligibility, placed applicants in tiers, assigned them to activities, and connected them to benefits. They exercised extraordinary discretion in performing this job.

In a marked divergence from AFDC, in which case managers were instructed to notify applicants of the full range of benefits for which they might be eligible, the state promoted a "light touch" policy, advising case managers to notify women of their eligibility for services only if they asked.[23] Once the state and federal governments had abolished the entitlement to benefits for those meeting income criteria, the Thompson administration rescinded due process protections if benefits were cut off or reduced. The only remedy the state guaranteed was a fact-finding process administered by the welfare agency itself, much like an employment relationship in a nonunion company, where disgruntled employees must take up their grievances with a human relations representative working for the same employer. As Thomas Kaplan has suggested, this "one-way street" in terms of contract accountability was intentional:

> The primary focus of W-2 is on the participant's obligations to follow the employability plan, or if considered ready for an unsubsidized job, to secure one. The emphasis is not on the responsibilities of the state or

the W-2 agency to find jobs for participants or to train them for emerging opportunities.[24]

By revoking the statutory right to social provision, policymakers pressed poor mothers into exchanging certain civil rights for cash assistance.

In New York, the implementation of workfare was accompanied by vigorous struggles over the legal definition of participants—that is, whether they were workers with the rights and protections that accompanied that status.[25] In Wisconsin, the debate was relatively subdued. The Hudson Institute argued that workfare participants could be considered trainees, and therefore exempt from the provisions of labor law. The Thompson administration agreed with this interpretation. Democrats, however, took issue with it; Milwaukee mayor John Norquist led a coalition that argued that these positions should pay the minimum wage and conform to labor law. When the Clinton administration's Department of Labor issued guidelines advising payment of the federal minimum wage (see chapter 5), the state argued that they were already in compliance: the cash payment of $673 a month, officials claimed, was remuneration for thirty hours a week of required work; the additional ten hours of required activity did not not count as work and thus required no compensation.[26] But some communications from the state asserted that the "the training grant is not a wage and therefore is not affected by changes in the minimum wage laws."[27] Thorny questions regarding the applicability of other federal labor laws and protections to individuals performing mandatory work activities remained.

Consistent with a market-driven agenda of remaking government in what Wendy Brown calls "market terms,"[28] the Hudson Institute's "99 Group" had recommended contracting out welfare program administration to private agencies. The policy designers saw this as fostering competition and market efficiencies and abolishing existing state bureaucratic arrangements, which they perceived as backward-looking and intransigent. In keeping with these recommendations, Wisconsin introduced a new competitive contract system and drafted new marketlike agreements to govern the local agencies that would win them. In most parts of Wisconsin, county social service agencies and job centers applied for and won the contracts.[29] In Racine, for example, the state selected the county's Workforce Development Center to administer W-2 programs. But in Milwaukee, the Thompson administration selected four community organizations and one private-sector firm: Employment Solutions, a nonprofit division of Goodwill Industries that specializes in serving individuals with barriers to employment; YW Works, a for-profit collaboration between the YWCA of Greater Milwaukee, the Kaiser Group, and Community Response Networks (CRN);[30] Opportunities Industrialization Center of Greater Milwaukee (OIC-GM), part of a national network of self-help organizations started by the Reverend Leon Sullivan in 1964 to bring employment training and economic development to African American communities; United Migrant Opportunity Services (UMOS), a nonprofit organization established in Wisconsin in 1965 to assist Hispanic migrants and seasonal farm-workers in the state; and Maximus, a national for-profit firm that provides program management services for state and local governments. (Maximus's multimillion dollar contract with the state of Wisconsin provided it the boost it needed to take itself public in 1997.[31]) OIC-GM, UMOS, and the YWCA had some experience providing employment services in Wisconsin, as the state had contracted with all three agencies under earlier jobs programs.[32] These private agencies assumed the responsibility for managing welfare participants' access to state programs in conjunction with county workers.

To oversee the five agencies, the Department of Health and Social Services chose Milwaukee's Private Industry Council (PIC). The PIC, dominated by large Milwaukee employers, had previously provided the city with employment-promotion services for hard-to-serve populations. Its chair at the time of W-2 implementation was the president and CEO of a local temporary services agency. Members of its board of directors included a vice president for Marcus Theaters Corporation, which owns and operates hotels, motels, theaters, and KFC restaurants in southeastern Wisconsin; representatives from Rockwell Automation/Allen-Bradley and Aurora Health Care; and members of education, labor, and community groups.

Under W-2, caseworkers placed participants who met financial and nonfinancial eligibility requirements, and who were not caring for newborns, into one of four employment-related tiers. These levels, which policymakers conceptualized as a "ladder," varied in the degree to which their work placements resembled "real world" jobs (see figure 3.1). At the top of the ladder were unsubsidized positions. If the agencies implementing W-2 deemed individuals to be "job-ready," even if they had been looking for work and been unable to find it, they could place them in this tier and require them to continue searching for a job.

From 1997 until 2007, individuals in this tier (sometimes called "case management only") received no cash assistance but might receive child care subsidies, food stamps, medical assistance, or other kinds of state aid. In June

---

Unsubsidized employment
Case management only; no cash grant

Trial job
Subsidized employment; minimum hourly
wage
Job-ready but unable to find work

Community service job (CSJ)
$673 a month
Not job-ready

W-2 Transitions (W-2T)
$628 a month
Not job-ready; self or family member
incapacitated

FIGURE 3.1. The W-2 employment ladder. *Source:*
Wisconsin Department of Workforce Development,
"Wisconsin Works (W-2) Overview" (1999), http://
www.dwd.state.wi.us/dws/w2/wisworks.htm.

2007, in an abrupt reversal of previous interpretations of W-2's enabling legislation, a state appeals court ruled that denial of financial benefits under this
category was inconsistent with the state's welfare reform statutes and required
that agencies help place those who were otherwise eligible for services in jobs.[33]
Nevertheless, the financial exigencies caused by state budget cuts meant that
in practice, many individuals were still turned away.

"Trial job" placements, intended to provide experience for individuals perceived as close to being ready to work, occupied the rung just below unsubsidized employment. Agencies were to place trial job participants in private
employment subsidized by the state. Private employers would pay partici-

pants directly but would receive a stipend of up to $300 a month from W-2. In practice, because of difficulties in managing employer participation, very few individuals were assigned to trial jobs and this placement category rapidly fell out of use. In 2003, for example, there were only five such placements in Milwaukee County and one in Racine.[34]

The next rung down the employment ladder was filled by community service jobs (CSJs), intended to provide work experience to "individuals who lack the basic skills and work habits needed in a regular job environment." These placements were meant to provide "real work training opportunities, but with the added supervision and support needed to help the participant succeed."[35] The state required community service job participants to work up to thirty hours per week and to participate in an additional ten hours of education, training, or employment search in order to receive $673 a month. Rules limited participants to six months in any one community service placement and placed a lifetime cap of twenty-four months on participation in the CSJ tier.

Community service jobs, the positions known informally as "workfare," are the heart of Wisconsin's welfare program. This is the tier that most forcefully moves women into jobs. Welfare programs from the 1960s to 1996 had emphasized training for productive employment. In contrast, workfare programs, with their work-first philosophy, assign education and training a very limited role. While every state implemented some version of workfare, only five placed more than 50 percent of their clients in its programs. Wisconsin was one of those states. More than three-quarters of all mothers receiving cash assistance in Milwaukee County for July 1998 held community service jobs, and the number dropped below 50 percent for the first time only in 2005. By then, however, many other states had increased their workfare positions, and the National Employment Law Project was predicting that the 2005 reauthorization of welfare reform, with its even more stringent work rules, would require at least thirty-nine states to increase the percentage of their caseload participating in workfare programs.[36]

The lowest (least marketlike) rung of the employment ladder was made up of W-2 Transitions placements. Caseworkers assigned individuals to this tier if they or a family member were severely incapacitated by illness or disability or if they were incapable of working for other reasons, such as drug or alcohol addiction. Agencies required women in this tier to participate in (or accompany their children to) alcohol and drug abuse counseling, mental health services, doctor's appointments, or physical rehabilitation for up to twenty-eight hours per week, and to engage in education, supported work, or training activities to reach a total of forty hours per week.[37] Participants received $628 a month, and as in community service jobs, they faced a twenty-four-month limit in these placements, although extensions could be requested in extreme cases.

In response to an investigation by the Office of Civil Rights of the Department of Health and Human Services for failure to accommodate women with disabilities, the state introduced a "barrier screening tool" in the summer of 2003 to help identify women who were eligible for the W-2 Transitions program. Caseworkers asked an exhaustive series of questions about the applicant's health, family members' health, personal habits, and relationships. They requested extensive documentation from doctors and sometimes from courts or drug treatment programs. "Diagnosis" of barriers to employment did not always translate into appropriate remediation or treatment, however. In some cases, parents prevented from working by mental illness or substance abuse refused treatment; in others, the caseworker recommended placement in an alcohol and drug abuse treatment program that turned out to be unavailable or that the agencies did not have resources to pay for. As caseworkers placed women in the four tiers of the program, they operated within the parameters of state and agency guidelines, but also under the constraints of available funding and the need to meet benchmarks for progress in reducing caseloads and moving clients into work. Apart from these four tiers of the employment ladder, the state provided a $673 per month caretaker-of-newborn benefit to mothers of children up to twelve weeks old, and did not ordinarily require these mothers to work for their aid.

MOVING MOTHERS INTO JOBS

While Wisconsin's welfare caseload had declined dramatically in the period of Thompson's welfare experiments, state officials still faced the daunting task of moving approximately twenty thousand "job-ready" people into unsubsidized employment during the six-month transition from AFDC to W-2.[38] At the time of the program's inauguration in September 1997, thirty-one thousand families remained on the AFDC caseload. Though we do not know how many of these individuals found employment and how many simply left the rolls, by December 1998, the number of parents claiming cash assistance via the new W-2 program had dropped to just over nine thousand.[39] These are statewide figures, but approximately three-quarters of the mothers participating in W-2 in March 1998 resided in Milwaukee and Racine counties. As the number of participants enrolled in the program continued to decrease over the next four years, the remaining cases became more concentrated in the southeastern part of the state, where poverty rates and unemployment were highest. As a result, the labor market impact of this influx of workers was concentrated in these cities. The large number of women moving into employment in Milwaukee and Racine created challenges for mothers looking for work and for welfare agency job developers charged with finding placements for participants for whom work was mandatory.

Researchers at the University of Wisconsin's Institute for Research on Poverty (IRP) found that 31 percent of single mothers who entered welfare between September 1997 and July 1998 were placed in one of the two upper tiers.[40] Given the low numbers of trial jobs, most of these mothers must have been placed in unsubsidized employment and required to look for jobs without cash assistance. When IRP researchers asked a subsample of the mothers if they thought that the W-2 program had helped them to "get a job or get a better job" in 1998, nearly three-quarters of the respondents living in Milwaukee said it had not.[41] Of those who left welfare for employment in 1998, over 35 percent worked in the low-wage service sector as nursing aides, food preparation and service workers, cashiers, and cleaning and building service workers.[42]

Many women required to work by the new welfare rules turned to temporary agencies to secure employment, some referred by the W-2 agencies and others on their own. In the earlier experiments that had pushed women to work under AFDC, 30 percent had found employment through temporary agencies,[43] and these agencies geared up to offer their services under the new wave of reform. New York–based Accustaff and Milwaukee-based Manpower Inc., as well as several smaller firms, developed programs in Milwaukee targeted at W-2 participants, as did P. A. Staffing in Racine.[44] Maximus set up its own temp services subsidiary and then contracted that entity for placement services. Despite their initial popularity with caseworkers, temporary assignments posed some intractable problems for W-2 participants. By their nature erratic and unpredictable, temporary placements did not work well for parents who had not only to arrange for child care but to secure vouchers from the state (based on an agreed-upon work schedule) to help pay for it.

In the first years of reform, policymakers had high hopes that the majority of women they required to work could find positions in regularly advertised private-sector jobs. The private sector itself seemed ready for the challenge. The month before the policy changes were to take effect, the *Business Journal of Milwaukee* carried the story of Serigraph, a lithographic firm:

A shortage of available labor in Washington County is forcing West Bend–based Serigraph, Inc. to move a portion of its operations to Milwaukee County. . . . "We have run out of labor in Washington County," said Michael Stoecker, chief operating officer for Serigraph's Specialty Group. "Milwaukee has a rich pool of available people, including W-2 workers, and it is our intention to tap those talents."[45]

Another business journal reported on the experience of the *Milwaukee Journal Sentinel* in using W-2 labor. The paper had established a training program for workfare participants, and its human resources manager gave an overall positive assessment of the experience. "We had a perfect place to put them and that was in our production and distribution areas," she said. "What we learned . . . is that people who are coming off welfare are the same as those who have had regular, permanent employment in terms of reliability and job performance."

The same manager noted, however, that there was "a definite stigma attached to the former welfare cases" at the *Journal Sentinel*, and it was not simply the stigma of race or of having been on the dole:

The former welfare recipients were joining the paper just after it had completed a wrenching merger of what had been the afternoon *Milwaukee Journal* and the morning *Milwaukee Sentinel*—a merger that meant layoffs or dramatic shifts in work for many employees.[46]

Although Wisconsin's W-2 program had "nondisplacement" provisions in place to prevent employers from using workfare participants to replace regular workers, the newspaper's restructuring in the context of the merger allowed it to lay off some regularly salaried workers and hire workfare participants without repercussions.

By 2000 Wisconsin's secretary of workforce development estimated that five thousand businesses in the state had hired W-2 participants. She claimed that the program was working because of "Milwaukee-area businesses that are begging for entry-level employees."[47] Summarizing the situation in this early period from a somewhat different perspective, the local A Job Is a Right campaign noted, "This is why state officials are telling the world that W-2 is a success. They have managed to create a pool of low-wage captive workers for the benefit of businesses unwilling to pay a living wage."[48]

Some W-2 agencies contracted out the creation and supervision of the new community service jobs to employment agencies. Others hired their own "job developers" to work with for-profit firms, public agencies, and community-based organizations to create positions. Assigned to work by agency personnel and provided cash benefits by the state, community service job participants essentially constituted a pool of free labor for the organizations where they were placed. Agencies expected private sites to hire participants after six months if they proved successful in fulfilling their work responsibilities—but most assignments ended without a permanent job placement, at which point caseworkers generally assigned women who had not exhausted their eligibility to a new site for another six months.

Many agencies sent community service job participants to work for community organizations or to perform child care or clerical work for for-profit firms. Goodwill Industries' Employment Solutions placed most of the women it served in its own warehouses, where they packed, unpacked, and sorted used clothes. Other contract agencies also sent participants to Goodwill's facilities. Some agencies assigned women to food pantries run by local charitable groups, such as Second Harvest, or had them perform filing tasks in agency offices.

YW Works director Julia Taylor undertook the most publicized innovations in creating community service jobs. Taylor solicited contributions from local investors for a venture capital fund that provided bridge financing until she was able to secure support from foundations and mainstream banks for a for-profit jobs creation program. Using these funds, she first bought a plastics factory to train workfare participants in injection molding and to house programs that taught women and men construction skills. She hired a clothing designer and set up an apparel operation called the Creative Workshop in which women took apart old sweaters and other clothing items and reknit them, producing "wearable art."[49] Women in the workshop also sometimes performed light assembly work subcontracted to the enterprise by retailers or manufacturers.

In the early phase of these ventures, the local press hailed Taylor as a star. Tommy Thompson called her Generation 2 Plastics "innovation at its very best" and took her to Washington to testify about her projects before the House of Representatives Subcommittee on Human Resources. While Taylor appeared before the subcommittee as an exemplar of entrepreneurial approaches to job formation, she took advantage of this opportunity to plead with committee members to allow service providers like the YWCA more flexibility to provide education and training. She called for some required work hours to be reduced or eliminated and replaced with training that would "address the barriers of this specific population."[50] By 2003, however, Taylor's projects had—in the words of the local press, "gone sour." The for-profit YWCA subsidiary was hemorrhaging financially, and Taylor was forced to close the plastics factory and Creative Workshop. As the Y slashed budget and staff, she left to head the Greater Milwaukee Committee, an organization that had represented Milwaukee's "captains of industry" since the 1940s.[51]

As the women who were best prepared to find employment left W-2 for the labor market, the challenges that kept the remaining mothers out of the workforce (such as illness, a sick or disabled family member, or addiction) also prevented them from attending their community service job assignments on a regular basis. These attendance problems caused some employers who had provided placements to sever their ties with the agencies. Several agencies moved to two-stage placements, requiring parents to participate in unskilled work like sorting clothes or shelving food for at least a month before they became eligible for more desirable work sites.[52] Based on the incorrect presumption that women's attendance problems were due to a lack of work experience rather than family or personal difficulties, these strategies placed women in jobs—any jobs—in order to give them labor market experience.

It would, of course, have been impossible to move mothers into work without providing access to child care. Initially, far too few slots were available in the Milwaukee-Racine area, and costs were out of reach for mothers whose checks were, at best, $673 a month. The state needed to foster and fund a dramatic expansion in child care capacity in the local market. This new program, called Wisconsin Shares, provided need-based subsidies to mothers of children under twelve for market-based care. In order to enroll, women had to be employed and earning less than 185 percent of the poverty line or to be participating in W-2.[53] The state reimbursed the day care provider at market rates ($12,012 a year for a child under two in 2002).[54] In providing these subsidies, the state hoped to entice new providers to enter the market. The program succeeded dramatically in this respect—by 2002 it had "produced a doubling of state-licensed group care and quadrupling of licensed family day care capacity in lower income central-city neighborhoods."[55] Ninety-eight percent of the subsidies paid by the program went to families who were then or had previously been enrolled in W-2. The state thus supported the purchase of child care services on the market, rather than offering them directly or requiring employers to provide or subsidize them. For mothers laboring under the solitary wage bargain, this program offered essential support.

Child care subsidies were extraordinarily expensive, particularly in Milwaukee County, where the state spent more than 50 percent of its child care budget.[56] From a modest beginning in October 1997, when the state enrolled 3,925 families in Milwaukee County, by 2003 the program had grown to serve 12,350 families at a cost of over $13 million per month.[57] In the 2003–2004 budget cycle, the statewide bill for direct child care subsidies was over $298 million, more than double the total paid to W-2 contracting agencies for all other functions.[58] Part of this money came from the state's TANF block grant, although sizable amounts also came from a federal child care fund and the state's tax revenues.

Standard 8-to-6 child care did not fit well with the kinds of jobs that women found when they left welfare. Many of these were second- or third-shift jobs, and many had irregular hours. In addition, for women without cars, moving children between home and day care, or day care and school, was extraordinarily difficult to coordinate with forty hours of work, education, and job search, often in different locations. This was especially true if there were several children who had different placements or schools. Under the leadership of the YWCA, the Milwaukee welfare agencies pioneered the use of transportation programs that shuttled children between sites. They also developed a program for sick and disabled children who could not be accommodated by regular day care facilities; child care providers learned to use a nebulizer, to interact with autistic children, and to carry out other tasks useful in meeting special needs. Over time, the market began to respond to the demand for these services. By 2002 more than 50 percent of Milwaukee's licensed family day care centers and 30 percent of licensed group providers offered door-to-door transportation services for subsidized children.[59] Providers also expanded the number of second- and third-shift slots. While some women continued to rely on informal child care arrangements with family and friends, most agencies considered these solutions less reliable and encouraged women to place their children in formal services, using family care as a backup.

While child care subsidies were an important starting point, the new programs did not address many of the other social reproductive challenges women faced in low-wage service sector jobs, such as the lack of sick leave or spotty coverage by workers' compensation and unemployment insurance. Women's ability to survive dilemmas of care and to maintain steady employment also suffered from the lack of any form of maternity leave and from the fact that they could not afford the unpaid leave to which they were entitled under the Family and Medical Leave Act. Without a broader array of supports for care, an incidence of disability and illness—their own or a family member's—frequently sent women working in low-wage jobs back to welfare.

DOWNWARD SPIRAL: NEGATIVE EVALUATIONS, FISCAL IMPROPRIETY, AND CASELOAD CUTS

During the boom years of the 1990s, many observers asked how much of the "success" of welfare reform (generally measured as reduction in caseload) could be attributed to the vibrant economy. The movement of women into work in the low-wage service sector was premised on the availability of jobs. And the provision of the support services they needed in order to be able to work, such as child care, depended on a strong state budget. As the nation and the region entered recession in early 2001, it became clear that the sands on which the program was built were shifting. These shifts exposed deep flaws in the program's institutional framework and practices.

In contrast to the pride with which the Thompson administration trumpeted early news of caseload declines, announcing new figures monthly in a press release, by 1999 the state's Legislative Audit Bureau, charged with evaluating W-2, was sharply criticizing both the governor and the local agencies. Most of these criticisms concerned abuses by the for-profit firms and community organizations that the state had contracted to administer the program in Milwaukee. The state, working with the Hudson Institute, initially had structured the contracts so that "efficient agencies"—those able to provide necessary services at a cost below the fixed contract amounts—could retain a portion of any unspent funds as profit and as restricted-use community reinvestment dollars to be used for initiating new services. The large reduction in caseloads took on new meaning when the 1999 Legislative Audit Bureau evaluation estimated that within the first year agencies had generated profits of $33 million and community reinvestment funds exceeding $47 million.[60] Poverty advocates in the legislature and in Milwaukee County argued that these caseload declines, which far exceeded the department's expectations, proved that the new program did not provide safeguards to prevent agencies from dropping parents who needed services from the rolls. Although the secretary of workforce development defended the arrangements, her department bowed to pressure from the legislature and poverty advocates to make future receipt of bonus payments contingent on meeting performance standards tied to service provision and moving participants into employment.[61]

These criticisms by the Legislative Audit Bureau came as businesses called for more emphasis on training and workforce development. In 1999 the *Business Journal of Milwaukee* published several articles claiming that the state was expecting them to solve its welfare problem "by just hiring people." One article noted:

> Unfortunately, this backward approach does not prepare the individual or the industry, and it does not provide long-term solutions to sustained economic health. The reality is that the economy has ups and downs, and we have shifts in technology and labor demands. Preparing the labor force to meet these challenges has actually become more difficult, due to welfare reform policies and strategies that emphasize or require "work first." These policies have resulted in job placement programs that de-emphasize and even exclude job skill training and education as eligible activities.[62]

Despite the state's roll-out of new performance standards, during the agencies' second contract period, the Legislative Audit Bureau released three more negative evaluations, which thrust market contracting and agency discretion back into the spotlight. In the first two reports, state auditors enumerated multiple fiscal improprieties and problematic employment and subcontracting practices at Maximus and Employment Solutions.[63] In the third, they shifted focus from agency practices to participant experiences, identifying large interagency variation in the types of services participants received across the state, the number of extensions granted, and the use of sanctions; it also pointed to the continued poverty and high recidivism rates of families who had left the program.[64]

By 2003 the recession that had begun in 2001 had turned into a jobless recovery. Caseloads climbed as women who had left the rolls during the strong economy of the late 1990s reentered the program. As figures 3.2 and 3.3 illustrate, the number of welfare cases closely tracked the unemployment rate, but state budget allocations, which had been dropping since 1999, continued to do so.

After sixteen years with Republicans at the helm of state government, Democratic governor James Doyle took office in 2003. Doyle began his term with a troubling $3.2 billion budget deficit inherited from the previous administration. His ability to maneuver was also hampered by the fact that the November elections that brought him to office gave Republicans control of both houses of the state legislature. In this context, his administration struggled with conservative legislators to maintain levels of funding needed to meet contract commitments. Emboldened by the reports of agency misspending, and anxious to close the budget deficit, the legislature cut welfare program funding. In May 2003 the state ran short of resources and the legislature's Joint Finance Committee released nearly $14 million in contingency funds to allow the state to meet its existing obligations to participants. Despite the shortfall, in its biennial budget bill in the summer of 2003 the legislature decreased service and benefit allocations. In a move demonstrating that conservative values trumped fiscal concerns in the legislature's agenda, it also vetoed Governor Doyle's proposal to extend caretaker-of-newborn benefits from twelve to twenty-four weeks, which could have saved the state money by reducing its expenditures on child care subsidies.[65]

At the end of 2002–2003, the administration declined to renew its contract with financially strapped YW Works. And it shifted contracts for one of two regions served by UMOS, which had been fined for failing to serve its W-2 clients adequately, to Maximus. Then in August 2004, OIC-GM's CEO was convicted of felony conspiracy for using TANF funds in a kickback scheme to direct contracts to the agency. This triggered an investigation by the legislature that uncovered additional fiscal improprieties and poor performance, leading the Doyle administration to reduce the size of that agency's contract in December 2004; the agency lost the remainder of its cases in February 2005 when the thirty-seven-year-old social service provider closed its doors.[66]

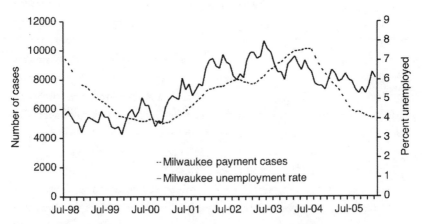

FIGURE 3.2. Milwaukee County payment caseload and unemployment rate. *Sources:* Wisconsin Department of Workforce Development, http://www.dwd.state.wi.us/dws/rsdata/w2data.htm; Bureau of Labor Statistics, http://data.bls.gov/cgi-bin/srgate.

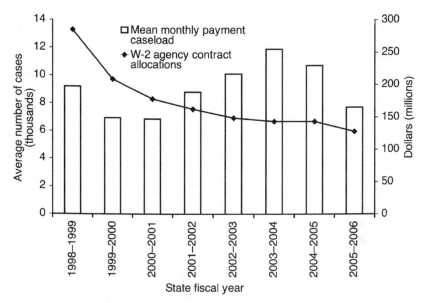

FIGURE 3.3. Annual changes in payment caseload and W-2 contract allocations. *Sources:* Wisconsin Legislative Fiscal Bureau comparative budget summaries, 1997–2005; Wisconsin Department of Workforce Development, http://www.dwd.state.wi.us/dws/rsdata/w2data.htm.

These moves created a "crisis" in the administration of reformed welfare. In July 2004 the Department of Workforce Development circulated an administrative memo advising the remaining agencies on how to reduce payment caseloads. These directives instructed staff to emphasize upfront workforce attachment, that is, to require those who applied for assistance to search for jobs in the local economy for some period of time prior to becoming eligible for benefits. The department estimated that agencies would have to use this means to cut the number of families receiving cash assistance by 40 percent by the end of 2005 in order to stay within budget.[67] The imperfect safety net provided by reformed welfare was now even harder for poor women to access.

THE EXPERIENCE OF SEEKING ASSISTANCE

Women applying for cash assistance in 2003–2004 faced a shifting landscape of agencies offering services and a bewildering array of new rules. They confronted a high likelihood of "diversion" into unpaid job search. Their cases were managed by agency workers who were under pressure to use their discretion to reduce caseloads by all means possible. Their experiences moving in and out of welfare thus reflected both the legislature's cuts to the programs on which they depended and the declining availability of jobs in the larger economy.

In Milwaukee, the sites where women applied for welfare were not government buildings or state-run service centers but facilities that community groups and private companies had established after receiving state contracts to administer the program. In an ironic twist, several of the agencies set up shop in buildings abandoned by manufacturers in the 1980s and 1990s. In 2003, not only was Maximus housed in a former Allis-Chalmers factory, but the offices of United Migrant Opportunity Services on Capitol Drive in Milwaukee occupied a giant warehouse. Other facilities, such as the Milwaukee YWCA's Sixth Street service center or Racine's new Workforce Development Center, sat alongside—in some cases literally in the shadow of—shuttered and decaying factories. These locations spoke to previous eras of stable manufacturing employment and seemed ill-fitted to their new purposes. While the buildings were public spaces, armed security guards monitored the entrances to limit entry to staff offices to individuals who worked there or had documented appointments.

Parents coming to these sites for assistance first met with a resource manager who gathered basic information, described the program requirements and informed them of other community resources through which they might address their needs without having to enroll in W-2. If they still wanted to apply, the resource manager referred them to a county social service worker, who assessed whether they met the financial eligibility requirements. If they did, they next consulted a financial employment planner at the agency who assessed their personal situation, education, and employment history to determine if they were "job-ready."

The financial employment planner (FEP) asked applicants a series of questions and entered their information into the state's data collection system. Having worked through a series of computer screens, there would be a pregnant pause while the FEP and the participant waited to see whether the computerized program determined that the person was eligible to enroll. Sometimes, if the FEP disagreed with the computer determination, he or she would consult a supervisor for advice on how to circumvent the system. But when women who were denied assistance became frustrated or angry, some FEPs tried to deflect their animosity by placing responsibility for the decision on the automated process. In truth, however, FEPs had great discretion in determining which applicants could receive cash assistance. Agency officials argued that this discretion was essential in addressing the wide range of circumstances presented by women applying for assistance. It also proved critical in regulating the caseload to meet changes in labor market demands and funding allocations.

Once caseworkers determined that they were eligible, applicants signed a participation agreement (see appendix E). The rules and responsibilities outlined in this agreement included naming and helping to locate the noncustodial parents of all children, providing requested documents in a timely fashion, reporting changes in income, assets, and family structure, making sure that children attended school, and paying back any disbursements made in error. It explained that failures to perform required activities without good cause would result in "strikes" against the participant, and that three strikes would end benefits. It also explained that refusing to accept a job placement or quitting or being fired from a placement would result in termination from the program.

Once the participant signed the agreement, the caseworker helped her devise an "employability plan" (appendix E). This plan included job goals, personal goals, and an activity schedule. The lists of goals and activities were often generated from preexisting sets of possibilities listed on the computer. State guidelines required the participant to sign the plan, including a statement that said, "I have agreed that I will do the activities listed in this employability plan. . . . I know that if I don't do these activities (including keeping all appointments, completing up-front job search, accepting a job, and keeping a job), my W-2 payment may be denied, ended, or go down $5.15 for each hour I miss."

The employability plan is an unusual document. State manuals describe it as "a 'road map' out of welfare and into self-sufficiency . . . a logical series of actions which become a blueprint for change." The manual says that the plan must place the participant in activities that will lead to the earliest feasible transition to unsubsidized employment, but that at the same time it can "be viewed as a means by which participants are able to articulate their aspirations and measure their progress."[68] Despite being called an employability plan, the document can establish "personal goals" that range from resolving parenting issues to seeking financial or psychological counseling to participation in support groups. While the plan is to be "developed jointly by the FEP and the participant," the state manual outlines circumstances under which a FEP alone may write the initial plan, even mailing it to the participant for her signature and return. The manual dictates that "each time the Employability Plan is changed, it *must* [emphasis in original] be printed, signed by the FEP . . .

and the participant must be given the opportunity to sign it." However, it also says that "if the participant refuses to sign the Employability Plan, the agreement is still considered binding because the individual committed themselves to W-2 participation when signing the [earlier] participation agreement." The participation agreement and the employability plan were the "contracts" poor women signed with the state that enumerated their responsibilities and the freedoms they would relinquish as a condition of participation. They were the statutory foundation for their loss of citizenship rights.

After women signed these agreements, many agencies assigned them to soft-skills training programs before placing them in a work experience position, even if they had extensive work histories. These programs were meant to offer help in nontechnical aspects of job readiness, such as timeliness, proper attire, interpersonal skills, and attitude. In developing these programs, some community organizations recycled training techniques that they had used in earlier incarnations of their mission, some dating back to the war on poverty. OIC-GM, for example, drew on a "Keys to Life" program introduced by Reverend Leon Sullivan and his compatriots in Philadelphia in the early 1960s. According to Sullivan's autobiography, this program helped participants to develop a renewed sense of self-confidence and focus before they started specialized job training. Other organizations developed programs that were informed by theories of cognitive behavioral therapy or incorporated principles from Alcoholics Anonymous that associated women's success in moving into work with their ability to change their environmental cues and their networks within the community.

But motivational programs were not limited to community organizations. On the first day at Max Academy—a soft-skills training program established by the for-profit firm Maximus, students were asked to chant, "I am somebody, you are somebody, we are somebody, because he don't make no junk." Later in the program, a trainer told the women, "You are unique. When you were born the mold was broken. When you learn to believe in yourself, love yourself, you will open the door to your future. Don't take life for granted." Among these positive affirmations were also admonishments to participants to take greater responsibility for their situations. The trainer said, for example, "When you are unhappy with your situation and pointing your finger at others, remember there are three fingers pointing back at you." U.S. congresswoman Gwen Moore, who represented Wisconsin's Fourth District and had once received welfare herself, was reputed to have referred to these classes derisively as "'You go girl' sessions."[69]

There was nothing subtle about the way these sessions sought to socialize women into new "work values." "In this economy, you have to be willing to start at the bottom, even if you have experience," trainers told women. "Instead of always looking out after others, it's time to put yourself and your job first now. It will allow you to achieve your dreams and to fulfill your responsibilities as a parent." Trainers counseled participants to take on responsibilities outside their job description if asked and to schedule their family responsibilities so that they wouldn't have to take time off from work. They told "success stories" and cautionary tales drawn from their own lives and those of others. Some of the narratives were dramatic, like the tale of a woman who had gone from struggling to keep her home after being abandoned by her husband to cofounding and managing a bank. Others ended with the protagonist securing a job at McDonalds or as a housing complex manager. These motivational programs seemed especially hollow in an era of economic downturn. Women who could not find jobs had little patience with programs instructing them how to dress, talk, and open a bank account. While in the past the introductory sessions would have been followed by technical training programs, these opportunities evaporated as funding for W-2 dwindled.

Caseworkers assigned women who had signed an employability plan and completed soft-skills trainings to work and work-related activities. They monitored their attendance at work by a system of punch cards. They imposed an hourly sanction on women who missed hours, unless they had a valid excuse. Negotiation over missed activities was a frequent feature of women's appointments, and caseworkers varied in how often they granted exemptions.

Women's lifetime and position-specific time clocks for benefits were activated when they received assistance of any kind through the agencies. By 2003 some agencies allowed women to enroll in part-time community service jobs, if their employer stated that they could not provide more hours. A woman who was employed between fifteen and nineteen hours per week could receive a cash benefit of $341 per month if she also completed her workfare assignment. Providing partial support to women in this situation allowed employers to keep workers on hand without guaranteeing them consistent hours. While women were enrolled in a partial community service job, however, eligibility was deducted from their time clocks at a full-time rate.

Women's time clocks were also ticking when they received child care subsidies during a period of job search. The following interchange occurred at one agency:

CASEWORKER: At this time, I deem you to be job-eligible, because of your education and your work experience. You said you need child care.... Do you need transportation?

APPLICANT: Yes.

CASEWORKER: The reason I ask is that it does tick time away on your sixty-month clock. You can job search on your own, but you wouldn't get child care or transportation. If you went through the [case management only] program, you would get assistance with job searching but you wouldn't get cash. You would go through assessments and a thirty-day intensive job search. We would see you weekly to monitor your progress. You would also meet with our job specialist, who will give job leads.... If you are not employed by thirty days, then you would be eligible for placement in a cash-generating position. Do you want to do that?

APPLICANT: I have to find employment. I need child care to look for work.

Time limits weighed heavily on women who had used their full twenty-four months of eligibility for community service positions to prepare for and move into employment. Unfortunately the last hired during the job expansion of the late 1990s were also the first fired when the economy entered recession. Reenrolling in W-2 required getting an extension, which was far less certain than securing assistance in the first place, and caseworkers simply turned away many women who had used up their time. One caseworker, who had served at a number of different agencies, expressed concern that this sometimes happened even when women were applying for the caretaker-of-newborn program.

Access to time-clock extensions varied depending on a woman's agency and case manager. One agency gave most applicants a three-month extension if they had used up their allotted time, but others were reluctant to do so. Women felt these differences across agencies most acutely when they transferred after a move. Anita Knowles faced this situation when she moved and her new case manager refused to continue her in the W-2 Transitions program despite the fact that she was caring for her sick daughter. The caseworker based her decision on the fact that there were child care centers that would accept her daughter despite her health issue.

Women who received W-2 Transitions support to care for an ill family member were not guaranteed an extension, even if the health issues that had made them eligible were ongoing. During the twenty-four months of their Transitions placements, agencies required them to obtain doctor's evaluations for their spouse or child at regular intervals in order to determine whether they could be accommodated in some institutional context. Approaching her twenty-fourth month in a Transitions position, Maria Calderon's case manager warned her:

> This is an arrangement that the state will ask about. . . . They may ask your doctor. They may ask me how seriously ill your husband is. . . . If your husband could get care by an agency for adults, the state may tell me to do that.

As one woman, who was caring for a son with a severe head injury, told us:

> It's like twenty-four months in your lifetime that you can collect W-2, or something like that. I mean, who's to say if in twenty-four months he's gonna be back to his age. And if he's not, and he needs care, well, too bad. I guess I just have to get a job and he can't have the care he needs.

As the labor market tightened after 2000, it became harder for agencies to develop new work experience placements and several began allowing participants to count voluntary positions at their child's school, a preschool, or a church as community service jobs. During this period, they also sent large numbers of women to Goodwill work sites where they sorted clothes and stocked shelves for the entire time they received assistance. Some FEPs bemoaned the fact that without high-quality placements to offer, they were sending women to make-work assignments, adding to their burden of responsibilities without advancing their skills or experience.

By 2003 budget cuts had forced an end to most training programs. Agencies dropped most of their subcontracts for job-specific training and supportive service programs that could accommodate workers with physical limitations or complex schedules. Pressed by poverty advocates, the Doyle administration had instructed agencies to accommodate disabled parents, but funding cuts limited their ability to do so. By the summer of 2004 it was clear that the agencies could not serve everyone claiming assistance. Unable to secure additional contingency funds from the legislature, the Doyle administration distributed new guidelines, instructing agencies to reduce their caseloads by closing the cases of women deemed most likely to be able to find work, even if they had not done so at the time, and had not exhausted their time limits. As figure 3.3 demonstrates, agencies responded rapidly.

At this juncture, W-2 became—even more than before—a stepping-stone to the bottom. Far from a haven for poor mothers seeking to regroup or to prepare themselves for family-sustaining work, the program shunted them into make-work assignments and then low-wage jobs that left them unable to adequately support and care for their families. In contrast to the promises of "independence" made by welfare reformers and agency trainers, these mothers remained poor and subject to the state paternalism that came with their continuing need for government subsidies, despite their participation in full-time work. By this point, the degraded conditions of W-2 participation truly mirrored those of the low-wage labor market that the program was meant to emulate.

Policymakers and pundits around the country extolled Wisconsin's welfare reforms for the way they encouraged and supported workforce attachment. This was clearly the program's primary goal. What outside evaluations largely missed was the systematic way the reforms disadvantaged the workers sent out into the labor market. They did so by providing inadequate support for women's family care, leaving them with insufficient resources to weather crises of social reproduction. And they made receipt of state aid contingent on relinquishing rights to choose the kinds of jobs in which women would work, and the hours and locations of labor. In a further blow to economic citizenship, it set those jobs outside the framework of labor rights and protections, claiming they were tutelary assignments designed to train women for work. While policymakers may not have fully anticipated the results of these disadvantages, their terms were written into welfare reform from the very beginning.

In response to workfare programs, many new day care centers offering service seven days a week, from 6 AM to midnight, have opened in central-city Milwaukee.

Because they serve many women who do not have cars, many day care centers now offer transportation.

As if illustrating the transition from manufacturing to a service economy in southeastern Wisconsin, the welfare office managed by Maximus, Inc., is housed in a former Allis-Chalmers factory, in space shared by Kmart and other retailers.

Racine's welfare services are housed alongside the county's Department of Workforce Development offices in a "comprehensive service center."

Boarded-up factories in Racine (above) and Milwaukee (below) speak to the loss of good jobs in both cities.

Much of the central-city housing stock in Milwaukee and Racine dates from the turn of the last century.

In 2002, nearly 60 percent of working-age black men in Milwaukee were jobless, by far the highest rate of any city surveyed by the Bureau of Labor Statistics.

The south side of Milwaukee, which used to be home to Polish immigrant working-class families, is today predominantly Latino.

CHAPTER FOUR

TYING THE FIRST HAND

THE SOLITARY WAGE BARGAIN

> The family is a gendered institution for privatizing social costs.
> **LISA DUGGAN,** *THE TWILIGHT OF EQUALITY*[1]

WELFARE AND CRISES OF SOCIAL REPRODUCTION

On a hot summer day in 2004, in a McDonald's on Milwaukee's near north side, Delia Carter sat before the tape recorder. Her narrative took a turn that was by now familiar to us—echoed by every woman to whom we spoke:

> It's hard, you know. I got to do all this by myself. I got to come up with food by myself. I got to come up with clothes by myself. If [the kids] need anything, I got to come up with the money to get it. It makes you want to give up. It's beyond hard. . . . You know we have everyday situations, and these situations are not small.

In listening to Delia's story, it became evident that when she said "it's beyond hard," she was not just complaining about the onerous work that is endemic to participation in the low-wage labor market, but rather pointing to dilemmas that could not be resolved in a way that guaranteed safety and well-being for herself and her children. When she said, "I have to do this by myself," she did not just mean that she had no help from the father of her children or her family, but also that neither her employers nor the state offered the assistance she needed. She was referring to the fact that she received little support to help her manage a situation that would have been considered an unfortunate necessity in earlier decades but now is held up as a norm: to combine full-time work with the care of three young children. These kinds of narratives about shouldering the burden of caring for their families alone were the most prevalent and poignant in the interviews we conducted: "You can't ask anybody. You got to get it yourself." "You can't rely on anyone else but yourself." Over and over, nearly every woman to whom we spoke addressed, in some way, the issue of their fundamental isolation in providing and caring for their families.

Conservative policy analyst Lawrence Mead has written about the isolation of women on welfare: "A class of Americans, heavily poor and nonwhite, exists apart from the social mainstream. . . . This social separation is more worrisome to most Americans than the material deprivations that go along with disadvantage."[2] But Delia Carter *had* been working. It was the conditions of her work that had deepened her sense of isolation—the fact that she did not have resources to help her meet her various, and conflicting, responsibilities to her employer and her family. Neither the state nor her employer provided them, and her job did not pay enough to permit her to purchase the help that she needed on the market. One welfare agency manager summarized this dilemma:

> These are resource-poor people. And part of the job of a case manager is to help establish an artificial network of resources, like middle-class people take for granted. You know, if I have a problem, I get on the phone, I call my relatives, I call a friend, I borrow a car—whatever it is, I've got backup all over. Poor people have other poor people for friends, so their systems are resource-poor. It's important to make sure that they're networked to resources that are necessary to survive and to move on.

This is a very different version of isolation than the one enunciated by Mead, but it echoes Delia's sentiments exactly.

By far the largest factor leading the women in our study to turn to welfare was their inability to balance work and care for their families. Nearly all—94 percent—applied for benefits as a direct result of a dilemma of social reproduction, which we defined as a problem providing care for themselves or someone in their family. In each instance, they found the demands of their jobs incompatible with their ability to provide a bare minimum of care.

For many of these women, welfare served, in the absence of employer-provided programs, as a version of maternity leave. Forty percent of the women we interviewed turned to welfare to receive caretaker-of-newborn benefits for a maximum of twelve weeks after the birth of a child. Several women who had difficult pregnancies or birth experiences also received a month or two of W-2 Transitions support immediately before or after their child was born.[3] A few women actually referred to these benefits as "maternity leave" and said that their employers had encouraged them to apply for the benefits.

Heidi Luttenburg's experiences provide an illustration of how women used caretaker-of-newborn assistance. Heidi lived with her two younger brothers in a run-down and chaotic two-flat in a decaying neighborhood of Racine. The apartment was strewn with boots, old clothes, dishes, and boxes at the time we visited. Heidi's father and a friend were watching television, while her daughter, dressed in pink overalls, stood at a coffee table tearing up paper. Heidi did not seem to mind the disarray and was grateful for the free place to stay. "My brothers are a big help," she said. "I don't know what I would do if I was an only child. I would be so lonely. I mean, sometimes I get mad and wish they weren't there, but if something ever happened to them, it would break my heart."

Heidi had worked as a cashier for a large grocery chain for nearly five years—until her daughter was born in 2002. The company had no provision for maternity leave so she applied for the caretaker-of-newborn program. Until her daughter's birth, she had been living with her boyfriend, but he was jailed immediately after the birth for a driver's license violation. Heidi was unable to afford the rent on her own, so she moved in with her two brothers and cooked for them in return for a place to live. She remembered this as a difficult time. She had had trouble staying on her feet as a cashier during the last two months of her pregnancy.

After the baby was born, Heidi's checks from the state were delayed inexplicably for two months. During this period she sold plasma in order to buy diapers and a car seat for the baby. But the $1,300 she eventually received from W-2 helped her to buy a baby bed, clothes, and other necessities and gave her the opportunity to stay home with her daughter for eight weeks. After her state support ended, she went back to work, this time as a waitress at a local country club. With tips, she averaged about $12 an hour, much better than the $7.60 an hour she had earned at the grocery store (although this put her income above the limit for food stamps, so she lost that support). The waitressing job also allowed her to work evenings and leave the baby with her mother, who worked day shifts. Still, she said, "I don't want a whole forty hours right now because that's just too much time away from Tammy [her daughter] and I miss her so much." Heidi, who had completed high school, hoped to enter a licensed practical nursing program at the local technical college in the fall.

For Germaine Epps, caretaker-of-newborn benefits were essential in allowing her to deal with an unexpected pregnancy. At the time we interviewed her, she was supporting her three children, her mother, and her adolescent brother on the salary she earned as a certified nursing assistant. "I have a lot of people depending on me to make ends meet," she told us. Her mother was an alcoholic and had been unable to care for her brother, and Germaine felt she could best deal with the situation by moving them both into her home. She went to court to gain custody of her brother so that she could make decisions about his schooling and care. Germaine had started working as a nursing assistant when she was just sixteen. She was in foster care at the time, and had dropped out of high school. She completed both her graduate equivalency degree and a nursing assistant certification course at the local technical college. She had worked in nursing ever since, except for a brief period in 1999 when she left to take a job as a forklift driver. She found that work easier and the pay better, but she was laid off after two years and returned to nursing jobs.

Germaine applied for caretaker-of-newborn benefits after the birth of her youngest son in 2003. After six weeks, however, she decided to return to work because the state check was about half her usual take-home pay and she could not get by on it. She was not able to get her old job back but found a similar position at slightly less pay. The highest hourly wage Germaine had earned in nursing was $9.50 an hour and she did not receive benefits through her job. Although her current employer offered health insurance, family coverage cost $100 a month, and her salary was low enough that she remained eligible for medical assistance.

Germaine's work life had become measurably easier two years before when she bought a car of her own and no longer had to organize rides or take the bus. She remembered taking her kids to day care and school by bus in the period before the car: "I had one in a stroller and one on my hip, and a diaper bag. . . . I had to catch the bus to the day care and then to Avery's school and then to work. . . . It took two hours." She spoke wistfully about the surprise of her new baby, whom she adored, but whose birth had set back her plans to return to school to take business courses. "I had it good for a minute," she said. "I was on a roll, because they were at school all day, but then I had this little baby. Now I've got to wait for him to get in preschool or kindergarten. But I mean, I'm cool, 'cause I see this is just how I'm gonna be for a while. I just chill." Fortunately, now that her brother was older, he was proving to be a big help. He coached her son's basketball team, and his girlfriend at times watched the baby.

For Alba Ramírez, newborn benefits, combined with W-2 Transitions funding, allowed her to stay at home with her daughter Leticia, who was born prematurely. Alba had moved to Wisconsin from Puerto Rico in 1998 after one year of college. She came to Racine, where she had family, and eventually found a job in the warehouse of a local publishing company. At the time of our interview with her, Alba lived in a neat frame house on a relatively quiet street in the downtown area. She shared the house with her mother and sister; to-gether they had taken advantage of a city program for first-time, low-income home buyers and had purchased the small white bungalow where they shared expenses and chores. Their pride in the house was reflected in an enthusiastic domesticity: wind chimes and hanging baskets of impatiens plants decorated the front porch, and crocheted doilies protected the furniture inside.

Alba left her job at the publishing house temporarily in 2002 when her daughter was born early and needed to be kept on a monitor. She had done light assembly work for this firm for three years prior to her daughter's birth and had recently been promoted to line supervisor. Because her employer did not offer any sort of maternity leave, she quit her position and enrolled in the caretaker-of-newborn program after the birth. She was not eligible for un-employment insurance (UI) under the state's guidelines, which ruled out preg-nancy, birth, illness, or providing care to a family member as "good cause" for leaving employment. When doctors told her she would need to stay home with her daughter for the first six months, she requested transfer to the W-2 Transitions program. Once her daughter was off the monitor and able to be in day care, her former employer rehired her, although not in her former super-visory position; she returned to the line where she earned about 60 percent of her previous income. Compared to many of the women with whom we spoke, Alba was in a fairly secure position financially. Still, at $8 an hour, her wages were below the poverty level, and she continued to qualify for many forms of state aid: food stamps, a 60 percent child care subsidy, medical assis-tance, and WIC. Her ultimate goal was to enroll in night school to study for a job as a medical or clerical assistant, but she felt she would have to wait until her daughter was older and her English-language skills were better before she could take that step.

A 2005 legislative audit of Wisconsin's W-2 program noted that the num-ber of women receiving support under the caretaker-of-newborn program had increased markedly over the preceding years—from 18 percent of welfare cases statewide in 1998 to 34 percent in 2004. The report speculated that "the reason may have been that some of these individuals were already employed before they entered W-2 and were using the program as a form of paid ma-ternity leave, which W-2 agencies told us is occurring."[4] For these low-wage working women in their reproductive years, the state caretaker-of-newborn program substituted for paid maternity leave, a benefit that most industrial democracies provide but that neither all U.S. employers nor the U.S. govern-ment make available.

Care for newborns was not the only reason women turned to welfare. Nearly a third of those in our study—29 percent—did so in order to be able to stay home with children who were ill. Carina St. Clair had combined work with care for her two children from 1991 to 1998. She had held jobs on the assembly line at a wire factory, as a clerk at a grocery store, and at a cookie shop in the mall, as well as in telemarketing. Her highest wage in these jobs was $7.50 an hour. In 1998 her youngest son was born with kidney and lung problems. At age six, he still required a catheter and diapers and was confined to bed most of the day. Carina managed his medical equipment and took him for weekly checkups. Caseworkers had managed to gain extensions for her so that she could remain on W-2 past the time limit, as there were no day care options for her son, and placing him in a skilled nursing facility would have cost roughly fifteen times as much per month as Carina's check.

Carina's two older sons played with her youngest and helped her move him around, but caring for him appeared to be taking its toll. "Lately, he's been a little too much," she admitted. She spoke of not wanting to leave the house and alluded to untreated depression. "I've been on my own since I had my kids," she said:

> I know I didn't make 'em by myself, but I've been dealing with them since they've been born by myself. And it's hard when you ain't working no jobs. You got all these bills, and yet your income is only a certain amount, so it's hard.

Her oldest sister, who had raised her when she was little, had been her greatest source of support. "She used to get on the kids," Carina remembered:

> When she'd hear them talking smart she'd say, "Don't you do your momma like that!" She showed me the ropes even though she didn't have kids, because she took care of *us* when our momma was at work. She always had our back.

But four years previously, her sister, at age thirty-eight, had been found murdered behind a suburban Milwaukee hotel.

The biggest issue that Carina faced was not being able to get housing assistance. She was on the waiting list, but due to funding cuts the prospects were not good. While she received $628 a month from W-2 and a little over $600 a month in Supplemental Security Income (SSI) for her son, her rent in the upper-floor apartment of a shabby north-side two-flat was $875 a month. Food stamps helped, but not enough to balance the budget. Certainly Carina could not afford a car, which made transportation to doctor's offices difficult. She was currently investigating rumors she had heard about a local charitable program that might help her purchase an old car and a new bed for the kids.

Tamyra Calloway of Racine also used the W-2 Transitions program to be able to stay home with a sick child. Tamyra was a mother of four whose marriage to a man in the military had disintegrated a few years before, and she had a solid record of work as a certified nursing assistant. More than anything else, Tamyra wanted to go back to school to get a nursing degree. But she had to put that plan on hold when her two oldest children, within a year of each other, were diagnosed with bipolar disorder. Tamyra had worked for a regional medical center for over three years, one of a short series of long-term nursing assistant jobs, when her daughter was hospitalized for an acute psychiatric episode in August 2003.

Tamyra's daughter, Eluria, was eight years old and extremely bright—the school had moved her ahead a year based on her test performance. Perhaps for these reasons, doctors had trouble identifying her problem. "My daughter went almost three years without being diagnosed," Tamyra told us:

> They kept on saying she's just stressed, she's just stressed. So I kept on changing her doctors and trying to find somebody that could tell me something different. A child that's stressed don't attack clothes, don't do bodily harm to herself or to others.

When the acute episode occurred, Eluria was hospitalized for over a month, and Tamyra did not have enough accrued leave to cover her absences. She quit work and applied for W-2 Transitions so that she could stay with her daughter in the hospital and care for her at home afterward. Eluria faced several shorter periods of hospitalization over the next six months, as doctors experimented with new medicines. During this time, Tamyra built up tremendous debt. Some of this was medical debt—even though she had health insurance through her previous employer and was able to keep it for several months after leaving work, her deductibles and co-pays added up to nearly $12,000. And her W-2 check of $628 amounted to only half of what she had been making, so she also fell behind on rent and other living expenses. She applied for food stamps, and was eventually authorized for $115 a month for her family of five. By the time she went back to work in January 2004, Tamyra had accrued a debt burden that would take her years to pay off. To add to her distress, the medical center where she had worked had refused to hold her job, and when she was ready to come back, they had instituted a hiring freeze. The new job she was in Milwaukee, about twenty-five miles away. Still, without W-2 to provide some income during the period of Eluria's acute illness, things could have been even worse.

Carina's and Tamyra's experiences were not unique. Jasmine Delp's son was born with a physical disability and received therapy through Easter Seals. Jocelyn Brill's son was born with a herniated esophagus that caused projectile vomiting and made him ineligible for day care. Sandra Cho's son, who had fallen out of a second-story window while in a babysitter's care at age two, required nine physical and cognitive therapy sessions and several other medical appointments a week. As many studies have demonstrated, children in low-income families have a higher incidence of chronic health problems and special learning needs—these are closely linked to the nutritional, medical, and other deprivations of poverty.[5] For some of the women in our study, the family health issues were short-term, and they could return to work after several weeks or months; in other cases, the problems were of longer duration, or chronic. All of the women caring for sick children received support through the W-2 Transitions program, which was designed to meet the needs of parents who had barriers to immediate employment. During this period, their assigned activities were to manage their children's therapies and medical appointments. In all but one situation, caseworkers told the parents that once their children had progressed enough to be placed in specialized day care, they would have to return to work.

Some women turned to welfare, not because their children were sick or disabled, but because they were ill themselves. Around one-quarter of the women in our study initially received assistance during a health crisis. This was the case for Della May Collins. Della May grew up in a poor area of Chicago. She had strong parents but, by her own admission, "had a bad choice in men." Wanting to get her five children, aged four to thirteen, out of the inner city, she accepted an invitation in 1997 from the mother of her youngest children's father to come down to Arkansas for a while. Living with her partner's mother in a small town there, she was able to work two jobs—as a certified nursing assistant and as a kitchen assistant for a group of nursing homes. "In Arkansas," she said,

> that's where me and my kids really had it going on. We had it together. I was able to take them everywhere, you know, things like game rooms, parks, and stuff like that. Stuff little kids need to be at. I was able to pay for YMCA for them so they didn't have to be hanging all out in the street. I had my bank account established, where I was able to pay my

bills and have extra money to put aside for bad times. If my kids needed something, I could just go right to the bank and get it out and go get them shoes or something.

Things were going well until her partner moved from Chicago to Arkansas to join them; they fought, and he began beating her. She put up with it for a while, but after one particularly bad incident, she feared for her life and went to a shelter. The shelter workers cared for her and arranged for her to be moved, clandestinely, to Milwaukee. Because they feared the man would come after her, they arranged for her to receive food donations so that she would not be listed on the state's food stamp rolls. And they helped her find an apartment and a job at a local Pizza Hut.

Della May adapted to her new setting and enjoyed the work:

> I liked that job. I got to be around different people, new people, stuff like that. Me and my manager, we was close. I did all they gave me, all their overtime—when some of the college students couldn't make it and stuff. It was helpful to me and my kids.

She worked at Pizza Hut for two and a half years. Then, in the summer of 2003, she began to experience strange feelings: dizziness and weakness and tingling in her arms. Doctors began doing tests and eventually diagnosed a pituitary tumor. They performed surgery to remove it in February 2004. Despite having worked at Pizza Hut for nearly three years, Della May was not eligible for unemployment insurance or disability pay. While she had often worked more than forty hours a week, earning overtime, she was classified as part-time and her hours were irregular. So in August 2003, she left her job to go on W-2 Transitions. Like many other women whose casualized work relations denied them access to programs such as unemployment insurance, she had no access to elements of economic security that had been standard for U.S. workers since the Depression.[6] Without access to these entitlements, she was forced to turn to the state for need-based welfare.

In July 2004 Della May's doctor was still urging her to limit her activities. Nonetheless, her case manager told her that she was well enough to work and that he could move her into a community service job. Della May assessed the situation in this way:

> When they told me I had to go off medical leave—when they felt like I was feeling fine—I went out looking for a job, 'cause they can't pay my bills if their little time clock runs out on W-2, you know. The doctor

will tell you, "You don't need to do this and you don't need to do that." I wouldn't drive or nothing like that, but I sure looked for a job 'cause he ain't the one that's gonna pay my bills for me and my kids.

Through a temporary placement service, Della May took at job as a packer for a large biochemical firm. She said: "I'm hoping they'll hire me in. That's something I could hold on to for a long time. He [the manager] jokes around with me and says, 'Hopefully you'll be here twenty-five, thirty years,' so hopefully he's saying he's gonna hire me in." Unfortunately, Della May ran up against the informal "ninety-day rule" that characterizes many temporary positions, in which employers cut off contracts before workers become eligible for permanent positions. Her employer terminated her rather than hiring her as a regular employee. Early in 2005 her health problems resurfaced, and she returned to the W-2 Transitions program for a few months. By the end of 2005 she was off welfare again, but we were unable to locate her to find out if, or where, she was working.

Shireen Hull had worked in fast food retail since she left high school and married, around the time of the birth of her first child. She had not really wanted to get married at sixteen, but her parents insisted, and reflecting back on the experience, she argued that it probably was a good thing because it made her give up "partying" to concentrate on work. She held a series of positions over the next four years as a cashier and cook, sometimes doing inventory or helping the restaurant manager.

Shireen's moves from one job to another—from Burger King to Chik Filet to Taco Bell—were almost always occasioned by her oldest daughter's health problems: pneumonia, an undiagnosed condition that required a spinal tap, multiple ear infections. This discontinuity in employment, along with the state's other qualification requirements, meant that she was not eligible for unemployment insurance in early 2002, when during a prenatal checkup, doctors found a tumor on her pancreas and performed surgery. During her recovery, her husband, who had a drug problem, beat her badly, and she was taken unconscious to the hospital. She filed for divorce and moved in with her mother and father. She described this as "the hardest time I had" because her parents lived in a one-bedroom apartment, and "being pregnant and trying to sleep on the floor wasn't working out too well." Her husband was jailed, and according to Shireen, took these events as a wake-up call and gave up drugs.

During her surgery and recovery, Shireen received W-2 Transitions support for four months. Once her daughter was born, she received caretaker-of-newborn benefits for an additional three months. Throughout this time she supplemented her check of $628 a month by selling plasma to a blood bank and ice cream on the street. Once her newborn benefits ended, Shireen found a job at Burger King and coordinated her shifts with her mother and her ex-husband so that they could provide day care for the new baby. She planned to start working toward her graduate equivalency degree once her work schedule stabilized. She continued to experience back and leg pain from the beating, which made it difficult for her to sit through our two-hour interview, and her daughter had just been diagnosed with a learning disability caused by high levels of lead in her blood. When asked about the challenges she was facing, she had clearly put both illness and divorce behind her: "Just the economy," she said. "I need a nice job and a reliable car. That's just about it. Everything else is fine. I just got to work harder for things now. And not having a high school diploma or GED makes it harder." Thinking of her personal life, though, she became sad. "With three kids, it's gonna be hard to find a guy that's actually gonna love me for me and not try to use or abuse me or be into drugs and gangs. Someone that I would be able to trust my kids around. . . . Maybe I can think about it twenty years down the line when my kids are out of the house and I don't have to worry so much."

While Shireen demonstrated considerable resilience in the face of surgery and domestic abuse, Ebony Walker's case demonstrated how the gradual accretion of these kinds of problems could become overwhelming. Ebony was forty-three at the time of our interview with her—one of the older women in the study. She had held an impressive array of jobs over the years, although none for very long. She had worked as a model for a department store and as a secretary, had bound books on an assembly line and driven a school bus, had sold housewares at Sears and flipped burgers at Burger King. In her estimation, her best job had probably been as a certified nursing assistant, but she had injured her back after two years of lifting and moving patients. She quit the job, but did not recover from her injury, and continued to suffer back pain.

Ebony's parental responsibilities grew with the birth of additional children. She was raped by a stranger in 1986 and struggled with a difficult relationship in subsequent years that involved dangerous episodes of domestic violence and rape. She began to suffer from depression and post–traumatic stress disorder. When she bore twins in 1995, one of them died. Over time, her health problems increased and became more complicated: she suffered from diabetes and a thyroid condition, but more significantly a heart condition that required surgery in 2003. Any one of these problems might have been manageable. The combination, however, pushed Ebony past the point where she could cope. By the late 1990s she found herself unable to hold a job and turned to the state. She said that she wanted to work but that, in her assessment, a part-time job would have been optimal. Unfortunately, that was not an option under W-2.

Ebony had applied for Supplemental Security Income—which provides support for individuals suffering disability—but with federal claims processing slowed to a snail's pace, she was not hopeful.[7] "I didn't get on W-2 because I was on drugs or a criminal," she said. "That's the wrong, stereotypical image people have. The majority of people who are on welfare, they are disabled. You need income to care for these children and they should not be stigmatized in this way. And so far, society has not seen that."

These women were not unusual. As their stories indicate, combinations of crises were common. Shireen Hull faced pancreatic surgery, pregnancy, a child's ill health, and domestic violence leading to divorce. Ebony Walker had several complex health problems combined with post–traumatic stress disorder from multiple episodes of rape and violent abuse. Della May Collins faced a pituitary tumor and domestic violence so severe it required her to relocate to another state. Divorce, or the end of a long-term relationship, figured in many of these crises, although no woman ended up on welfare because of divorce alone. But combinations of problems were far more likely than single incidents to lead women temporarily to drop out of the labor market.

All of these women were workers, and some, like Della May Collins and Tamyra Calloway, had demonstrated a long-term commitment to a job. But their employers did not show the same commitment to them, and they did not have access to the kinds of leave that would allow them to recover from acute illness or care for family members who were seriously ill. None was covered under unemployment insurance programs. Some were excluded because of the casualized terms of employment—they were not considered full-time, career employees. Others were not covered because the programs were designed, from their inception, around male norms. They provided income to allow breadwinners to continue to support their families when they lost a job, just as workers' compensation covered them if they were injured at work. But they did not compensate time away from work to provide care when those same family members were sick.[8] Workers like Della May and Tamyra had demonstrated the work values that state and federal policymakers were claiming would set them on the road to independence. But illness thrust them back into a system that doled out benefits as means-tested welfare rather than entitlement—failing to provide a support that would allow them to combine care of self and family with their commitment to work.

"STEALING FROM KIDS TO WORK": WOMEN'S PERSPECTIVES ON THE CARE DILEMMA

Women's recourse to welfare was shaped, not just by their family dilemmas, but by the structure and rules of the jobs they found in the low-wage service sector—jobs with some of the toughest work rules in the economy. Much ink has been spilled on the problems that professional women experience in combining work and family, but the challenge is even tougher at the bottom of the labor market. As Shulman notes,

> Approximately one-third of Americans work night shifts, but while twenty years ago these shifts were fairly evenly distributed amongst high- and low-wage workers, today that has changed. More than 75 percent of the cashiers, food prep workers, nursing aides, orderlies and attendants, retail sales, and waitresses work non-standard hours. Now it is workers with the fewest resources that confront the difficulties of these schedules—added health risks, exposure to violence and accidents, and more expensive and less available child care.[9]

Many low-wage jobs in hospitals and retail also involve mandatory overtime to fill in for coworkers when they are ill or absent.

To contend with these work rules and continue to give their children the care that they need, women in low-wage jobs use strategies that Lisa Dodson has called "making their own flex time."[10] This entails leaving work as necessary to care for their children or to handle personal affairs, even though employers may consider them tardy or censure them for unexcused absences. While this strategy raises the risk of being fired, it makes sense, Dodson argues, given that most low-wage jobs offer no long-term security or career ladders. In fact, research indicates that workers who voluntarily leave one low-wage job for another may not lose much in the process, and some may see their wages improve as a result.[11]

Exploring the reasons for job turnover among the participants in our study provides evidence of this strategy and calls attention to the rigid schedules and rules of positions at the low end of the labor market. In speaking with the women about their employment histories, we asked about their reasons for leaving each of their past five jobs. Most commonly, a woman left a job because it was temporary, either because she had acquired it through a temporary agency or because it was seasonal work. Nearly 80 percent of the women had had this experience. The second most common reason, cited by three-quarters of the women, was that they were pregnant or ready to give birth and did not have maternity leave. The third reason (mentioned by 57 percent) was to take a better job. But almost as frequently, in 55 percent of cases, women left jobs because they needed to take more time than their bosses permitted for child care or some other family responsibility.

These women had a variety of views on parenting. Some of the most moving segments of the interviews we conducted were those where women articulated their goals and aspirations for their children and their own visions of what it meant to be a good mother. As Gwendolyn Mink reminds us, for many women of color, the right to have and care for one's own children is a touchstone.[12] The memory of conditions of domestic servitude, and before that of slavery—of leaving one's own children in order to care for the children of white employers or masters—was an unarticulated backdrop to current struggles to parent well for many of the African American women with whom we spoke.

Memories of their own childhoods also shaped women's views. As in any group of individuals, these experiences varied. Some had warm memories of time spent with parents or grandparents, and often their goals as parents were shaped by a desire to emulate those relationships. Della May Collins recounted, "My role model is now deceased, and that's my mother. She was a sweet mother always. She was very loving. She raised us in church. And she always got on us if we did something wrong. . . . She just wanted us to do right, you know." Rowena Watson, who was raised by her grandmother, said, "My grandmother never raised her voice at us. She never called us other than by our name. She always instilled good things in us. You know, 'Baby, you go to school every day' and 'You act like a young lady.'"

The more difficult and poignant situations were those where women had to invent their own ways of parenting because the ones with which they had grown up were harmful or inadequate. Delia Carter explained:

My mother was a drug addict. My mother was in the streets. We had to be around molesters. We weren't going to school. We were sat in front of a TV. When my mother came back is when she came back. That's not a mother. . . . You know, she tried to keep our hair done, but I'd have given anything just to walk down the block with her, holding her hand. So being a good mother to me is—your kids knowing that you love them through good and bad, ups and downs. They should never feel like they come second you know.

In their testimony, women spoke of remembering what they had wanted and lacked, as children, and using those memories to construct a model of positive parenting. As Regina Shiflett put it, "Everything I wished my momma would do, she didn't, so I know what kids be missing and be wanting. 'Cause I wanted that. So I'll do everything she didn't do." But most frequently, in discussing parenting, women spoke of the stress of being the one who had to do everything. Delia Carter explained, "All the stresses in the world, but in the end, you got to put all this aside to be a mother to your kids. And not just any mother, but the *right* mother." Vanetta Brown told us, "So it's kind of hard. I have to be there for them, to control what they do. But then I won't have an income and won't be able to provide the things they need. It's really hard."

Rowena Watson eloquently described the trade-off between putting bread on the table and providing day-to-day care:

> To be a good mother takes time, patience, understanding. To be a good mother is to be consistent with your children. To build a rapport with the child that's old enough to understand. A good mother respects her children, you know? You got to show love with your kids, talk to your kids, and build a relationship with them. But then, it's hard financially. . . . When you find a job and when you're looking for a job, sometimes you're tired and you can't spend the time that your kids want you to spend. You're stealing from your kids to do something else. You're taking time away to be able to provide for them. And then you have to send your kids off to child care with people you don't know anything about. It's just hard you know—financially, emotionally, spiritually.

For Shalimar Hall, achieving the right balance between work and her children led her to quit a very good job as a clerical at a telecommunications firm to work for another company. She had just gotten out of an abusive relationship and was losing her house because she couldn't afford it on one income:

> When I left [firm A] it was because of them [the children]. The reason why I'm at [firm B] is because of them—so I don't have to work those hours. I was working till around eight o'clock and just coming home, giving them a kiss, and going to bed. Didn't know how the day went, didn't know who helped her with her homework. And it's a sacrifice because I was

making good money with [firm A], but time just became more important. Yes, I make less money, but I'm able to spend time with my children. I'm just going to have to replan my budget and have a roommate now. I asked my daughter, "Do you want your mom or do you want a house?" She said, "I want my mom." It just came down to where I couldn't afford the house. But at least I'm going to have time for them. I love being home when they come home from school, and making dinner and giving baths and putting them to bed, tucking them in. I love all that. I didn't like it when I had to come home at eight, nine o'clock at night.

Geraldine Anderson also sought some kind of balance:

I was able to stay home with my oldest daughter until she was three and a half. The second child I wasn't able to. I had to go back to work when she was ten weeks old and I hated it. I hated it because no one is going to nurture like a mother. There are times that I look back on that time I spent with my oldest daughter, I mean just watching her and having lunch with her and going to the playground—all these little things. When they're gone, they're gone, and you can't get them back. And not only that, but I have less problems with my oldest. She's more secure in herself—more stable. It's a necessary evil—that you go to work, you know, and some stranger is taking care of your child. It's a dilemma . . . I say dilemma because you're supposed to get ahead, but children, they are the main ones that should be considered.

These are familiar problems for women of all classes, given special urgency by these women's lack of resources and the politically constrained framework within which they make choices.

Each of our interview questions about job-leaving led to a story about the balance between work and family. The women's phrasing frequently ended with an upward inflection, suggesting a question, as though the women were asking, "What was I to do?" "What would you do?" Rachel Fernandez recalled working at Burger King forty hours a week, making $6.25 an hour. "But I was missing too much," she said. "I had to call in. Kids' appointments . . . I had school activities with my kids. And [the manager] was like, 'If you keep it up we're gonna have to let you go.' And I said, 'Well, just let me go then, 'cause I really want to participate with my kids.'"

None of the jobs held by the women we interviewed provided pregnancy or maternity leave; nor, in most cases, did they provide sick leave or personal days. Women who needed time off for these reasons had to take days without pay or, if they needed more than a few days off, to quit and try to find work again when they were ready. Darla Tanner reported, "I ended up suffering from severe depression and I was put on medication, so my doctor suggested I take a leave. And when I came back, they terminated me." Delia Carter had worked for several months for a cleaning firm that had contracts with several large hotels. She said, "With the chemicals we were using it wasn't agreeing with me being pregnant, so they let me go and they told me after I had my baby I could come back." Shalimar Hall reported, "They fired me from there because my son got sick and I needed to take off several days in a row because he has chronic ear infections. . . . He had to have surgery to get tubes in his ears." And Catherine LeBlanc recalled, "I ended up getting fired for taking my break fifteen minutes early because I had to use the restroom. And I was pregnant, mind you!"

Shakira Hall described an exchange with the supervisor in the day care center where she worked:

When my son was born, his lungs were underdeveloped. So when he gets sick he gets wheezy. One time he wasn't talking right and he got really flushed, so they called me and I had to leave work to take him to the instant care, so they could give him a treatment. She [her boss] had an attitude about it, but I still went. My son comes first.

Shakira had agonized over the decision to leave her son in a day care at all. As she said to us earlier in the interview:

You know Zach, he's already had so many problems since he was a baby, and he gets sick a lot. I mean, he almost died when I had him. So for me to leave him—I feel like I'm going to freak out. I have anxiety. . . . So they [her welfare caseworkers] made me go see a psychiatrist.

Case managers equated leaving one's child in day care with responsibility, a notion with which the women we interviewed struggled. A woman who had just completed an agency's soft-skills training program that emphasized this definition of responsibility tried to put into words what she had learned:

Being responsible for your child is—it's like taking your child to be in a day care so you can go to work, or you can go to the W-2 thing. . . . It's like you can't really use your kids as an excuse for not coming in for work. I understand sometimes that people's kids need them—that they be calling out sometimes. . . . Sometimes it's OK, but if your baby just has a fever, you know, maybe you can keep him with your grandmother, family, somebody, just until you get off of work. It's like sometimes, people make the excuse "My baby's sick. I got to go home." Well, sometimes you can't really go home right away. Sometimes work is kind of important. And I'm not saying that your baby is not important, but it's like kids are always gonna have problems. And you can't always take off work just because the baby is sick. Because it's kind of like you gotta take the responsibility to the point where you can still be a good mother. I'm pretty sure that people have, like grandmas and friends that can keep their baby until they get off work if they are sick or a little feverish. . . . I mean I have a baby. I am really not going to go home if it's something like a little headache. Then I would be calling up my mom so I can see if she could pick him up and take him with her. But you know, if she can't, then I'm going to have to go home.

This woman was clearly still working through her feelings about the issue at the moment we spoke to her. Her words evidenced an internal dialogue between the new perspective she had learned in class and her own incipient critique of it.

Agency workers pressed women not only to put their children in day care, but also to find adult care for other needy family members. One manager talked about the reluctance of the Hmong women his agency served to place disabled husbands and fathers in adult day care:

We found a number of southeast Asian folks who were taking care of severely disabled family members. In some cases, those family members were former Hmong soldiers. They had participated in the Vietnam war and became disabled, and then the family immigrated here. So we thought—using an American model—that we would work with an adult day care service. What you would get is a place for the disabled family member to go, which would then free up the caregiving responsibilities from our participant, who could then work and should then ultimately be able to be a more productive member and bring in some more cash to that family. But there was all of this stuff that you don't think about in terms of what the family responsibilities in the Hmong culture are. So to have them go to an adult day care service is actually counter to their perception of what the subculture's requirements are.

Another caseworker told us that she had special difficulty getting Latina women to agree to arrangements for elder care. "That one is definitely a no-no," she said:

The thinking is that these people have cared for me all the time that I was a child. I can't put them into a nursing home now when they need me. I tell them that I understand but that they will have to make a choice to do that . . . because that's not an allowable activity [staying home to care for the individual in question].

Women who liked their jobs and desperately hoped to keep them spoke of the anxiety they felt when they received a call at work from the school or from day care. Della May Collins said, "What's hard is if there's a problem with day care, if one of my kids has to come home. And then I'm gonna have to come off my job. 'Cause I just got this new job, and that's a problem right now." Vanetta Brown told us, "There was a couple of times when I rushed to the hospital because he has asthma really bad. It was just so horrible. I'm like, 'Oh my god, I hope I don't lose my job.' One time he stayed in the hospital for three days. You know, I had to be there with him for three days. I was thinking all the time 'I hope I don't lose my job.'"

Anna Robles, who was suffering from gallstones, initially resisted surgery because she was afraid she would be fired for missing work:

I was working at [a grocery store] and I had these weird pains—sometimes it was just so bad I would have to bend over. So I went to the doctor and they did X-rays and stuff. Then I started working at [a big-box retailer]. The doctor called me and said, "You have gallstones, you have to have surgery." But I said no. It was a bad moment, and I tried to cancel it. And I told the people at [the store] that I would cancel it. I was so scared that I was going to lose my job. I had just started. But they said, "You go—your health is more important."

As a new employee, Anna did not have sick leave, but her employer allowed her to take to take leave without pay. Given the new norms of the low-wage labor market that had been ingrained in her, this seemed a magnanimous gesture.

As Shulman has noted, the hours of low-wage service sector jobs are notoriously irregular, leading to problems in scheduling day care. Many women did not know what hours they would be working until they read the schedule posted at the beginning of each week. Some were "on call" and could be asked to take an extra shift, or to change shifts, at any time. Some of the worst situations were those where they would go to work not knowing when they would get off. Delia Carter described her stint as an inventory specialist, counting merchandise for big-box retailers. "We had to be all across Milwaukee," she said, "and when you got there you didn't know when you were gonna leave. . . . You were liable to be there until four in the morning, until the whole store was counted up. Until everything was counted, you could not leave."

Wisconsin provided child care subsidies for women with preschool children and provided for after-school care up to age twelve. But many women worried about their adolescent children—how to keep them safe, keep them out of gangs and away from drugs and early sex. Rowena Watson explained:

> I've got a fourteen-year-old at home. I don't think she should be at home by herself, because she's at that age, you know. But I have to, you know—I have to. Even if I don't want to. . . . They need more for black children to do. You know, we have two kids killed every three weeks because there's nothing to do. Teenagers having babies—find something for these teenage girls to do! They don't even have summer school any more. They've got this "No Child Left Behind." Out here in Milwaukee, every child is left behind.

These fears for children were not unrealistic. On a hot summer day in 1998, DeAndre Reeves, a thirteen-year-old Milwaukee boy with cerebral palsy and mental disabilities, scalded himself to death in a bathtub while his mother was working at a local Pizza Hut. DeAndre's fourteen-year-old brother, who was watching him, had stepped outside for a few moments. His mother, Yvette Reeves, had once received Aid to Families with Dependent Children during the summer months so that she could stay home and watch over DeAndre when he was not in school. When welfare reform came to Wisconsin in 1996, caseworkers told her that she would have to work all year and that no child care assistance was available for children over the age of twelve. At the time of DeAndre's death, she had been on staff at Pizza Hut for two years, where her wages were so low that she remained eligible for food stamps and medical assistance. In response to public outcry over policies forcing the parent of a disabled child to work, officials from the state's welfare administration hastened to point out that there were resources available for mothers in this situation—that the system might have provided additional support had she known to ask for it. But others noted that these resources were not necessarily offered by caseworkers, and were not always provided even when someone asked.[13]

In a labor market environment where lack of flexibility was the norm, women valued the instances when bosses seemed to care. Catherine LeBlanc spoke about the issue of work rules and managerial flexibility. In her view, it had to do with whether managers were familiar with the problems of their employees and could identify with their dilemmas. She had worked for a big-box retailer at a time when the store was being refurbished to reopen as a supercenter. As she described it:

> We were putting in sixteen-, eighteen-hour days. There was guys that would work twenty-four hours. We could have as much overtime as we wanted when we were setting up that store. And it was hard. Nothing was together and they had to open. . . . And when the new management came in, they didn't know what we went through. They just looked at us as if we were slackers.

Once the renovated store opened and the new management team came on, Catherine noticed a change:

> When the old managers were there, they knew me and they knew that I was a hard worker and that if I did miss a day they could call me and I'd work a third-shift position for them if they needed me to. They knew that, they understood. They—like a lot of them were from the inner city, so they knew what kinds of problems all of us girls had. They would cut us breaks and we'd always pay them back, you know.

The new managers were "from the suburbs," she said, "and they didn't even know how to talk to anybody."

Catherine was not the only person to talk about the value of having an understanding boss. Vanetta Brown, who worked in a housekeeping position for a hotel, described how she felt when her son's babysitter would cancel unexpectedly: "I'm like, 'Oh my god, I'm gonna lose my job!' She's like, 'I can understand, it's really hard when you don't have anybody.' She was a very understanding boss and I was so happy, you know." In contrast, tough bosses could make life harder. Tawanna Marks told us: "I quit working at [a fast food restaurant] in January. That's the day my momma passed and I told the head manager I was taking two weeks off, 'cause we had to go down south and do the funeral. And the manager told me that was no excuse to miss, so I quit."

Because so few jobs in the local low-wage labor market at the time of our interviews offered sick pay or personal days, none of the women we spoke to explicitly addressed this aspect of job structure; the availability of such leave was simply beyond their expectations.[14]

Many of the women we interviewed struggled to articulate an alternative framework for thinking about care work, one that would explain the decisions they had made and the difficult choices that they faced. Some women argued, for example, that they should have the option of staying at home with their newborn children for a longer period. Denise Adkins said, "You have to send them off at six weeks, and I think that's too young. I don't think they give you enough time to spend with your children when they're first born." Natasha Castinelli concurred: "I think they should let you stay home with your kids until they're six months. It would be a lot better." Others criticized the pressure to use day care centers indiscriminately. Rowena Watson said:

> You know, you have to send your kids off to child care with people you don't know anything about. People you don't have time to investigate. You know, you go in one day and they want you to find a day care by three days later. So how can you go and look at these people? You can end up putting your kids in situations they shouldn't be in.

Shakira Hall said, "I just don't want them in day care. I worked at a day care, and I saw things that go on and I just don't like it. I'm just uncomfortable." She ultimately quit her community service job and began babysitting for children in her home in order to be able to care for her children herself.

One of the most powerful critiques of our society's failure to value the labor of care came in a story recounted by Delia Carter about her reasons for dropping out of high school:

> My sister was seventeen. And she decided that she didn't want to be a mother. So one day she brought my niece over and she said she was coming back, and she never came back. She did not come back. And like I said, for a minute, we thought she was dead. We lost all hope that we was gonna ever see her again. It was over a year before we heard from her. My mother, she was trying to get herself together at the time. She was still doing drugs, but she was trying to get off, you know. And my brother had already went to selling dope because my mom couldn't do nothing for him. She was on dope. What was she gonna buy for him? How was she gonna take care of us? She couldn't. So he had already left,

and it was up to me. I had to drop out of school to take care of my little niece. And I don't regret it. Sometimes I regret it now, because look how society treats you—like I just grew up and felt like I wanted to be a little whore and be in the streets. You know it wasn't like that! We had hard times growing up, you know. We had to fend for ourselves while we was little. My sister wasn't ready to fend for no child. And so I can't blame her for that, you know. I don't regret that. You know, I regret how I get treated now in 2004 because of that decision that I made back then, but I really felt like that was the best decision I could have made. My niece was two and a half years old when her mother came and got her back. Her daughter knew me as momma. I was momma, you know. I heard her first words. I taught her how to walk. I seen her crawl for the first time, speak for the first time. All of that. It was me, you know.

For Delia, there was no question in her mind that she had done the right thing in taking care of her sister's child, and the validation of that choice was the attachment that her niece felt to her. What bothered her was the fact that potential employers, her welfare caseworker, and others whose evaluation mattered to her current chances for success could not see the value in that choice—could not see that it was different than simply being "in the streets." Two years of care—years that had deprived her of the chance to live a normal teenage life and complete her high school degree—were simply invisible.

FROM FAMILY WAGE TO SOLITARY WAGE

Poor, working-class households, where no member earns a family wage, have historically faced the dilemma of how to perform the necessary work of social reproduction. The significance of domestic labor becomes more evident when there is, literally, no one at home to perform it. But it may be that we reached a turning point in this regard in the late twentieth century. Researchers have made clear the degree to which productivity growth and economic expansion in the second half of the twentieth century depended on women's labor. According to economist David Elwood, who drafted one of the Clinton administrations's early welfare reform bills, nearly half of the growth in income in the United States since 1973 has been paid to women. In fact, the productivity of the economy throughout that time has been sustained by dramatic increases in women's waged work.[15] Twenty-four percent more women worked outside the home in 1996 than in 1973, and their average weekly hours had increased 15 percent, meaning that overall, women were contributing 40 percent more work hours than in 1973.[16]

For sociologist Susan Thistle, these data are the surface signals of a far deeper transformation in the U.S. economy, marking a decisive restructuring of the relationship among the domestic realm, the market, and the state. As women move into the labor market in larger numbers, she argues, something else happens. The family begins to purchase on the market many of the services formerly performed at home: child care, elder care, meals, laundry services, cleaning. A number of feminist researchers have made this point, but Thistle compiles and analyzes data from the Bureau of Economic Analysis and the Bureau of Labor Statistics to measure how much the movement of these essential services into the market realm has contributed to economic growth over the past four decades:

> Economists have long recognized that the development of new regions and the conversion of nonwage workers into wage workers can create great profits, leading corporations to set up factories overseas. To understand the gains of the past forty years, we must realize that a similar lucrative process was happening within the United States itself, in the very center of American homes. As the market reached into kitchens and bedrooms, turning many domestic tasks into work for pay, and as women themselves applied labor freed from domestic chores in research labs, hospitals, factories and fast food restaurants, productivity rose greatly and a large new pool of income was created.[17]

Thistle's analysis shows that women's turn to paid work since 1970 created more than one-fifth of the growth in private-sector GDP.[18] Not surprisingly, this growth was most marked in services. Overall, she shows, about a quarter of employment in the service sector involved tasks that were performed at home in earlier decades.[19]

But Thistle argues that something even more fundamental has changed in the relationship among state, home, and market over the past forty years, and this is the darker side of the story of women's contributions to productivity. The upsurge in women's contributions to economic growth coincided with the removal of provisions for care. All of the key supports for women's household work—marriage as a lifelong institution, the family wage paid by (some) employers, and an entitlement to government assistance for poor single mothers—had disappeared by the late twentieth century. While social scientists make much of the breakdown of marriage, they often forget that support for tasks of household maintenance via the family wage were part of the old agreement between capital and labor that began to break down in the 1970s. The union wage was a family wage, and as workers lost power vis-à-vis their employers, those employers ended old agreements that committed them to pay well enough to provide for the care of children and other chores necessary to sustain and reproduce families. Similarly, at midcentury, the state offered a safety net for women without partners, but this support too had been eroded by the end of the 1990s.[20] Thistle points with irony to the fact that "employers and conservative politicians loudly championed the male breadwinner even as they simultaneously denied men the means to support their loved ones, . . . trying to hold onto the gender division of labor while at the same time rejecting the private and state support needed to sustain it."[21] By the mid-1990s, she argues, all of the key supports for care within the home were gone and no one—not the state and not employers—was willing to commit resources to support family maintenance.[22]

But perhaps the fact that policymakers spoke with two voices was not merely ironic. There is a case to be made that women's entry into paid labor was, at least in part, *impelled* by the erosion of the family wage. In other words, as the family wage system was broken, employers not only benefited from the decline in working-class men's real wages. They also gained by the entry of these men's wives, at even lower wages, into the labor market. Capital in the second half of the twentieth century was having its cake and eating it too, at least in this regard, as every decrease in the real wages of men propelled more low-wage women into work (and led to the marketization of more services formerly performed at home). As economists have acknowledged, cutting off welfare had the same effects, by removing poor single mothers' option to remain at home with their children and propelling them into the low-wage labor market.

Thistle alludes to these linkages when she notes that a feared shortage of health care workers in the 1990s never materialized, due to the growing pool of poor women workers. "Behind the availability of these women's labor," she notes, "lie stories of the loss of traditional support." Her analysis shows that new workers filling low-wage service sector jobs in the 1990s were almost all unmarried mothers with a high school education or less, "whose turn to the workforce was accompanied by a drop in the share on welfare." She also points to the fact that welfare agencies steered women "toward job training in the care of children and the sick or work in fast-food restaurants."[23]

The 1996 welfare reform radically reconfigured the boundaries among market, state, and family, but not in service of a coherent vision of how responsibilities for work and care should be divided. Conservatives talked a great deal about promoting marriage and family values, but they did not allocate resources that made it easier for families of any kind to stay together. Instead, they bought into the model of the individual as a market actor that said that even mothers of preschool children should work. They understood that no family could live on a single minimum wage. "One income earner alone cannot support children unless her job pays considerably more than the minimum wage," the *New Consensus* noted. "Two persons working full-time at the minimum wage can earn enough . . . to lift a family of four above the poverty line; a single parent obviously cannot."[24] But these policymakers did not object to this situation; rather than advocating an increase in the minimum wage or the provision of government support, they promoted "dual provider marriage" as a solution to the problem of poverty. They did not advocate paid family or medical leave. Instead they supported establishing paternity and inducing fathers to pay child support—without acknowledging that unemployed men, imprisoned men, or those making under $10,000 a year could do little for their children. They let employers off the hook, eschewing regulation of wages and benefits. And they saw the role of the state as one of instructing the poor in self-reliance, rather than providing insurance or support.

In all of these ways, welfare reform failed to address basic issues of social reproduction for poor families. The federal government did provide block grants crucial for child care services and subsidies, but these proved expensive, particularly since many of the children involved were infants, who require the most intensive care. Conservatives had initially suggested that this care could be provided by family members. "The logistics of work for these mothers are no doubt difficult," Lawrence Mead opined, "but lack of *government* child care seems seldom to be a barrier; most prefer to arrange child care with friends or relatives informally."[25] When family advocates demonstrated that family members were often working, deceased, ill, or living far away, policymakers agreed to include subsidies.[26] But they ignored many other issues surrounding work and family, including sick leave, family and medical leave, and flexibility in work schedules.

As we have noted, the solitary wage bargain is premised on the notion of the worker as an abstract individual who is neither embodied nor encumbered. In this market-driven view, families are seen as constraints that interrupt education and employment and prevent some people from building their "human capital." How the next generation is to be provided for—indeed how new workers and consumers are to be produced—is a separate market question, as is the issue of how the needs of the sick or disabled are to be met. In the economic models that inform free market policies, these are externalities, not the intrinsic concern of the labor market.

An example of this kind of reasoning is found in the *Economist*'s 2008 treatment of the issue of immigration. A special issue on the topic proclaimed, "When a foreign worker first arrives, usually as a young adult, fully educated and in good health, he makes few demands on schools or clinics. . . . If growth weakens, migrants can go home."[27] This is another way in which employers and the state have been divesting themselves of responsibility for social reproduction. As Michael Burawoy wrote several decades ago, temporary labor migration shifts the costs of social reproduction "outside the system." Employers have access to healthy, educated workers in the prime of life, while young children, the ill, the elderly, and the disabled are cared for in villages of Mexico, the Philippines, or Burkina Faso. Burawoy argued that the bracero program that brought Mexicans to the United States as guest workers from 1942 to 1964 was premised on the notion that these workers could fill a need for labor without taxing our social system with the costs of raising children or caring for people when they became too old or disabled to work.[28]

We cannot all be migrants—we have to go home sometime. Yet the solitary wage bargain treats wage work as a purely individual contract between the employer and the worker. It presumes that the individual is supporting him or herself alone and that the worker and the employer are the only two parties who have an interest in the outcome of the negotiation. These presumptions structure the amount of the wage, the hours of work, and the benefits provided—or not provided. Unlike the family wage system, in which employers (through their payment of collectively bargained wages) and the state (through its compensatory programs) supported a particular set of family arrangements, the "solitary wage bargain" is premised on an instrumental amnesia. It externalizes the costs of social reproduction by shifting them onto individual workers.[29] This is our new free market version of family policy.

The women in our study recognized and commented on this gap. Darla Tanner said:

> With the new welfare reform, it's understandable that they want to push people to work. No one needs to sit home and collect a check while working people are paying for them to do that. . . . But the real problem is, we don't have enough child care and we don't have enough health benefits. . . . If they could just make sure we have enough health care and

child care benefits, then it might change the outcome. If I had the proper help when it comes to my children, that would allow me to go out and make money so I could pay the bills.

Darla's own life story provides many examples of these dilemmas of social reproduction. Over a long afternoon interview she described a series of events that clearly continued to haunt her. They involved her abduction and abuse at age eight and the death of her mother when she was eleven, followed by long years of being shuttled from one relative's house to another. She had her first child—a little girl—and dropped out of high school at age seventeen. The baby's father was murdered shortly afterward. Now twenty-seven, she had three children: Shemeka, ten; Demetri, seven; and Aaliya, four. Her struggles to care for them bore the mark of her own trauma. There were times when she could hardly bring herself to leave them at school, because she was afraid something would happen to them, and other times when she felt too helpless to care for them at all.

But despite setbacks—some of her own making, others not—Darla had a remarkable work record. When we checked back two years after this first interview, she was one of only two of our study's participants to be earning over $20,000 a year. She had held a number of jobs, including working in auto sales on one of the largest new car lots in Milwaukee. Her highest monthly paycheck at that job was $5,000, and her lowest –$250 (when she had taken a cash advance against her pay). She had enjoyed many of the jobs, but in all of them she struggled to combine the demands of work with the care of her three children, fighting the voice inside her head that said that she could leave them home unattended "just this once" in order not to lose a shift. And in all of her jobs, from time to time, she had struggled against a depression so dark that she didn't want to cook, didn't want to clean, didn't want to spend time with her kids. Darla's big gamble was enrolling in an associate's degree program at a local business school, despite receiving no state support to do so. "You've got to spend money to make money," she told us. "I'm investing in my education right now."

But this is getting ahead of the story. What Darla wanted to get across to us, and to our readers, was welfare reform's failure to support family care. By her own account, her success came despite—not because of—the state's strict workfare policies. In her assessment, and her stories of her own life, she traced the consequences of public policies designed to foster labor market participation for the private workings of home and family. What are the real consequences of requiring a mother of young children to work forty hours a week? What happens when there are gaps in care? When there are more responsibilities than hours in the week? When the weight of all the conflicting demands comes crashing down? Speaking of state officials, she said:

> They look at the numbers and say, "We got so many people off welfare," you know. They're celebrating. They're happy. But look at the number of children that have been removed from their parents' care since then. I wonder why they don't notice that child abuse and neglect rates went up since welfare reform? These are things they need to consider.[30]

It has become something of a truism, among observers of all political persuasions, to point out that public support for welfare eroded as women's labor market participation increased. "A program that was designed to pay mothers to stay at home with their children cannot succeed when we now observe most mothers going out to work," the *New Consensus* noted.[31] According to sociologist Ann Orloff, welfare "seemed to make possible staying at home to care for children at public expense for poor women—exactly what isn't guaranteed to any other mother or father."[32] This point belies the fact that poor mothers have been pioneers in working outside the home, doing so even when middle-class citizens considered it shameful. Since the earliest days of industrialization, they have left their own children to work as live-in domestics and caregivers for middle-class families. They have labored in factories, fields, and mills. As Kathryn Edin and Laura Lein have shown, even in the days of Aid to Families with Dependent Children, when "welfare-dependency" was held to be at its high point, women on welfare worked to supplement their checks.[33]

Women's workforce participation has increased markedly since 1970, and their work has in large part sustained the productivity of the economy since that time. But educated middle-class and poor women have participated in these trends in different ways. Unlike most other industrialized countries, the United States has not offered supports for care as women move into work but instead presumed that individuals will seek market solutions. Thus, the ability of women of all classes to afford the services that replace their household labor has depended on low wages in certain parts of the service sector. Employers have kept child care, elder care, cleaning services, and restaurant meals affordable by paying workers in these sectors less than a living wage and by rolling back benefits. As consumers of services, middle-class women have come to depend on other women's receiving low wages to bolster their ability to enter the labor market. Poor women, to the extent that they too are consumers, also benefit from those low wages, but they also suffer since they are the workers who are so poorly paid. Simply put, this is a case where the "haves" doing well depends on the "have-nots" having less.

Men and women with skills and education, who can command regular work at decent salaries, have options when a need to provide care arises: their employers might offer paid leave or, more likely, they might use savings to cover salary while taking time off under the 1993 Family and Medical Leave Act. In two-parent households, one partner might forego income and stay home to provide care when children are young or someone is ill. These adjustments are not easy—the trade-offs are sometimes painful. But a compromise can usually be crafted. For those who are poor, there are far fewer options. Employers in the low-wage service sector have abrogated their responsibilities, offering no sick leave, no maternity leave, and no health insurance, while imposing insecure but inflexible working conditions. Living in poor neighborhoods where mortgage and insurance redlining are still facts of life and predatory lending abounds, it is hard to build savings or assets.[34] There is no such thing as a 401(k) if you work in fast food retail or even as a certified nursing assistant. When the poor single mothers in our study needed time off to care, they came up short, quit their jobs, and ultimately turned to the state for means-tested assistance.[35]

Locating women's labor market strategies—and their decisions about how to combine market work with care for their children—within this larger context of withdrawn state and employer support makes it clear that they face choices that are both unprecedented and largely not of their own making. These choices are historically conditioned—related to the erosion of the family wage, the loss of employer-provided benefits, the end of an entitlement to welfare benefits, and in the case of many inner-city labor markets like Milwaukee and Racine, the prosecution of a war on drugs that incarcerates the majority of black men and releases them with felony convictions that prevent them from working. These processes have forced poor mothers into the labor market, which has absorbed them hungrily in times of economic prosperity and left them struggling to find work in periods of recession and stagnation. But the market has not provided adequate means to care for the young, the old, and the ill, and it has not made sufficient provision for the reproduction of the next generation of workers.

In *The New Consensus on Family and Work*, the policymakers behind welfare reform wrote that the "most disturbing element among a fraction of the contemporary poor [identified as low-income single mothers] is an inability to seize opportunity even when it is available. . . . Some may have work skills in the normal sense, but find it difficult to be regular, prompt, and in a sustained way, attentive to their work. Their need is less for job training than for meaning and order in their lives."[36] Like thirty million other Americans, the women in our study sought to feed and clothe their families. Like eighteen million other low-wage working mothers, they struggled to balance their time on the job with providing the care that their children need. They did so in a new world of jobs that offered little flexibility and no supports for family care, and on wages that left no cushion for hard times. Unlike the authors of the *New Consensus*, their definition of meaning and order included not just their work performance but also their ability to ensure that their children had clean clothes and got to school on time. With employers withdrawing the benefits that had sustained families through much of the twentieth century, and the erosion of government social programs, they struggled to maintain jobs in a recession and jobless recovery. Without sick leave or savings, unable to count on financial support from partners or parents, women struggled with the ups and downs of parenting, bearing the full responsibility for the well-being of their families with one hand tied behind their back. This is the market-driven paradigm of social reproduction—the solitary wage bargain.

CHAPTER FIVE

TYING THE SECOND HAND

CHALLENGES TO ECONOMIC CITIZENSHIP

> The welfare recipients who are told that they must work at whatever job is available see the specter of slavery and indentured servitude come to haunt them again, returned from a not so distant past. And the persistence of racism makes that fear plausible.
>
> JUDITH SHKLAR, *AMERICAN CITIZENSHIP*[1]

> This is what *inmates* do, inmates who have had their freedom taken from them.
>
> W-2 CASEWORKER, MILWAUKEE

The following interchange took place during an informational session in late 2003 at one of the private agencies that the state of Wisconsin had contracted to implement its welfare programs. A caseworker was explaining to participants who were having trouble finding employment that they must first engage in a supervised job search; if they did not find a job on their own, then the agency would place them in a community service position, for which they would receive a welfare check. This placement would last six months, at which point, if all had gone well, their employer was supposed to offer them a longer-term position on terms and at a wage negotiated by the welfare agency staff. If a woman did not agree to those terms and quit the job, she would be dropped from cash assistance. The tension grew in the room as the discussion proceeded.

AGENCY REPRESENTATIVE: You will do twenty hours of work experience, ten hours of basic education if you do not have a high school diploma or equivalent, and ten hours of employment search. . . .

WOMAN IN AUDIENCE: What if you already have work experience?

AGENCY REPRESENTATIVE: The state says that everybody must donate twenty hours per week. You are placed for thirty to ninety days. You must stay a minimum of thirty days at a given site, unless you experience significant harassment. We encourage the sites where you'll be placed to hire you. That happens about 60 percent of the time. We negotiate for $7.15/hour [postplacement wage].

This last bit of information set off murmurs throughout the room.

SECOND WOMAN IN AUDIENCE: What if the pay isn't what you would like?

AGENCY REPRESENTATIVE: It's not me; Madison [the state capital] says you cannot refuse a bona fide job offer. You cannot quit a job and expect to come back into a payment position. You would be placed in a CMS [case management services] position for thirty days—a nonpayment position. If you don't participate, then the FEP [financial employment planner] has the discretion to extend the CMS placement to ninety days. If you're having problems with a site, tell us you are having a problem and don't stop going. We will investigate the problem. If you just stop going, you will be sanctioned . . .

THIRD WOMAN: What if you haven't been hired within ninety days?

AGENCY REPRESENTATIVE: We will move you into a new site.

FOURTH WOMAN: What kinds of work sites do you have?

AGENCY REPRESENTATIVE: Mostly child care and clerical. We've been trying to create some positions at hospitals, but we're running into resistance from the hospital workers' union.

FIRST WOMAN: Is there a way to find out at what rate each place will be hiring?

SECOND WOMAN: Can we see the list of sites?

AGENCY REPRESENTATIVE: No, based on our meeting, I'm the one who decides where you'll be assigned.

The politicians and policymakers who reformed welfare believed that unemployed single mothers raising children needed to be made "less free" in order to "become something closer to the disciplined workers the economy demands."[2] They argued that it was legitimate for welfare agencies to require poor women to give up certain freedoms and to submit to the tutelage of the state as a condition of receiving aid. Here we explore some of the ways that women became less free as a result of their experiences with the welfare system, trading their civil and labor rights for their community service jobs. This is how the "second hand" is tied in the cases of women struggling with conditions in the low-wage labor market.

The framers of welfare reform made clear the kinds of jobs that they believed workfare participants, and women leaving welfare, would be filling. The *New Consensus on Family and Welfare* was explicit: "Among other kinds of work for which such mothers can be trained (which would, in turn, assist them in bringing up their own children) are child care and preschool education. In most cities, where female heads of families tend to be concentrated, hotels and other service establishments have many needs for entry-level employees." The authors add to the list, at various points, hospital workers, maintenance workers, cashiers, and restaurant staff. They point out that many experts tend to think in terms of middle-class jobs and therefore to prescribe training for factory or office work for poor women "while overlooking the opportunities that immigrants find so helpful in gaining a foothold."[3]

Lawrence Mead provides the following account of congressional debates over work requirements in the 1980s:

> The moderates insisted that at least low-paid work was generally available to recipients, despite high official unemployment. . . . The fact that they were menial jobs was no excuse for not taking them, said [congresswoman] Martha Griffiths.[4]

According to the framers of reform, in accepting workfare placements in these kinds of jobs, participants might not be acquiring specific skills but they would be building the competencies and sense of self-reliance that are the prerequisites of citizenship.

WORKFARE IN WISCONSIN

Community service jobs—CSJs, better known as workfare—have been the hallmark of Wisconsin's welfare reform. The Wisconsin Works program prescribed mandatory work experiences for women deemed to be capable of work but to "lack the skills and work habits needed in a regular job environment." Community service jobs, then, were intended as an opportunity to "practice" work under supervision.[5] While most women in our study entered welfare as a result of a crisis of social reproduction, which qualified them for caretaker-of-newborn or W-2 Transitions assistance, most exited through the prescribed work experience of one of these community service positions. In Milwaukee County in 2002, about 60 percent of welfare participants were in community service placements. These assignments required thirty hours of work and ten hours of job search or educational activity.[6] (The only allowable educational programs in 2004 were classes leading to the graduate equivalency degree or a few approved technology courses.) The most common job placements were in office, light industrial/housekeeping, thrift store, and care work. Based on a job site survey of participants, Andrea Robles and her coauthors reported that women felt that they gained the most valuable skills and experience from office work and the least from assignments in thrift stores and housekeeping.[7]

As we have seen, the staff of the agencies contracted to manage Wisconsin's workfare programs in Milwaukee and Racine determined whether workers were "ready" for employment and assigned them to activities, including job placements. Staff members identified work sites where they could place women and monitored their performance in these positions. The nature and quality of these job placements depended on an agency's resources and its networks in the community. In 2003 Milwaukee caseworkers placed 68 percent of CSJ participants with private nonprofits, 21 percent with private, for-profit firms, 6 percent with public agencies, and 4 percent with combined nonprofit/for-profit enterprises.[8] While finding appropriate jobs and short-term training programs for women had always been a challenge for the agencies, the quality and variety of placements had diminished considerably as a result of the state budget crisis that began in 2001.

In Racine, the Workforce Development Center integrated the activities of workfare with other programs for job seekers and employers. Located in one large building, and overseen by the county's Workforce Development Board, the center incorporated representatives from technical and community colleges, the Racine Area Manufacturers and Commerce Association, the Economic Development Corporation, Goodwill Industries, and the YWCA, as well as the state Department of Workforce Development and the county Human Services Department. The county emphasized that the center was "the focus of a comprehensive service initiative that seeks to meet the needs of both job seekers *and* employers serving as a critical component of larger efforts to improve the economic health of the county."[9]

As described, women placed in community service jobs signed an employability plan that committed them to participation in certain work activities for a specified number of hours each week. While some caseworkers listened to participants' needs and tried to make appropriate matches, others did not give women opportunities to express their preferences or to make choices.

Program evaluations suggested that caseworkers based assignments more on the availability of work slots than on the background, skills, or goals of participants. Depending on their contacts, some agencies placed more women in thrift store work, while others placed the majority in housekeeping and light industrial tasks.[10]

Many of the women we interviewed complained about the combination of rigid rules and poor placement opportunities in community service jobs. Consider Rachel Fernandez. Rachel was born in Puerto Rico, but her parents moved to Milwaukee when she was still a baby. She had four children, three of whom were living with her at the time. She was on parole from a drug conviction at the time we interviewed her. She was grateful to have gotten her children back and was working hard to reestablish a stable home for them. She had turned to W-2 after a mental health crisis—she had attempted suicide—and she was hoping that caseworkers would help her to get her graduate equivalency degree and to find an office job. But at every step she seemed to be running into walls.

First, she wanted to take classes for her GED at Milwaukee Area Technical College, because the "classes" at her assigned agency had no instructors—people were simply placed at a table and directed to make their way through workbooks. "My FEP worker said no," she said. "So now I'll be going to UMOS [her assigned agency] two hours a day. . . . I had to give up MATC." "Is it just that they didn't want to pay MATC for the classes?" we asked. "No," she replied, "'cause I was paying for the classes. I was paying for them. But he was like, 'No! You've got to consult me, whatever you want to do.'"[11]

In a similar way, Rachel butted heads with her caseworker over her work activities:

> I do what they want me to do. Things I don't want to do. . . . Like right now, they gave me an activity to work at a pantry shop [food pantry] that I'm not interested in whatsoever. My interest was computer and office assistant classes, and they don't want to put me in that. My worker tells me, "Well, you have to do it because our supervisor tells us for you to do it."

Finally, Rachel had difficulty with the fact that her employment plan required her to put her nineteen-month-old son in day care even when he was having trouble with asthma. It had been difficult to find a provider who would take him and when she did, it was on the condition that she would pick him up if he had an attack. "So I go to pick him up and [my caseworkers] don't understand that," she said:

The things they want you to do that we don't want to do! But they force us to do it just to get our little paycheck. And it's not worth it. Sometimes I feel like saying screw W-2. You know? But I can't, because I can't afford my rent or my bills, so I have to do the things they want me to do.

Rachel felt that the lack of choice was just wrong:

The main thing . . . I think we should be able to do what we want to do and not what they want us to do. I think we should be able to choose our activities and our job skills and education. . . . Just let us choose what we want to do.

Serena Clark also complained about this lack of choice. We have seen her dilemma. She had grown up in a house where family members used and sold drugs and had started selling them herself when she was eleven. But when she was sixteen, a religious organization took her in and got her off drugs, and she traveled around the country for a while giving testimony about her experiences. After she returned to Milwaukee in 2001, she married and gave birth to a son. She applied for caretaker-of-newborn benefits then; in 2003 she returned to the welfare office to see if she could get support while training as an AODA (alcohol and drug abuse) counselor.

Serena had been accepted into a minority training program at a reputable drug and alcohol treatment center in Milwaukee. She believed that she had found her calling. Comparing the work to the "preaching" she had done with the religious organization, she said, "in counseling you can relate, rather than just having a good speech or good words to say. . . . It keeps me home. It keeps me real." For Serena, this was a tremendous accomplishment, not only because she had overcome a drug addiction, but also because she had been born with a disability:

I'm grateful for life, because I was born paralyzed. I was born with a brain abscess and they said I would always stay that way. I had brain surgery. I've always had, like, ADHD classes. So it was just like getting out of that . . . getting people to acknowledge that I can do something for myself. I'm trying my hardest. I have my right mind, you know. I'm not slow, as they would categorize me. Especially [my caseworkers]. I never told anybody that I had those types of problems. Or about being abandoned. You know what I mean? But having social skills was something that I had to learn over the years because of the violence and abuse that I had as a child. I'm able to talk, to socialize now. I'm not kept away where my voice has been stolen from me. People telling me, "Shut up." "You're stupid." "You're slow."

The problem was that Serena's caseworker didn't consider her counselor training a legitimate community service job activity:

> She says I shouldn't be wasting my time at it. That I need to make more time to do my job logs or I need to find a full-time job, you know, like working as a waitress, rather than having a part-time job and doing what I want to do for my future. She wants me to give up my hopes, my dreams. What the hell am I gonna do that for? Give up all this I accomplished just to be a waitress? . . . They require me to hand in job searches. It totally interrupts my schedule, because first of all I have to study, and then I have to be at my work activities, and then I have to pick up my son. . . . I'm not going to go out every week and look for twenty jobs.

We will return to Serena's case in a later chapter to see how she resolved this dilemma.

For Shakira Hall, the number of activities the state required her to perform in return for her check—working at a community service job, attending classes, searching for an unsubsidized job, and caring for her kids—was also a big problem:

> I just want to cut my activities down . . . so maybe I could just go to school right now. I mean, that would be so much better—if they would let you do one thing at a time. But then it all got too complex and too hard, 'cause I was going to school, going to work, coming home, and I was stressed. I'm trying to do four things, coming home stressed out 'cause I can't pay the bills, stressed out because Gordon and I don't see each other. I mean it rips a household apart! And I know I'm not the only person that thinks that. After your two hours of school, you do four hours of CSJ, and then they want you to spend two hours a day looking for a job.

Shakira fantasized about what she considered the ideal work situation:

> My ideal job would be preschool. That would be perfect. And especially if it was a school where she [her daughter] went and he [her son] was going. So I wouldn't have to worry about day care. I'd be working and I'd have summers off with them. I'd have the same days off with them.

For Delia Carter, the problem was that she was assigned to work sites in the neighborhood where her former partner lived—a man who had beaten her badly and against whom she had a restraining order. (He was eventually jailed for his abuse of her.)

> I was in an abusive relationship. This man almost killed me one time— and in front of my son. He threatened to kill me again—in front of a lot of people this time. So I really felt in my heart that he was serious. You know, you don't say that in front of all these witnesses if you don't mean it. And I let my [case] worker know that I was scared to leave the house. I mean it got so bad I wouldn't even go to the store—I would pay little kids around the neighborhood to go to the store for me. So I'm not going to do no activities in that neighborhood. You know, I'm not going to die at the hands of this man because ya'll want me to come and sit in a class that's supposed to be a GED class for two hours and then go clean up somebody's bathrooms. You know, I'm not gonna risk my life for that. And I tried to get them to put me somewhere else on the other side of town. Nobody could do that. You know what I'm saying? None of them could put me nowhere else. I was just sanctioned.

Caseworkers from another agency told us that their agency had introduced new policies for battered women after a similar case in which a man had, in fact, tracked his partner to a workfare site and killed her.

Other women complained about training programs that never materialized. Geraldine Anderson told of attending a program at Goodwill Industries:

> I was required to go and attend this job training program. And I went, and I did all of their preliminary stuff—being on time for work and all those other things, OK. And it lasted for two weeks, and I'll never forget, at the end of those two weeks, the man came in and told everyone that they didn't have the funding or job training programs available. I went to another [training] through OIC [one of the contract agencies]. They talked about budgets and they talked about saving money. And then after going through all of this you're supposed to transition into some job training, but it never happens. We did what we were supposed to do in hopes that it would lead to something better, but it never did.

Delia Carter told a similar story:

> I was trying to get into CNA [certified nursing assistant] classes. [They said] you go these classes for thirty days and we'll put you in a training.

You just got to show that you will come and you will be on time for thirty days. I go for two and a half months. It was work experience classes, where you go and do work everyday . . . you know? And then I hear there's no trainings available.

Vanetta Brown said:

I left the day care job because they told me I had to go through some classes [to get certified], and I went to W-2 to get into their classes for that and they told me their classes were gonna be booked up for like three months. They put you in programs, but the programs they put you in is not helping you toward anything. It's not helping you toward the career you want to go to or the job you want to be in. They didn't give me any skills.

Others simply complained about the quality of the jobs. According to Denise Adkins:

I was told if we had a lot of job experience, we shouldn't have to do one of those assignments that's just basically to see what it's like to work somewhere. I've had so many jobs, I just thought that was a waste of time for me. I think they should do more training, getting people involved in classes so they can get better jobs.

These women, like so many others, were convinced that there was something wrong with the state's being able to dictate the kinds of work they would perform and the conditions under which they would do it. As one W-2 participant told a *Milwaukee Journal Sentinel* reporter, "That's all they want to do, push you into something you don't want to be . . . like working at a fast food restaurant."[12] Another woman tried to explain how she felt about the program to researcher Andrea Robles:

You love your research . . . what you're doing. What if your boss came to you and said "now your CSJ assignment is to pick up garbage?" You wouldn't like that. If you put people in a CSJ that they don't care about, they won't learn. . . . It won't work.[13]

The women who participated in W-2 were not the only ones who perceived and discussed this lack of freedom. One caseworker told us: "That's what *inmates* do, inmates who have had their freedom taken from them." She suggested that the program might work for more women if it had better placements to offer participants—real jobs with private-sector firms. But as it stood, she argued, "We're not helping anyone. We're just another burden, another barrier like everything else."

THE DOWNWARD MOBILITY MACHINE: CHURNING WORKERS TO THE BOTTOM OF THE LABOR MARKET

Participation in community service jobs for the women we interviewed was, in a disturbing number of cases, associated with a pattern of downward job mobility. A number of women in our study had previously held responsible clerical or managerial positions. When they turned to W-2 in a crisis and began to transition back to employment, they were placed in CSJs that involved unskilled, manual work.

Rowena Watson was one such case. Rowena had two daughters when we met her, one fourteen and one a few months old. She had worked from 1998 to 2001 as a manager of three independent living facilities. The job, as she described it, was

> to assist people who have developmental disabilities in daily living activities: cooking, cleaning, checking their mail . . . teaching them how to be successful in a home atmosphere. I supervised different staff members that worked hands-on with the people. I supervised three different houses, maintaining the clients' money, paying their bills, buying them clothes, buying them furniture, buying them food . . . like a mother!

She had started the job as a personal care assistant and had been promoted to supervisor. She attributed her promotion to her "willingness to do things that other people didn't want to do, like taking them on an outing. When I first started there, I didn't have a car, so we went places on the bus."

As a supervisor Rowena made about $11 an hour, and the job had good benefits, including health and life insurance. She described this period of employment as the best time in her life:

> Me and my kid were doing well. I didn't have to ask nobody for nothing. I didn't have to kiss nobody's ass. I could do things with my daughter that we have not done in so long. . . . I worked a lot, but she was always taken care of by my grandmother. We had a car. We went out to eat every Friday. You know, I even took my daughter to work with me and she would sit at the kitchen table and do her homework . . . just like a family.

While Rowena enjoyed this job, she eventually quit after several experiences of what she interpreted as racism:

> Well, I was a young, black supervisor in a big company with a bunch of Caucasians. . . . They started doing little things to me. They would come and get my time sheets, and they wanted to see receipts . . . like they were just trying to find something to fire me about. I got really tired of it. And I know me, and I think they knew that eventually I was going to say something, so I resigned from my position so that I could keep my supervisory title. Because I thought, "I can go anywhere and become a supervisor," you know, especially as a caregiver.

From 2001 to 2003 Rowena worked in several certified nursing assistant jobs and in home health care. Then, during a pregnancy in 2003, she began to experience high blood pressure, and her doctor told her she would have to take medical leave. Because that was not an option offered by her employer, she turned to W-2. When we interviewed her, her baby daughter was seven months old and she had been assigned to a community service job. "They send me places to work," she said:

> One of them is on the north side—you help them cut down their rubbish and their trees. Another one—they send me down to the City of Milwaukee Department of Public Works and you help them fix the streets. Or that island out there, you know—they have people from W-2 go out there and water the grass and plant the flowers.

"What am I going to do cutting down bushes?" she asked. "Am I gonna put that on my résumé?"

Ebony Walker provides another example. Ebony was a mother of five children, two of whom were grown and three of whom still lived at home. While she had completed high school and had taken some college courses, her working career had been interrupted by serious health problems, as we learned earlier, including several heart surgeries, herniated discs in her back, diabetes, and post-traumatic stress resulting from domestic violence. In 1996 she worked as an office manager for a community development organization in Milwaukee. A caseworker had placed her in this position under the former welfare program, Aid to Families with Dependent Children. She loved the job, which required considerable administrative and clerical skill:

We helped the senior citizens clean their houses and make repairs, picking them up, taking food to them. . . . That was very fulfilling. I started out as a clerical aid and worked my way up to executive secretary. I already had the secretarial skills, but I didn't have computer literacy yet and I learned a lot there. I learned to do payroll, calculating percentages, helped with audits, learned how to do inventory. And my boss trusted me to handle money, so I went to the bank for the company.

Ebony lost this job when the organization's funding was discontinued.

When she returned to the welfare office for a new placement, W-2 had been implemented, and Ebony was assigned to a trial job with another community development agency. Again, she found the work enjoyable and challenging:

It started off that they were trying to use me as a joke [because she was a workfare placement]. But they didn't understand that I'm a hard worker. I started off as a clerical aid and worked my way up to executive assistant for a skilled trade apprenticeship program. I did job recruiting, secretarial work, document production, ran errands. . . . I did a lot of things in that office. I enjoyed that job because I could see that the community was receiving help that they needed.

Nevertheless, despite state rules, she was never hired on a regular line:

As a [trial job] participant, you are supposed to be hired [on a regular contract] after six months, legally. I didn't know any of that. I just kept working because I liked working. But the company took advantage of me because the label "welfare recipient" was tagged to my head, so they refused to hire me regardless of the skills and talent that I had. I had a stigma once I got on the program.

When the state discovered that her boss at this organization was embezzling large amounts of money, they shut down the agency, and Ebony lost the job she had held for over a year. Unable to pay her rent, she ended up in a homeless shelter. There, the depression she had been battling all her life became worse. She had experienced numerous episodes of abuse and domestic violence in her life and had seen a psychiatrist off and on to help her, as she put it, "stop being afraid." At that time, she said:

I was having nervous spells and I didn't know why. I took medicine to keep me from shaking because I had that much fear in me. I had nightmares. My children were affected, and I couldn't think clear. I wound up having to get on welfare.

Ebony's caseworker placed her in a W-2 Transitions program for a while, where she could continue to receive counseling, but after some months she was assigned to a CSJ placement that required both job search and employment activity. Here, she said, "they stuck us all in factories and had us doing jobs nobody else wanted to do. And that's the honest-to-god truth—from picking up trash on the street, like the people at the county jail had to do, to working in the Goodwill with the disabled people."

In Ebony's own assessment, she would do best, given her health problems, if she could work part-time:

> I have a combination of illnesses. Let me work four hours a day. I love working. I like helping people. Give me a choice to do that and help me find a place that will hire me. I don't want that stigma tagged on my head: "OK, she's a welfare recipient, she's unemployable."

In both Rowena's and Ebony's cases, women who had accrued significant skills and experience exited the labor market for a brief period and reentered through W-2 programs. Their experience provides a vivid illustration of what Peck calls "churning workers back into the bottom of the labor market," "creating workers for jobs nobody wants," and the construction of "a new category of forced labor, compelled to accept low wage work."[14]

Catherine LeBlanc's experience reveals a third example of downward mobility in a CSJ, and a novel response to it. Catherine was a mother of three children under the age of four. At the time that we interviewed her, she was working off the books as an exotic dancer. This was a choice about which she was very ambivalent, a condition reflected in the several explanations she gave for it. At first, she said that she had taken the job so that she wouldn't have to depend on her boyfriend, who was earning a living selling drugs:

> He's like, "Woo-hoo! Look at me! I have this and I have that!" But he's been to jail on a gun charge. He's not nickel-and-diming it no more, so he's gonna get some time. Now he's like a hero to the kids 'cause he can take them shopping more. I want my daughters to know they don't have to put up with that. And I want my son to know that he doesn't have to do that either.

Catherine's concerns were also financial, and how she came to a situation where exotic dancing looked like a good option requires some explanation. Most of her childhood was spent on the road with her Native American mother and her grandparents:

> They have family everywhere, like on reservations and stuff, and they had an RV and they would just go. And my mom's the baby, so she'd just call them up and she'd be like, "Where are you guys?" And they'd send her money to get to wherever they were. We lived in Vancouver, Washington, Arizona, Virginia, Michigan, Alabama, Florida, even Mexico City. But when I was fifteen, we came back to Milwaukee and I moved out of my mom's house and got an apartment with another girl.

While this peripatetic childhood left Catherine with only an eighth-grade education, she managed to get a job at a drugstore by claiming to have a high school diploma. She started in the photo department, then moved to another store to take a job as cosmetics department manager. After three years, she moved to a position as a department manager at a large local retailer for $8.65 an hour and after fifteen months moved again, this time to Walmart. There, she was offered $9.50 an hour as a department manager with a full-time, Monday through Friday schedule—no nights, no weekends. She was thrilled, and even more thrilled when they promoted her to claims manager. She sounded almost wistful recalling that job:

> I had my own little office and my own phone and my own computer—it was just like my own little area. I did my work, and it was fast-paced. It wasn't like I was just sitting at a desk. Everything that people returned was my responsibility. And I liked helping out with the receiving stuff too, and I used to have fun unloading the trucks. I like working with stuff like that. I like to use my hands. I'd rather do hard work.

After about a year and a half, Catherine became pregnant with her youngest child. She was having a hard first trimester, and the store's managers would not allow her to move to part-time, even temporarily, in the claims manager position. So she asked to be shifted to a part-time cashier's job, at a cut in pay, until after the baby was born. What happened to Catherine next was a classic example of the impact of harsh work rules. She was fired for taking a break fifteen minutes early to use the restroom. Despite the fact that she was pregnant and doing a job that required her to stand on her feet, her action was called "time theft" because it wasn't her scheduled time to take her break.

Catherine filed for unemployment, and collected it for seven months. During that period her health insurance ran out, and she accrued over $10,000 in prenatal medical bills, leading her to file for bankruptcy. At the time her unemployment insurance ended, her daughter had just been born and she collected caretaker-of-newborn benefits for three months. When those benefits ended, she was still breast-feeding and not ready to go back to work yet, and her boyfriend offered to support her. But the state was continuing to manage her case, and partly because she didn't want to take her boyfriend's drug money, she accepted a CSJ placement. Despite her experience as a claims manager and department manager, she was placed in a job as a clerical aide in a day care center. She described the job as less than challenging: "I really didn't do anything. I'd just sit and watch TV and eat. . . . Occasionally I'd type up flyers for her or something. I would answer the phone sometimes."

Ultimately, with her monthly income cut to less than half of what it had been, she realized she couldn't make it. Speaking of her work as an exotic dancer she said:

> Sometimes I feel like a hypocrite. I used to think "I would never do *that*. I would *never* do that." But I was just so tired of being broke. . . . And a few of my friends had done it and they go back to it once in a while when they don't have a lot of money or they're trying to get something they really want or they need to make a car payment or something. First, I was gonna do it just so I could take my kids to the Dells [a popular Wisconsin recreation area]. . . . And that week, I ended up making so much money that I was like, "I'll do it another week and then I won't have to ask my dad for my rent money."

One advantage the job presented over going back to retail sales was that she could work nights, after her kids had gone to bed, and her boyfriend or his mother would watch them. "They don't even know I'm gone," she said. And the money—from $300 to $1,000 a week—was tax-free.

Jocelyn Brill provides yet another example of downward mobility in community service jobs. Jocelyn had worked as a receptionist, as a sales associate for a clothing store, and then in a clerical job at a small podiatry firm for two years. She made $9.75 an hour at this last job. "I basically ran the office," she said. "I needed computer skills, people skills, patience." She quit her job to receive caretaker-of-newborn support after the birth of her son in 2003, and after that her caseworker placed her in a community service job learning to sew. Frustrated with her $673 a month check and with the work, she turned to "her own business"—a combination of selling hot home-cooked meals and less legal activities, and she also enrolled herself in business school.

The list goes on. Joanne Benitez, who had formerly done clerical work, found herself sorting clothes at Goodwill Industries for her CSJ placement: "Taking 'em down, putting 'em up, cleaning up the store, the restrooms." Darla Tanner, who had worked in auto and other sales positions, and sometimes pulled in over $30,000 a year, was working for the city cleaning apartments. Tawanna Marks and Nicole Harrison had both done factory work in the past, but Tawanna was assigned to cleaning the W-2 offices and Nicole to a job placing stickers on boxes in a training program for the handicapped. Nicole complained:

> I don't have no problems working with the handicapped, but they came down on my back because I wasn't getting my quota in, because you have to be helping them and redoing their stickers and what-not. I had to stop what I was doing [to help the others] and they was like, "Well, you're not making your quota. You're supposed to have twenty-five boxes."

Of the thirty-three women we interviewed, nineteen, or nearly 60 percent, had held a community service job. *None* of the women placed in these positions worked in activities that they found appropriate or challenging, or felt they were acquiring new skills. As Delia Carter put it, "Either they got you cutting up fabrics for their clothing line or you are cleaning up, doing janitorial work. If you're lucky—if heaven's done moved the earth—you get into a training." While some of those who had been assigned to community service jobs in earlier years had placements they felt built their skills and improved their job prospects, these experiences had dwindled over time, especially as the number of agencies administering welfare declined and the state's budget allocation for the programs shrank.

Geraldine Anderson offered this critique of the way that community service jobs shaped women's subsequent work:

> So they give a woman a . . . community service job, she goes into a hospital for six hours a day—free labor for the hospital—she learns some skills for four months and now she's got a six- or seven-dollar-an-hour job working in that same hospital—in the cafeteria, though. Not where she may have done her community service job. That was the success part—she's got a job. . . . But there's the whole illusion that if you do this program the way we have it set up, it will teach you how to get to work on time, it will teach you responsibility, it will teach how to work with your money. And not looking at the other end—the other end

being that there needs to be a way where you can step higher, where you can elevate, you know what I mean?

How common was this pattern of downward mobility in community service jobs? Of the women placed in CSJs, six had not held very responsible jobs in the past, having worked mainly in fast food or cleaning. For these women, an assignment sorting clothes or cutting brush was arguably a formative experience. But for thirteen of the women (68 percent of those placed in CSJs) the placements led to downward mobility in the labor market. Women who had worked as certified nursing assistants were placed in fast food jobs, a woman who had worked as a security guard and inventory technician was assigned to cleaning a mental health facility, a sales representative for a communications firm was placed in a housekeeping job, and factory workers were sent to clean vacant apartments. The work sites that state policy said were meant to help them acquire the "skills and work habits needed in a regular job environment" placed them in jobs that entailed far fewer capacities than they had used in their prior employment.

Participation in community service jobs undermined women's labor market trajectories in other ways as well. Once women were enrolled in W-2, had signed their employability contract, and were working with a financial employment planner (caseworker), the rules of the workfare program and the stigma attached to it could undermine their attempts to reenter the labor market at their former level. Ebony Walker alluded to this problem when she said, "The label welfare recipient was tagged to my head." She expressed the sense that she was not viewed as a "real worker" because she had been sent by the welfare agency: "It started off they were trying to use me as a joke." Because she had been assigned to the job by the state, Ebony could not forge a direct contract with her employer, who preferred to continue using her labor on a subsidized basis. At the time of our last interview with her, Ebony had been engaged in a job search as part of her W-2 assignment, and told us:

I had been offered a position through a temp service as an executive secretary, which is what I used to be. I let one of my caseworkers know that I had the job, but that I had to go in for my second interview. She called the temp service that I had signed up with and told them, "Well, she's on welfare, so we want to monitor her for a year . . ." Now, I hadn't told them that I was a welfare recipient, and because they found out, I couldn't get the job for $15 an hour. They decided to give it to someone else and started offering me jobs for $6 an hour, which was not enough for me to actually get off welfare and stay off. You know, I know what I'm worth and what I'm capable of doing, and $6 an hour was like a slap in the face. I tried to go for some of the $6 jobs, but they were so far across town to where I couldn't commute on the bus, so I got depressed again and was ready to give it up, till I looked at my children and said, "Well I've got to feed my babies."

She added: "There ought to be a law passed that you can't check a person's socioeconomic status. If they come and you find out they are ready to do the job, let them work. They shouldn't have to know that you were on welfare."

Serena Clark told a similar story. She had been assigned to job search and had called a number of companies that seemed promising, when she found that her caseworker was calling them as well to verify her log entries:

She was calling the places that I had written on my job logs. That's like lowering me. How is the W-2 gonna call the place? Then they're only gonna think I'm qualified for getting $5.15 an hour. . . . If they see that I'm getting a W-2 check, you think they're gonna give me a job? No, they're gonna look at me as a statistic!

In both of these cases, the monitoring required by the program and the stigma attached to participation compromised the women's ability to reenter the labor market at their previous level of skill and wages.

THE LABOR MARKET STATUS OF WORKFARE PARTICIPANTS

What are women doing when they participate in workfare? Are they workers who happen to be placed in their jobs by the state, or are they welfare recipients who are required to perform activities as a condition of aid? Are they trainees? What exactly is their relationship to the private firms and public agencies for which they labor? What rights and protections normally associated with work pertain to them? These questions have not yet been definitively answered in law or in the courts, leaving workfare participants in a never-never land of ambiguity.

In Wisconsin, policymakers designed workfare programs to imitate the rewards and sanctions of private-sector jobs. Nevertheless, women assigned to work activities still receive "welfare," in the sense that the time clock that limits their benefits is ticking and the state, through its contracted agencies, monitors their work attendance and imposes sanctions if they miss hours. While women work thirty hours a week for public or private sector employers, the fact that they have signed a contract with the state committing themselves to these activities creates a complex new relationship involving state, employer, and worker/citizen. As Goldberg has emphasized, workfare participants are both "anomalous figures who seem to be situated on both sides of the worker/ relief distinction" and "liminal figures who seem to be situated on neither side of the distinction."[15] The issues surrounding workfare participants' relationship to existing labor laws have proven so complex that the Congressional Research Service regularly produces reports summarizing current law and administrative rulings regarding the applicability to their labor of the Fair Labor Standards Act (FLSA), unemployment insurance, Social Security, state workers' compensation laws, the Earned Income Tax Credit, OSHA, and various civil rights and nondiscrimination statutes.[16]

The participation agreement signed by workfare participants in the state of Wisconsin does allude to the existence of rights and protections, but it does not specify what they are. It says that W-2 work assignments will meet all federal and state labor laws and rules "that apply" without clarifying which do and which do not. It says that the assignments will meet all federal, state, and local health and safety standards, will be free of discrimination, will not require the participant to give up labor or union rights, and will not replace a worker who is on strike, locked out, or involved in another bona fide labor dispute. Nevertheless, as subsequent sections will show, these claims have neither been bolstered by enforcement nor clarified by litigation in the state. Exploring the ways in which welfare reform has affected participants' rights in Wisconsin thus requires some reference to legal and statutory struggles in other parts of the country, since precedent set in one location often affects legal framing and policy implementation elsewhere.

STRUGGLES OVER A MINIMUM WAGE

The first of these issues to be addressed at the federal level was whether the Fair Labor Standards Act requirement of a minimum wage applied to workfare participants. The original text of the PRWORA did not address this issue, but in May 1997 the Clinton administration's Department of Labor issued a set of administrative guidelines entitled "How Workplace Laws Apply to Welfare Recipients." This document held that most workfare participants were covered by minimum wage laws. Since administrators determined the hourly "wage" by dividing a participant's monthly benefit by hours worked, and since PRWORA set a minimum work week of twenty hours, this created a problem.

Only in Alaska, Wisconsin, and parts of California and New York were TANF benefits high enough to provide the required wage. The Department of Labor guidelines permitted administrators to add food stamps to the calculation of monthly income, but some states still found that they needed to increase cash benefits to reach the minimum wage.[17]

The National Council of State Human Service Administrators and some governors protested the Labor Department's guidelines, worrying that the ruling would dramatically cut back the number of hours they could require welfare recipients to work. Organized labor applauded the new interpretation, however, arguing that unless benefits were pegged to the minimum wage, the entry of large numbers of workfare participants into the labor market would depress wage rates for entry-level jobs in both the public and private sectors.[18] Democrats in Congress tried to attach an amendment to the 1997 Balanced Budget Act that would have extended workplace protections to workfare participants, thus providing a more durable legal basis for such an interpretation, but this measure was defeated. Republicans, in turn, announced their intent to pass legislation exempting participants from labor protections, but in response to Clinton's threat to veto the measure, did not proceed. Six states have subsequently passed laws extending the minimum wage to workfare participants.[19]

In September 1996 welfare policymakers in Wisconsin argued that they were not legally bound to pay workfare participants the minimum wage. They labeled a woman's check her "training grant" and declared that it "is not a wage and therefore not affected by changes in the minimum wage laws."[20] After the Department of Labor issued its guidelines, state officials were forced to change course, calibrating benefits and hours worked to insure payment of a minimum wage. In order to make these calculations work, they had to exclude all hours spent in mandatory activities except for those in the work placement itself.

The new federal guidelines provided a basis for workfare participants to appeal their assignments on grounds that they violated minimum wage requirements. While there were no such cases in Wisconsin, welfare advocates watched with interest when, in 1998, the Southern District Court of New York ruled that participants in a New York City work program were entitled to a minimum wage, specifically finding participants to be "employees."[21] Encouraged by these developments, the Welfare Law Center, the Legal Aid Society, and the National Employment Law Project tried to push the wage issue another step forward, arguing that participants should be paid the *prevailing* wage for the kind of work they performed in the local labor market, in accordance with requirements of New York State welfare law. When the Southern District Court of New York agreed with the plaintiffs, the state legislature quickly repealed the prevailing wage provisions of the welfare law and substituted new language requiring localities to use the minimum wage.[22]

When the federal government issued its final TANF and welfare-to-work regulations in April 1999, it solidified the interpretation that minimum wage laws applied by stating unequivocally that the Fair Labor Standards Act (FLSA), the Occupational Safety and Health Act (OSHA), unemployment insurance (UI), and nondiscrimination laws "apply to TANF beneficiaries in the same way they apply to other workers."[23] This interpretation appeared to shift in 2002, when the Bush administration generated proposals for PRWORA's reauthorization that entailed increased work requirements without more funding; many people assumed that this meant abandonment of the minimum wage standard. Their concern amplified when a lower level official in the Department of Health and Human Services indicated that this was indeed the proposal's intent. Tommy Thompson, then secretary of health and human services, intervened quickly, however, to insist that the Bush administration was committed to guaranteeing a minimum wage for hours worked, although he did not clarify how states could ask participants to work more hours without receiving funds to increase their cash benefit. In practice, most states achieved this by cutting their rolls.[24]

One troubling, and as yet unresolved, aspect of minimum wage enforcement is how to handle states' garnering of some or all of mandatory child support payments as compensation for benefits. With the passage of PRWORA, states had been given greater latitude in deciding how to treat money collected from noncustodial parents. Wisconsin officials elected to experiment with, and later adopt, a full pass-through of all support collections between 1997 and 2005. This was in contrast to most other states, which retained part or all of payments. However, beginning in 2005, a custodial parent performing a workfare assignment was forced to give up the child support to which she was entitled in return for her check, and was effectively uncompensated for her work. The same is true when the state claims a participant's retroactive awards of federal disability benefits or other income.[25] While welfare administrators in Wisconsin and elsewhere recognized this problem, no complaints or lawsuits concerning this issue have been filed.

As time passed, Wisconsin benefit levels began to diverge from the minimum wage. Cash benefits did not increase between 1996 and 2008, even when the city of Milwaukee set a minimum wage higher than the federal standard, and when the federal minimum wage rose. PRWORA guidelines prevented administrators from reducing required work hours. Thus, in a context of persistent budget shortfalls and limited political support for welfare, they allowed the "wage" of workfare participants to slip below the level required by both local and federal ordinances.

ANTIDISCRIMINATION LAW

With minimum wage coverage resting on still-fragile statutory grounds, workfare participants' rights to other kinds of protections remained unclear. One area of concern was whether women performing workfare assignments were protected from discrimination and sexual harassment. Legislators had included certain protections in PRWORA, including prohibitions against age discrimination under the Rehabilitation Act and coverage by the Americans with Disabilities Act and by Title VI of the Civil Rights Act (outlawing discrimination by organizations receiving federal funding). The applicability of Title VII protections (outlawing discrimination by private organizations) was not clear, however, leaving some to suspect that by listing statutes that *were* applicable, Congress had intended to exclude coverage by all others.

In 2002 Legal Action of Wisconsin, the American Civil Liberties Union of Wisconsin, and the NAACP's Milwaukee chapter asked federal civil rights officers to investigate the way the program screened and assisted disabled participants. In a complaint filed with the Office of Civil Rights of the U.S. Department of Health and Human Services, they alleged that disabled participants, and women who were raising children with disabilities, were not being given the accommodations required by the Americans with Disabilities Act. The complaint pointed out that a significant portion of individuals on the rolls had disabilities and that caseworkers were requiring them to perform workfare assignments that were beyond their abilities or were declaring them "job-ready" and ending their benefits.[26] In response to this complaint, HHS required the state to implement a "barrier screening tool" that would provide greater opportunity to discover disabilities at the time of intake.

Another discrimination issue that surfaced in Wisconsin concerned the imposition of sanctions on workers who did not complete all of their assigned activities. When participants failed to complete every hour of their assignments, caseworkers were authorized to deduct money from their welfare benefits for each hour missed. In 2002 the ACLU and the Milwaukee branch of the NAACP filed another complaint with the Office of Civil Rights, this time pointing to racial disparities in the imposition of sanctions.[27] A subsequent study by the state's Department of Workforce Development confirmed these disparities and recommended training for case managers and supervisors, restoration of a fair hearing process (which would have required a statutory change), and continued monitoring of the situation.[28] In this case, as in the disability case, the complaints did not reach the courts but were resolved through the state's agreement to revise its bureaucratic procedures. In contrast, lawsuits filed on behalf of workfare participants in several cases in New York State were re-solved in ways supportive of the claim that antidiscrimination law applied.[29]

In 2000 a number of workers filed sex and race discrimination complaints against Maximus, one of the state's contract agencies. One widely covered case concerned two women who complained to the Equal Employment Opportu-nity Commission about their treatment at Maxstaff, the temporary services subsidiary of the firm. Maxstaff sent Tracy Jones and Alfredia Parks to an un-subsidized employment position in the warehouse of a private retail appliance chain in Waukesha, Wisconsin. After talking with their coworkers, the two women found that their pay for work as "furniture preppers"—workers who prepare furniture to be shipped to customers—was $7.01 an hour—far less than the $8.13 an hour earned by the men with whom they worked.[30] Jones previously had worked as a machine operator, a warehouse carton packer, and a building maintenance worker. "It was my prior experience as a union steward that helped me recognize this was wrong," she reported. Jones was fired by Maxstaff ten days after she filed her complaint with the EEOC. In September 2000 the EEOC found in favor of the two women, instructing Maximus to engage in remediation.[31] As a result of these incidents, the state Legislative Audit Bureau called on all W-2 agencies to develop affirmative action and civil rights compliance plans, as required by law, as well as to designate a coordina-tor for equal opportunity policies and to develop appropriate complaint and grievance procedures.[32]

OTHER LAWS AND STATUTES

Despite the fact that the final TANF regulations stated that the Fair Labor Standards Act and the Occupational Safety and Health Act applied to work-fare participants, many employers continued to commit grievous health and safety violations. In New York City, the press documented several cases of workers laboring without safety training or access to toilets, potable water, protective clothing, or safety equipment, and several deaths of workfare par-ticipants there drew public attention.[33] Advocates for workfare participants noted that while administrative rulings tended to guarantee them the same protections as others who work under similar circumstances, if there were no "comparable others," it was difficult to establish a protection standard. Also, the administrative rulings were not self-executing and were difficult to enforce, leading the National Employment Law Project to conclude that "many workers continue to suffer terms and conditions of work which are vastly inferior to those of the paid employees with whom they work side-by-side." NELP lawyers also pointed out that workers who complained, whether about unsafe conditions or sexual harassment, were especially vulnerable to losing their benefits and, in many states, had no access to an appeals process. They concluded that the complexity of the employment laws that apply to participants and their intricate interactions have worked against their enforcement, leading to situations where workers are "subject to unfair and illegal treatment on the job."[34]

Workfare participants unevenly benefit from and contribute to the various social insurance and tax programs in which workers normally participate. For example, they are not required to pay into unemployment insurance and Social Security funds and do not pay federal income taxes as long as their welfare check is their only income, is based on demonstrated need, and does not equal more than minimum wage when divided by hours worked.[35] Their earnings, in turn, cannot be counted toward the Earned Income Tax Credit (EITC). While being exempted from these programs saves participants payroll taxes in the short run, in the long run, these exemptions can prevent participants from receiving Social Security coverage and other benefits; they also deprive them of the immediate benefit of the EITC.[36]

Workers' compensation coverage is especially complex because it is a state-run benefits program, with almost no federal involvement, and so eligibility conforms to the laws of individual states. According to the Welfare Law Center, some states have extended coverage to workfare participants while others have not, and some states offer workfare participants coverage at the same levels as their peers while others cover them at a lower rate. In 1996 the Ohio Supreme Court required that the state pay workers' compensation to the spouse of a worker who died from an illness caused by contact with pigeon excrement during a workfare assignment. The state had argued that providing inferior compensation to survivors of workfare participants who died as a result of their jobs was a means to discourage reliance on public assistance. The court ruled, on equal protection grounds, that the workfare participant was entitled to the same benefits as other workers.[37] In states where participants do have coverage, disputes have arisen between employers and welfare agencies over who is liable for a claimant's injuries. In Wisconsin, the state determined that workers' compensation was the responsibility of the W-2 contract agency for workers assigned to community service jobs.[38]

In theory, workfare participants are eligible for unemployment insurance (UI), provided they meet the earnings history requirements, show that they lost a job for reasons that were not their fault, and are willing and able to accept a suitable job. However, several courts have rejected the argument that workfare cash payments can be counted as wages to qualify for UI. While these cases were based on pre-PRWORA programs, they are presumed to hold for current workfare placements as well. Thus, in practice, workfare participants are not "insured" against loss of a workfare job.[39]

Finally, there is the question of the labor-organizing rights of workfare participants. The welfare-to-work regulations of PRWORA prohibit placement of participants in work sites where their presence as non–bargaining unit members would violate an existing collective bargaining agreement. The American Federation of State, County and Municipal Employees (AFSCME) successfully tested this provision in an administrative court in 1998.[40] Beyond this, welfare reform legislation and regulations do not address the issue of labor rights; in particular, they do not clarify whether workfare participants themselves have rights to free association and collective bargaining. State and local government employees, agricultural and domestic workers, and several other classes of individuals are excluded from NLRB protections, so the law would not cover workfare participants who labor in public agencies or perform excluded types of work. But its provisions do not specifically exclude workfare participants, though because of their temporary status, many administrators have understood them to be outside the law. This stance was given weight by the failure of the New York state legislature, in 1997, to approve a measure that would have allowed workfare participants to unionize.[41]

As federal guidelines, state laws, and court cases have accumulated, they have moved in the direction of establishing that workfare participants are employees entitled to a broad range of rights and protections. Nevertheless, ten years after the promulgation of welfare reform, the ground for this interpretation was still shaky. As one legal scholar noted in 1999, many administrators and lawyers believed that Congress may have intended "for the courts to determine on a case-by-case basis whether a particular workfare program or situation was within the FLSA's definition of employment."[42] Congress never delegated to the Department of Labor the power to interpret PRWORA; that authority remains in the hands of the courts.[43] The Department of Labor guidelines were helpful, but the document itself noted that they were "a starting point" and could not "provide answers to the wide range of questions that could be raised regarding specific work programs."[44] The upshot of this is that the coverage of workfare participants under existing state and federal statutes, has been, in the words of one legal scholar, "spotty at best."[45]

TRADING CIVIL RIGHTS FOR SOCIAL PROVISION

In *Coppage v. Kansas* in 1915, the U.S. Supreme Court made a clear statement about the rights of the individual to choose when, where and under what conditions to labor. It says:

> Included in the right of personal liberty and the right of private property . . . is the right to make contracts. Chief among such contracts is that of personal employment, by which labor and other services are exchanged for money or other forms of property. If this right be struck down or arbitrarily interfered with, there is a substantial impairment of liberty in the long-established constitutional sense.[46]

As historians have pointed out, this freedom to dispose of one's own labor has not been absolute. Emerging as a right in the mid-nineteenth century, it was significantly curtailed by Progressive Era protective legislation for women and children and by New Deal protections for a broader set of workers. Even after the end of slavery and indentured servitude, it has never applied to everyone; women, the "vagrant" unemployed, immigrants, and others have found their ability to negotiate contracts abridged by law.[47] Both craft unions and employers initially resisted minimum wage and maximum hours provisions, as well as health and safety rules, because they perceived them as interfering with the right to dispose of one's labor as one saw fit, and the courts upheld this view fairly consistently through the early years of the twentieth century. Beginning with its decision in *Muller v. Oregon* in 1908 (upholding a statute mandating a ten-hour day for women in factory jobs) and continuing with its 1937 ruling in *West Coast v. Parrish* (upholding a minimum wage for female workers), however, the Supreme Court began to interpret protections for "vulnerable" workers as permissible—a view that laid the groundwork for more broadly distributed protections under the Fair Labor Standards Act in 1938.

By the end of the New Deal, courts were consistently upholding the view that the government could regulate the terms under which individuals negotiated with employers. Even in this new context, however, the dominant view remained that men (if not all individuals) were not only permitted, but required, to contract freely in the labor market. Thus, in his famous midcentury essay on citizenship, T. H. Marshall could still proclaim that "the ability to follow the occupation of one's choice in the place of one's choice is a key aspect of citizenship."[48]

Few legal scholars believed it would be possible, in the legal climate of the early twenty-first century, to challenge workfare's mandatory placements on constitutional grounds. Nevertheless, several have outlined ways in which the programs might be considered unconstitutional. Vadim Mahmoudov, for example, notes that "government is not obliged to offer a particular benefit. However, once offered, the government may not condition the receipt of that benefit upon the recipient's forfeiture of a constitutional right."[49] It is fair to ask then, he says, whether, once the government establishes a program that requires participants to work for their benefits, there are any reasonable limits to the working conditions it may impose. Mahmoudov suggests that the rights in question are equal protection rights under the Fourteenth Amendment, since employee protections offered to regular employees are denied to workfare participants. Because the majority of workfare participants are single mothers, gender distinctions may also come into play.[50]

Similarly, legal scholar Charles Bogle has suggested that workfare assignments might subject participants to "unconscionable conditions." He premises this claim on the legal doctrine that the government should not regulate its citizens' conduct through the distribution of benefits in ways that would be unconstitutional if mandated directly. He argues that this concept of unconscionability has deep roots in Anglo-American jurisprudence: an unconscionable bargain is one that "no man in his senses and not under delusion would make, on the one hand, and no honest and fair man would accept, on the other."[51]

Contemporary U.S. unconscionability doctrine draws on commercial law, which allows courts to refuse to enforce contracts that violate this principle. According to Bogle, "recipients of public assistance benefits to which rights-pressuring conditions have been attached are in a situation similar to those who discover themselves on the wrong end of an unconscionable contract."[52] They are similar in that they have little opportunity to bargain over the terms of their benefits and are "asked to tender something of tremendous worth, a protected constitutional right, as a quid pro quo for the benefit." While Bogle believes that this is a reasonable way to understand the situation of work-fare participants, he notes that unconscionability interpretations have been controversial, that the case law based on the doctrine is incoherent, and the Supreme Court's standards for it are murky.[53]

Most legal scholars argue that the contract that workfare participants sign with the state represents their acceptance of the conditions of their employment in return for support. By signing an employability plan, then, and by accepting state services, the women we interviewed have given away their right to determine when, where, and under what conditions they will work. The state has presented them with a dilemma—a Faustian bargain—that historian Alice Kessler-Harris says has long troubled women's citizenship. They have gained social rights at the cost of civil rights—gained a measure of protection from the vagaries of the labor market at the cost of certain aspects of legal personhood.

WELFARE AND ECONOMIC CITIZENSHIP

Many theorists have noted the tight connection between citizenship and labor in American political culture. As Judith Shklar has put it, "We are citizens only if we earn."[54] In *American Citizenship,* she explains that this fixation on wage earning is not a remnant of the class values of preindustrial artisans but dates to the Jacksonian period of the 1840s, reflecting the emerging ideology of citizens "caught between racist slavery and aristocratic pretensions." Independent wage work became the emblem that distinguished the true citizen from the slave, as well as from paupers and the idle rich.[55] As Gordon and Fraser have pointed out, it also distinguished him from housewives.[56] In Shklar's words, "this vision of economic independence, of self-directed 'earning' as the ethical basis of democratic citizenship, took the place of an outmoded notion of public virtue and it has retained its powerful appeal."[57] Because of this tradition, Alice Kessler-Harris has argued that the U.S. government has "attached its most valuable benefits not to families but to wage work. Tying benefits like old age pensions and unemployment insurance to jobs affirmed the status of recipients as independent and upstanding citizens and delineated the secondary positions of those without good jobs or any at all."[58]

Women who are put to work through the institutions of welfare stand in an ambiguous position with regard to these discourses. They may labor forty hours a week, but they are not considered workers and their coverage by protective statutes and labor law is under contest. Those who accept this kind of aid are treated as "dependents" and give up their right to choose when, where, and under what conditions to work, as well as their rights to sue for fair treatment. Furthermore, participating in these programs propels them into the labor market with a stigma. No matter how many jobs they have held, how many years they have worked, or what skills they possess, they are marked as deficient workers. As Marshall said of sixteenth-century British Poor Laws, welfare reform has "treated the claims of the poor, not as an integral part of the rights of the citizen, but as an alternative to them—as claims that could be met only if the claimants ceased to be citizens in any true sense of the word."[59]

Writing about New Deal social programs of the 1930s, historian Alice Kessler-Harris has said:

> Work, wage work, had long marked a distinction among kinds of citizens: intimately tied to identity, it anchored nineteenth-century claims to political participation. But when the federal government linked wage work to tangible, publicly provided rewards, employment emerged as a boundary line demarcating different kinds of citizenship. Casual laborers, the unskilled and untrained, housewives, farm workers, mothers, and domestic servants all found themselves on one side of a barrier not of their own making. Their own benefits not earned but means-tested, classified as relief, not rights, many protested what seemed an artificial division and demanded inclusion. Their voices were quickly stilled.[60]

From the 1930s to the 1990s, "the idea that some people (generally women) would get benefits by virtue of their family position and others (mainly men) by virtue of their paid employment" distinguished the U.S. system of social provision. The "two channel" welfare state addressed men as workers and women as mothers.[61] Progressive Era reformers such as Jane Addams and Florence Kelley had constructed notions of Republican motherhood in which white women's citizenship was seen to be attained through keeping orderly homes, rearing healthy children, and applying their domestic skills and moral judgment to social reform in their communities. Such concepts provided the ideological basis for New Deal programs that granted women a "kind of social citizenship, but at the cost of equality."[62] Ruth Lister has called this concept the "mother-citizen."[63]

Other kinds of benefits, most notably health insurance, but also unemployment insurance and workers' compensation, came to American workers through their jobs. Both Cold War anxieties about large state programs and the opposition of business and insurance interests stymied the development of federal health insurance programs over the course of the twentieth century. By the 1950s, according to Katz, "America had a nascent system of health insurance that—uniquely among industrialized nations—tied benefits to employment.... Public policy had rejected the idea of medical care as a right of citizenship. Instead, it remained a consequence of income and class."[64] As Katz documents, women were generally left out, unless they were married to an insured worker, and agricultural and household workers were not covered. But between 1940 and 1966, the percentage of people covered by employer-provided insurance in the United States grew from 9 to 81 percent.[65] Both unemployment insurance and workers' compensation, while administered by state governments, were funded in part by employer contributions and were earned through time spent on the job. There was no unemployment insurance for those who could not demonstrate a prior record of steady work, and disability coverage for those whose injury or illness was not work-related was increasingly hard to come by.[66]

The experiences of the women who navigated Wisconsin's welfare system do not fit easily into either of the paths just described. Reformed welfare offers no provision for them to stay at home keeping house and raising children as "mother-citizens." So they go out to work. But the jobs they get in the low-wage service sector do not provide benefits and are structured in ways that do not allow them to meet the eligibility requirements for state programs such as unemployment insurance and workers' compensation. So they are not worker-citizens either. Caught in the empty space between these two visions of citizenship, they turn to the state for help through stigmatized means-tested programs that mark them both as failed workers and as failed mothers.

The significance of this stigma is illustrated by a *New York Times* op-ed celebrating the tenth anniversary of welfare reform. In August 2006 policy scholar Douglas Besharov pointed to the fact that low-wage workers continued to need state services, not as evidence that low-road employers were depending on the state to provide what they would not, but rather as evidence that the poor were still receiving welfare in disguise. Even off welfare, he claimed:

> some of these families survive only because they still receive government assistance—through food stamps (an average of more than $2,500), the Women, Infants and Children program (about $1,800 for infants and new mothers), Supplemental Security Income (an average of over $6,500), or housing aid (an average of $6,000). Their children also qualify for

Medicaid. In reality, these families are still on welfare because they are still receiving benefits and not working—call it "welfare lite."[67]

Besharov misrepresents the amount of aid received; the "averages" for food stamps, WIC, and housing assistance are for those who specifically qualify for the various programs (and in the case of housing aid, those who rise to the top of long waiting lists)—not all welfare leavers. And a very small proportion receive SSI, a specialized federal program for those with documented disabilities, who by definition are unable to work. But an even more glaring misrepresentation in Besharov's account is the fact that the majority of welfare leavers who participate in these federal programs are, in fact, working, many of them full-time, year-round.

What is even more striking, and what Besharov also misses, are the ways welfare programs increasingly serve, not families who are outside the labor market altogether, but those who occupy its lowest rungs. This trend results from the intersection of two large political economic movements: the steady erosion of wages and working conditions in low-skilled jobs and the emphasis on moving welfare participants into work. The result is a situation where more and more workers are looking to the state to provide what formerly came with jobs. The unspoken rules of the new economy force them to rely on welfare agencies for basic benefits and for subsidies, like food stamps, that bring their income to subsistence levels. If a decent wage and health insurance were formerly rights that economic citizens earned in return for hard work, that route now appears closed to poor workers, no matter how many hours a week they labor. Instead, the benefits and subsidies that make survival possible are doled out to low-wage workers as forms of stigmatized state assistance.

Food stamps, subsidized housing, Women, Infants and Children,[68] and other means-tested programs not only support welfare participants; like medical assistance, they also aid the working poor. California assemblywoman Sally Lieber brought this to public attention in July 2003, when she held a press conference to unveil documents that Walmart gave new workers instructing them on how to apply for food stamps.[69] A number of books on low-wage workers document the dimensions of this phenomenon.[70] Less than 5 percent of Milwaukee County's food stamp recipients were receiving any kind of cash assistance through W-2 in 2004, meaning that more than 95 percent of those who used food stamps were working independently.[71] More than 83 percent of those receiving WIC in Milwaukee County were employed and receiving no cash aid.[72] The mean earnings for the women we interviewed in 2003 were just over $2,000, and the mean of their *best* year for earnings (over the past five) was $8,800. Neither of these amounts even approaches the federal poverty line of $15,670 for a family of four in 2004. Food stamps, along with WIC and subsidized housing, were disproportionately supplementing low wages and unstable employment, rather than supporting individuals who remained outside the labor market altogether.

As Lieber's Walmart documents demonstrated, employers have frequently taken the initiative in encouraging women to seek state aid. The women we interviewed talked about having such conversations with their employers. Several mentioned that the personnel officer at their job told them "off the record" that, with their salary, they would still be eligible for medical assistance and that that might be a better value. As Heidi Luttenburg recalled, "They said the insurance there is not great, so it's better if I stick with the state, you know." About half of the women we interviewed had the option of purchasing health insurance after a waiting period on their jobs, which averaged six months for those working full-time and two years for those working part-time. But in all but one case they felt that they could not afford the premium. Regina Shiflett said, "I could get medical, but it was like $20 a week that they would take out, so I didn't get it." Twenty dollars a week does not sound exorbitant, but it was more than 10 percent of Regina's after-tax earnings and would have left her with about $180 a week to spend on rent, utilities, transportation, food, and other necessities.

Food stamps, subsidized housing, child care subsidies, WIC—these were all important programs to the women we interviewed. None of them could have survived without these forms of support. Over and over they told us, "WIC really helps. Milk is expensive. Food stamps helps a lot too." Or more bluntly: "I get food stamps, so at least we get to eat. Even if we don't got a place to eat out of, at least we can go buy food! At least they make sure of that—you might be homeless, but you can eat!" One woman said, speaking of her housing subsidy, "Thank god I had the Section Eight program for housing. That's how I survived all these years, because rent assistance was there to help me have a safe place to live for my kids. Without that, we would have been destitute beyond belief."

For Sandra Russell, who was working at a fast food restaurant and was proud to be moving from a cashier position to a crew leader, benefits were still in the distant future. "I've been there almost ten months," she said. "I'm moving up." Her advancement would entail giving up a stable 10-to-5 schedule for a "flexible" one, in which she would work different shifts as needed each week, including night and weekend hours. She was eagerly anticipating the raise from $6.75 to $7.75 an hour. But she still would not be eligible for any benefits, which only came with a manager's position. In the meantime, she continued to rely on the state for the supports that made her work possible. Connie Olsen, who was paid by the state to provide in-home care for disabled patients, noted the irony of her low wages: "Now that makes a lot of sense—I'm working for the state but I have to go to the state to get food stamps and medical. Does that make a lot of sense to you?"

The women we interviewed spoke, at times, about the stigma and degradation they felt. "This isn't me," one said. "I don't like the feeling." They took pride in mapping out their work histories and frequently pointed out that they had started working at age fourteen or fifteen. In asserting these things, they were speaking against the elephant in the room: the assumption—so prevalent in our political culture both before and after welfare reform—that the women who turned to these programs were not workers and were therefore inferior citizens.

Women who reentered work through workfare programs not only lost the status and many of the prerogatives of independent workers. They also lost the means to protect themselves in the labor market. When they suffered discrimination or unfair treatment or labored under unsafe conditions, they were not clearly protected by federal and state laws and were not permitted representation by unions or other workers' groups. In fact, they were monitored by their caseworkers and sanctioned for acts of noncompliance. They entered work with none of the tools on which previous generations of workers have relied to negotiate or demand fairer and safer conditions. They thus moved into the swing shifts and poorly regulated spaces of the low-wage economy with a second hand tied squarely behind their backs.

CHAPTER SIX

BOTH HANDS TIED

THE RACE TO THE BOTTOM IN THE LOW-WAGE LABOR MARKET

Does federal law permit the creation of a two-tiered labor force?
And if it does, where is our labor market headed?

VADIM MAHMOUDOV, "ARE WORKFARE PARTICIPANTS EMPLOYEES?"[1]

TYING BOTH HANDS

In July 2008 Wisconsin governor Jim Doyle moved the administration of the Wisconsin Works (W-2) program from the Department of Workforce Development, where it had been housed since 1996, to a newly created Department of Children and Families. W-2, a program that requires women to participate in work or work-related activities for forty hours a week, is now housed in a social service agency that includes child support enforcement, child welfare, foster care, and domestic abuse services. The governor's stated goal in establishing this new agency was to provide "more seamless, integrated and family-centered services that are focused on accountability and results."[2] The same press release explained that the Department of Workforce Development would continue to focus on "training and strengthening the state's workforce."[3]

The new agency may achieve seamless integration of services, but it also reflects the tensions and contradictions in the broader social meaning of welfare reform. Mothers who continue to work as a condition of welfare lose their status as workers under these arrangements. While they will still be working, the new location classifies them as caretakers of children, not as wage earners. Their service provision is removed from a context of job training, employment counseling, and information on workers' rights and linked instead to programs for children. The women themselves disappear from view, incorporated instrumentally into goals for child welfare and family formation.

This paradoxical—one might say schizophrenic—handling of support for poor working mothers reflects underlying contradictions that we have described in the structure of welfare since 1996 and in our broadly shared ideas about work, citizenship, and care. It reflects the gaps and fissures in a new system of social provision designed in response to the economic crises of the 1970s and 1980s and inspired by the principles of free market fundamentalism. When, post-1973, profitability crises drove business to look for new models of work, conservative thinkers helped to construct them. The solitary wage bargain and contractual citizenship were two of their key reconfigurations of the rights and responsibilities of workers and citizens. They formed part of the radically altered, and heatedly contested, moral economy of the late twentieth century.

The solitary wage bargain, as we have described, resulted from a series of retrenchments in the rights and bargaining power of labor, including assaults on unions and changes in rules that made it more difficult for workers to organize. As employers dismantled their former bargains with labor, they undermined the ability of workers to secure a family-supporting wage and benefits package. Influenced by resurgent ideas of unfettered markets, and pressured by business, the government both loosened regulations and slashed resources for enforcement of the rules that remained. In this context, workers saw the erosion of norms governing safety, job security, discrimination, work hours, and overtime that they had long taken for granted. Work continued to be the most important mark and guarantee of citizenship, but our social consensus about the prerogatives and support that should attend it had changed. The solitary wage bargain described an unencumbered worker who could flexibly respond to the needs of employers. As market fundamentalists succeeded in shifting our focus to the bottom line, the short-term, and the individual, both government and employer contributions to social reproduction disappeared.

When policymakers devised welfare reforms that required mothers to work, they did not address the fact that norms and practices of the low-wage labor market continued to reflect the "ideal [male] worker norm,"[4] despite the fact that the majority of its workers were women. Programs designed to give male workers income during illness, disability, or unemployment remain largely unavailable to women working in low-wage service jobs who need time off to care for themselves or their families. In most states, including Wisconsin, unemployment insurance policies do not count family care responsibilities as "good cause" for leaving a job, and part-time workers are not eligible for the program. This leads to a situation, nationally, where women are 32 percent less likely to qualify for unemployment benefits than men. Only fifteen states have provisions that allow individuals who are ill or disabled or who quit work to care for an ill or disabled family member to receive unemployment insurance.[5] Many low-wage employers are either exempt from or fail to comply with the Family and Medical Leave Act.[6] Nationally, less than half of low-wage workers receive paid sick days, and only a third of low-wage parents are able to take time off to care for a sick child.[7] These gaps make it difficult for women to move back and forth between paid and domestic work as needed by their families.

In reforming welfare, policymakers attempted to construct a new system of social reproduction for low-wage families, with poor mothers at its center. Cash benefits remained at the heart of the project. Even with time limits and newly required activities, they made it possible for women facing crises to leave the labor market temporarily. The state subsidized child care for mothers while they were working and, through these subsidies, fostered the creation of more child care options on the market. Its child support enforcement policies also brought small amounts of additional income to female-headed families. Over time, the assumption that poor women with children would be holding full-time jobs led to a reorganization of resources and practices throughout the community, and thus structured the lives of women whose lives did not come in direct contact with the welfare system. But the sum total of these new institutions and practices proved to be both insufficient and corrosive to poor women's rights.

Central to the new policy initiatives was the notion that citizenship was not the birthright of everyone but had to be earned through productive labor. This doctrine drew on our nation's long-standing embrace of work as a key value, but it took the additional step of arguing that citizenship should be contingent on its performance. Written into the 1996 welfare reform law, and inscribed in the new institutions of welfare, the doctrine of contractual citizenship created a new disciplinary status through which women who experienced social reproductive crises cycled. Those who labored in these programs were not able to secure additional skills to improve their labor market position but were channeled back into unskilled and menial forms of work. And while they labored in "training" for these assignments, they did so without the rights and protections of other workers. The reforms thus created an enclave of disempowered and vulnerable workers at the bottom of the labor market.

Even the most prescient of conservative thinkers probably could not have foreseen the way in which these two models—once given life by social policy—would intertwine in the lives of welfare participants. The erosion of economic citizenship for women in workfare positions and the erosion of social reproduction supports for women working outside the home were inextricably connected through the institutions of reformed welfare. As our case histories showed, women could weather a few crises—a sick child, a divorce, an illness—while continuing to work, but combinations of crises generally required them to leave their jobs to engage in the social reproductive labor needed to get their families back on a sound footing. Each time they left work and relied on welfare supports, the new policies channeled them back into the workforce in ways that marked them as dependent and undermined their economic citizenship. In some cases, workfare proved to be a "downward mobility machine," placing them in jobs that were less skilled and less remunerative than the ones they had left. The lessons these women learned while working without rights—lessons about what they could expect from an employer, how a job should be structured, the rights and protections to which they were entitled, whether upward mobility was possible—reshaped their understanding of work. And it was a lesson that was not just visible to them, but also to those who worked alongside them, to employers, to community organizations, and to government agency workers.

The interplay of these two processes—the loss of economic citizenship rights and the solitary wage bargain—created extraordinary obstacles for women struggling to care for their families. Metaphorically, they entered the struggle with both hands tied behind their backs. With adequate supports for family care, those who were healthy and whose families did not have major health problems could have sustained their labor market participation in periods of intermittent illness or family disruption, allowing them to gain seniority and to become eligible for benefits (which often entailed a waiting period of six months to two years). They would no longer have needed to engage in "strategic quitting" to cope with children's ear infections or asthma, a parent's death or hospitalization, or their own illness. If they had entered workplaces that modeled respect for their economic citizenship—that paid a living wage, offered benefits, insured them against job loss and disability, and respected their right to know their schedule in advance, to have regular hours, and to be protected by health and safety rules—they would not only have had resources with which to weather crises but tools to defend themselves as workers. Like the Racine nursing assistants in the 1980s, they could have joined unions and bargained with their employers—rather than with caseworkers at the welfare office. Considering these alternatives clarifies the narrow and unsavory options faced by the women in our study and the way in which the solitary wage bargain interacted with their loss of employment rights to constitute them as a group of stigmatized and vulnerable workers at the bottom of the labor market.

THE RACE TO THE BOTTOM IN THE LOW-WAGE SERVICE SECTOR

As we have noted, the creation of enclaves of disempowered workers has effects that potentially reverberate far beyond the workers themselves—extending to other members of the labor market in which they participate and to the economy as a whole. To paraphrase the question posed by Vadim Mahmoudov at the opening of this chapter, if it is indeed legal to create a two-tiered labor force, where is our labor market headed? What are the broader social and economic implications of this shift? What does it mean, in an era when free marketeers seek to weaken labor protections, roll back health and safety rules, and cripple unions, to create such spaces "beyond the reach" of the law?

The answer to these questions requires placing the experiences of these Wisconsin women in the context of the broader dynamics of the Milwaukee-Racine labor market, and locating that labor market in the global economy. It turns on the fact that the vast majority of community service jobs are in the low-wage service sector and that the women who move in and out of welfare in response to crises labor predominantly in this sector. Women's experiences in workfare jobs are part of the larger drama of expansion of the low-wage service sector in the postwar period. As women of all socioeconomic and educational levels moved into work, families grew to depend on being able to purchase meals, day care, elder care, cleaning, and other services at reasonable prices on the market. The firms providing these services responded by placing downward pressure on the wages and benefits of their workers. Unable to threaten workers with the outsourcing of their jobs—which must be performed face-to-face or within the community—employers have relied on what Robert Thomas has called forms of "social and political inequality outside the enterprise," such as gender and citizenship status, to justify ratcheting down wages and working conditions.[8]

Welfare reform appeared on the U.S. national agenda in a period of, and as part of, the ascendance of a free market–led restructuring of the economy that dismantled many forms of regulation and the bargains struck between capital and labor in the decades following World War II. For manufacturing, this was a period of global expansion of operations and the construction of a new international division of labor. Escaping the boundaries of the United States, with its high wage rates, labor unions, and sophisticated regulatory framework, corporations were able to participate in what has come to be called a global race to the bottom, in which competitive forces were structured around cost-cutting rather than technological or labor process improvements. This race proceeded by eradicating differences across globally dispersed labor markets, as firms threatened workers in the United States and other high-wage regions with loss of jobs if they did not take wage and benefit cuts, and told localities they would move if they did not receive regulatory breaks and reduced tax burdens. By the turn of the twenty-first century, in industries such as apparel and other consumer products sectors, this process had resulted in the creation of "one big labor market" in which workers around the world competed for the same jobs.[9]

By the late twentieth century, services provided more jobs than manufacturing in the U.S. economy. But for service industries—particularly those hard-to-move personal services that constitute the low-wage tier of the sector—the "spatial fix" available to manufacturers was not an option.[10] While it is difficult to measure productivity in services, and while different types of service jobs have different profiles, economists agree that increasing productivity growth in many service sector industries is uniquely difficult for employers. As Iverson and Wren explain, "Teachers can serve more students, nurses more patients, and waiters more customers, but this is not easily achieved without a decline in the quality of the service." Thus, it is harder to achieve the "virtuous circle between falling prices and rising real demand" that characterizes the expansion of manufacturing.[11] The only way to achieve a similar pattern of growth in services is by lowering wages. According to Iverson and Wren and others, high rates of growth in market-provided services presuppose "a more *in*egalitarian wage structure."[12] New forms of labor market segmentation, because they create enclaves of workers to whom labor rights and protections do not apply, provide a tool—a "relational fix"—for firms to engage in a race to the bottom in services. Workfare is one of a range of practices that place workers beyond the reach of labor law.[13]

Both unions and employers have recognized that the relatively immovable nature of some services could, in theory, provide a secure bargaining position for unionized workers. The loss of manufacturing jobs from the 1970s to the present led U.S. unions to turn their attention to place-bound service sectors, and most of their successes in organizing in the 1990s were among hotel and restaurant workers, janitors, hospital workers, and others represented by unions like the Service Employees International Union (SEIU), UNITE/ HERE, the American Federation of State, County and Municipal Employees (AFSCME) and the United Food and Commercial Workers Union (UFCW). As one labor scholar has written, "All unions need to focus on those industries that are both profitable and immobile, that is, those that are not likely to move abroad. This leads to a clear focus on the service industries."[14] Thomas Edsall of the *Washington Post* points to the enactment of this strategy by the unions of the Change to Win coalition, which split from the AFL-CIO in 2005: "[Andrew] Stern and his allies cite as prime targets for organizing those workers whose jobs cannot be moved overseas."[15]

Despite the tactical advantage offered by place-bound jobs and the fact that unions have targeted them for organizing drives, wages in these positions have not risen in recent years. The reasons are complex. Skill levels in many of these positions—particularly retail and janitorial work—are not high. In other occupations, such as child care and health care work, gender norms depress the pay scale.[16] But several other processes work to undermine pay and working conditions in the place-bound service sector, including the compromised citizenship status of many workers who fill these jobs.

We have seen how this operates in the case of workfare. Women who labor in community service jobs, who are by definition poor and are often women of color, lose many of the prerogatives of other workers by virtue of the contracts they sign with the state as a condition of their participation. Their status as welfare recipients and the rules that govern their participation mark them as failed workers who have relinquished their claims to certain rights and protections. As a condition of aid, they submit to government enforcement of norms and behaviors that it claims are in their best interest. Their most important obligation is to work in whatever job they are placed, under whatever conditions. Having traded civil rights for limited social provision, they form a deregulated enclave that renormalizes working conditions otherwise long ago abolished. The workers who labor under these conditions suffer, but so do those who work alongside them. As welfare activist and sociologist Frances Piven has written, "[Workfare] workers, most of them poor mothers, are being hurled like hostages into the front lines of the campaign against workers."[17] Former AFL-CIO education director Bill Fletcher calls workfare "a giant sinkhole, pulling into it the rest of the working class."[18] Michael Reisch has argued that the presence of workfare participants "helps to drive down the wage scale by increasing competition for unskilled jobs" and "strengthens the drive for greater workforce discipline and compliance, particularly in the service sector."[19]

The logic of workfare's impact on the labor market as a whole can be better understood if we place it alongside a broader array of practices and arrangements segmenting the low-wage labor market. As Fletcher has noted, "The acceptability of forced labor through welfare repeal comes at a time when forced labor, as a category, is being rehabilitated generally."[20] In 1996, the same year that the U.S. Congress passed the Personal Responsibility and Work Opportunity Reconciliation Act, it also passed the Illegal Immigration Reform and Immigrant Responsibility Act. This bill intensified patrols of the U.S.-Mexico border, made it easier to deport immigrants, established an income test for those who wished to bring family members, stiffened penalties for undocumented immigration, and limited the social services immigrants could receive. Just as PRWORA and the campaigns that pressed for its passage generated public outrage over welfare mothers depicted as living off the taxes of working folk, IIRIRA fueled nativist hysteria over immigrants, who were portrayed as garnering unearned public benefits and being linked to crime.

IIRIRA made all immigrants, legal and illegal, more vulnerable. But this vulnerability was ratcheted up with the 2002 Supreme Court decision *Hoffman v. National Labor Relations Board*. This ruling stated that employers who violate federal labor law in their treatment of illegal workers cannot be required to pay back-wages. According to the National Employment Law Project and the Mexican American Legal Defense and Education Fund, the *Hoffman* decision has encouraged employers to engage in retaliation against unauthorized workers who claim violations of their workplace rights and has had a chilling effect on labor law enforcement in industries that hire many immigrant workers. When Peruvian farm workers asked for enforcement of minimum wage and overtime pay rules, Florida tomato workers filed claims for nonpayment of wages, and a hose maker who suffered kidney damage requested workers' compensation—courts decided that the *Hoffman* ruling disqualified undocumented workers from any rights or recourse under the National Labor Relations Act. In 2006 the American Civil Liberties Union filed a petition to the Inter-American Commission on Human Rights—an arm of the Organization of American States—arguing that *Hoffman* has denied protections to millions of illegal immigrant workers in violation of U.S. treaty agreements to respect core labor rights.

Like workfare participants, undocumented workers cannot bargain for wages. In addition, they cannot claim welfare support, workers' compensation, or unemployment insurance. The impact of the *Hoffman* ruling that the NLRA does not apply to them is to take away even more basic rights: now they cannot even complain about unsafe working conditions or violations of labor law. As in the case of workfare, these effects spill over to the broader workforce. When citizen workers and documented immigrants work alongside unauthorized workers, the vulnerability of the undocumented leads to a decrease in overall wages and a decline in working conditions. In the words of the AFL-CIO, the *Hoffman* decision means that industries where jobs cannot be exported have been "able to import the labor standards of developing nations into the U.S." Employers have been able to create an underclass of workers,

> which has effectively reduced working standards for all workers. Immigrant workers are over-represented in the highest-risk, lowest paid jobs, but the exploited immigrants do not work in isolation. U.S.-born workers who work side-by-side with immigrants suffer the same exploitation. The U.S. Department of Labor, for example, determined that the poultry industry—which is approximately half African American and half immigrant—was 100 percent out of compliance with federal wage and hour laws.[21]

Prison labor is another enclave of workers without rights. As Noah Zatz documents, well over six hundred thousand, and probably closer to a million, inmates are working full-time in prisons and jails throughout the United States, where they build office furniture, take hotel reservations, make body armor for the U.S. military, and sew uniforms (including their own). This makes prison industry one of the fastest growing segments of the United States economy. While they are highly regulated, limitations on their use by private firms have gradually been reduced over the past thirty years. Wage rates vary from $0.17 to $5.35 an hour but rarely reach the minimum wage. A 2007 *New York Times* business section article, titled "Inmates Will Replace Migrants in Colorado Fields," explained that "as migrant laborers flee Colorado because of tough new immigration restrictions, worried farmers are looking to prisoners to fill their places in the fields." This "pilot program" was run by the state Corrections Department, and the inmates were paid 60 cents a day. Individuals involuntarily committed to institutions as a result of mental or developmental disabilities also perform these kinds of work. In both cases, states consider the relationship to be tutelary or therapeutic activity rather than employment, and thus labor laws do not apply.[22] As Bill Fletcher has observed, it is impossible for workers on the "outside" to compete with the extraordinarily low costs of prison labor.

Or consider recent legal decisions affecting home health care aides. In the early days of the New Deal, in a compromise with southern states that sought to preserve gendered racial hierarchies, Franklin Roosevelt's Social Security and National Labor Relations laws excluded employees in agricultural and domestic work—the segments of the economy where most women, African Americans, and Latinos labored. Little by little, over the next seventy years, union pressure succeeded in amending the laws to cover many groups formerly excluded. But in 2007 in *Coke v. Long Island Care*, the U.S. Supreme Court ruled that home health care workers were exempt from minimum wage and overtime protections under the "companionship" exemption to those laws, even when they were employed by for-profit firms.

Similarly, the 1990s saw a rapid rise in the incidence of independent contractor status among low-wage workers. While this practice is often associated with entrepreneurship or highly skilled craft or information sector work, employers increasingly "contract" with construction day laborers, health care aides, and cleaners. Independent contractors are considered small businesses and so labor laws do not apply to them. This practice is sometimes called "1099ing," after the tax form an independent contractor receives.[23] It parallels the emergence of temporary services as an enclave of attenuated labor rights, which, as Erin Hatton has argued, has challenged both "union" and "civil service" models of stability and mutual obligation between employers and workers.[24] Each of these measures represents a "relational fix" for service sector firms caught in a competitive squeeze, akin to what Harvey has called a "spatial fix" in the case of firms that can relocate.[25]

Independent contracting and temporary work are less stigmatized than workfare, prison labor, or undocumented immigrant labor, but in many cases ethnicity, race, and immigration status also may come into play. For example, the majority of home health care workers are African American or immigrant women, and many immigrant workers in these jobs are undocumented. And while temp service agencies operate across the spectrum of skill and wage levels, they are the primary institution organizing day labor for domestics, gardeners, and construction workers in many parts of the country, as well as one of the primary employers of workfare participants in Wisconsin. Many individuals in such insecure work arrangements also rely on state supports, such as food stamps and child care subsidies. The exclusion of workers from rights and protections operates in distinct ways, deepening and reproducing inequalities in each of these cases. But in each case—in ways parallel to workfare—new laws and policies cordon off and isolate groups of workers, deny them fundamental citizenship rights, and then hold them up as object lessons for labor market restructuring.

For women who labor in community service jobs—workfare participants—the fact that they are poor, often of color, and receive welfare feeds long-standing stereotypes of welfare mothers and the idle poor and makes their loss of civil rights more palatable to the public. As Lauren Berlant has written, citizenship "is constantly being produced out of a political, rhetorical and economic struggle over who will count as the people and how social membership will be measured and valued."[26] What Ange-Marie Hancock has called "the politics of disgust" in popular and political culture has given women who turn to welfare few allies and little voice and has stifled debate about the erosion of their rights.[27]

The creation of enclaves of disempowered workers can be understood as a new form of labor market segmentation. In the 1970s, sociologists found it useful to conceptualize the U.S. labor market as divided into a primary sector characterized by good jobs with stable firms and a secondary sector marked by unstable, poorly paid, dead-end jobs outside of key industries.[28] This model has less relevance today, as many of the characteristics of the secondary labor market are now common in all jobs. The new forms of labor market segmentation described here are distinct from these older forms because they establish distinct castes of workers, often marked by race, gender, ethnicity, or nationality, outside the law.

The designers of Wisconsin's welfare programs meant to construct a powerful social message about work as much as they meant to design a social program that addressed the needs of the poor. From 1996 to 2002 the manual for the program opened with the words "For those who can work, only work should pay." The "philosophy and goals" section of this document stressed the importance of creating a sense of urgency among participants that would propel them into work at the earliest possible moment. It emphasized the value of making individuals self-sufficient through work and of helping them to enjoy the pride of self-reliance.[29] It is clear that designers of the program *intended* to create a group of workers who operated outside of a traditional framework of rights and protections in order to teach these values. The message was not simply about the importance of work in some abstract sense, but that work in any job, under any conditions, was preferable to dependence on the state. Caseworkers encouraged workers to accommodate employers' demands and schedules, however challenging they might be. And these messages were sent, not just to those who participated in welfare programs, but to the broader community of which they formed a part. To argue that the newly reformed welfare served to discipline workers and to structure their ideas about work is not hyperbole—it was the avowed intent of those who designed and implemented the program. To argue that it served as a demonstration project for market-led restructuring borrows the vocabulary and expressed desire of its founders.

We have seen, however, that welfare reformers profoundly misread the barriers to work faced by mothers of young children living in poverty. They did not address the incompatibility between the terms and conditions of low-wage employment—its uncertain hours, its shift work, its lack of leave and benefits—and women's social reproductive responsibilities. While Wisconsin made subsidized child care available, it did not design other supports that could have fostered continuity in jobs. Working women who ran up against harsh rules and inflexible schedules "made their own flex time," and then reentered welfare to find themselves "churned to the bottom of the labor market" by its programs and placements. As one woman told us, with heartbreaking simplicity, "I wish they would have found a better way to help people out to work, because this is not the way."

CHAPTER SEVEN

CONCLUSION

UNTYING THE HANDS

Serena Clark never got a job as a waitress. For six months after we interviewed her, she kept her off-the-books job cleaning a Milwaukee restaurant, worked her part-time community service position, and turned in the logs from her job search to her case manager. She continued to attend training sessions to become an alcohol and drug abuse counselor, and in December 2004 she received her certification and the center where she had interned offered her a paid position. During her interview with us, she had recited a poem she had written, and when we learned this news, the closing words took on new meaning:

> That's why you don't play the game too fast.
> You make it last.
> And most of all, you don't make your future your past.

Serena had managed to use nine months of cash assistance from the welfare office, along with subsidized child care, to obtain the training she needed for a job that paid more than $20,000 a year. The grand irony was that she had to break program rules and mislead her case manager in order to do so.

Looking at state employment records two years after the interviews, we found one other case of success. Darla Tanner, who had been secretly taking business courses while working at a community service job, was also making more than $20,000 a year. "I know they don't think school is important," she had told us, "but it's very important. It's the window of opportunity that's gonna help a person change the rest of their life." Della May Collins was not hired permanently at the temporary factory job she had taken after her pituitary surgery, despite what she had felt were encouraging words from the manager. By 2005 a recurrence of her health problem led her to reapply for (and receive) W-2 Transitions assistance. Delia Carter was neither working nor on welfare, though she continued to receive food stamps; perhaps she was still living with her mother and sister and caring for her children and her niece.

As we analyzed state data on the employment and social program use of the women in our study in 2006, we could see evidence of the pattern we had identified in 2003: a period of work would end, and in that quarter a woman would receive benefits through the caretaker-of-newborn program or through W-2 transitions. This pattern suggested that women continued to work until childbirth or a health or care dilemma led them to turn to the state for aid. After the immediate crisis or need was resolved, caseworkers would move them to a community service job; most would then return to work. There were some exceptional cases, like Serena and Darla. And, as in the major quantitative studies of welfare leavers, some women simply disappeared from the records. We could not determine whether they had moved out of state, were being supported by family or friends, were working in the informal economy, or had died. Trends in the state data, like our earlier interviews, spoke to how closely work and welfare were intertwined. This connection was apparent in the lives of participants, but it emerged also from policymakers' visions of how the two *should* be connected—from their vision of welfare as a tutelary institution.

In this book, we have argued that to understand welfare in any era, we must pay attention to changes in the low-wage labor market. Since 1980 these labor markets in the United States have been shaped by two trends: one economic and one political. The economic trend is an explosion of low-wage service sector jobs, fueled by the growth of fast food chains, big-box retailers, day care centers, cleaning franchises, and other businesses that replace the labor of women in the home. The political trend is the ascendance of a particular mentality, a free market orthodoxy that eschews regulation and has provided the rationale for dismantling many of the labor protections built up over the course of the twentieth century. These two developments have shaped policy in arenas of welfare and work—affecting both what Karl Polanyi called "the protective covering of cultural institutions" and the kinds and conditions of work available.[1]

These trends were part of a *global* reconfiguration of working arrangements and social safety nets. In the 1970s manufacturing industries faced with declining profits began to lobby government for a rollback of regulations and the right to renegotiate their bargains with workers. They experimented with sending jobs overseas. This started a global "race to the bottom" in wages and working conditions in the manufacturing sector, as employers used the threat of closing plants and moving jobs to extract new bargains from industrial employees, and then often left anyway. These events devastated industrial cities like Milwaukee and Racine. But during this period, service sector industries experienced profitability crises as well. Many low-wage service sector jobs—like cleaning hotels and serving food or caring for children or the elderly—cannot be moved. Faced with the challenge of "achieving the virtuous circle between falling prices and rising real demand,"[2] service sector employers found other ways to prosecute the race to the bottom. We argue that the welfare reforms undertaken in 1996 need to be seen in the context of this process. By placing women in low-wage service jobs, attenuating their rights as workers, and "reschooling" them in what to expect from low-wage employers, the programs' designers fostered a race to the bottom in the service sector as well.

All women who entered these low-wage service sector jobs faced declining conditions.[3] But women who entered through the institutions of reformed welfare faced a double burden. It was the combination of eroding societal support for social reproduction—the solitary wage bargain—and placement in mandatory work assignments beyond the reach of law and protections that undermined their attempts to gain a secure foothold in the labor market.

The solitary wage bargain is a market-driven reconfiguration of responsibilities for the social reproduction of the next generation of workers—one that emphasizes the short-term over the long and individual over collective arrangements. Beginning in the 1970s and continuing into the new century, employers demanded new "flexibility" in setting shifts, successfully blocked efforts to raise the minimum wage, and strategized to limit their responsibilities for unemployment insurance, workers' compensation programs, and benefits provided under the Family and Medical Leave Act. Fewer offered benefit programs and sick leave; almost none explored new programs such as maternity leave. At the same time, the state ended the statutory entitlement to welfare and set lifetime and program-specific limits on its receipt. It also gave states more discretion to limit access to food stamps, medical assistance, and other supports. All of these changes presumed a worker who was healthy and able and who had no responsibilities at home. The family wage bargain had enacted a gendered model that distributed obligations across a broader array of actors; under the solitary wage bargain, by contrast, social reproduction became an "externality" (in economists' terms) or an "absent presence" (in those of literary critics). These changes effectively devolved all responsibilities onto the shoulders of workers.[4]

If crises of social reproduction drove women to welfare, workfare practices undermined their status and rights as workers. Mandatory placement in community service jobs nullified women's right to freely contract their services. The interstitial status of women who occupied these positions (between citizens with rights and paupers with none, to paraphrase Chad Goldberg)[5] placed them in an awkward and uncertain relationship to laws and employment protections, and barred them from joining with other workers in unions. The nature of the positions—in extremely menial, low-wage service sector work—led to experiences of downward mobility for women who had previously worked in more skilled or responsible positions.

What are the alternatives to such a punitive and ineffective system? An outpouring of work from scholarly collaborations and think tanks has addressed this question.[6] Many of the reforms they suggest could begin to address the dilemmas outlined here, for example, providing universal health care or health insurance; offering paid family medical leave or expanding unemployment insurance to cover extraordinary family care needs; improving subsidies for child care; expanding the Earned Income Tax Credit; raising the minimum wage to a reasonable level; making unionization easier; instituting new ways to promote asset ownership; or expanding education and training opportunities; and properly funding and modernizing the social security disability system for those who, permanently or temporarily, cannot work. Notably, none of these suggestions entail expanding our current system of TANF. All potentially provide supports for social reproduction in ways that do not require the trading of civil for social rights. This book is not a social policy tome, and it has not weighed the pros and cons of such programs. But its detailed analysis of what is wrong with the system that exists—and of the way its failures play out in the lives of individuals, suggests two key premises or starting points for any program of change.

First, such programs must be based on the recognition that *poor women with children are already working*, and wage work must be compatible with the care they must provide. In some cases—for example, if a woman is disabled or caring for a seriously ill family member—work outside the home will not be practicable. Stuart White, Joan Tronto, and others have suggested that caring for children or those who are ill is civic labor—the shouldering of a community burden. Eva Kittay has expressed this especially clearly. Speaking of infants and young children, the frail elderly, and those who are ill or significantly impaired, she says:

> At these times we need care, frequently total care, care so extensive that the people who care for us cannot attend to their own needs. . . .The dependency worker requires others who will see to it that resources are available to meet the needs of both herself and the needs of her charge. She also needs assurance that when her care for another impedes her ability to care for or fend for herself, she can depend on another for sustenance and aid and that when she is unable to care for her charge another will. . . . No society can exist beyond one generation unless its youngest dependents survive and mature into adulthood, and no decent society can neglect those who become dependent during the years that intervene between birth and death. Yet . . . the inevitably dependent individual and those closest to her in the chain of dependencies are the most exposed members in a social order.

Kittay has also pointed out that supporting this care "always seems to be expensive." She notes that this is so for two reasons: because it is labor-intensive, and "because to date so much of this labor is gotten for free."[7] She notes, however, that costliness was previously used as an argument against environmental protections, and yet we have since learned that this is a cost worth bearing. Perhaps investing in the care of citizens may come to seem reasonable in some near future.

Second, new programs to replace workfare must be premised on what Alice Kessler-Harris has called economic citizenship.[8] She uses this term to refer to the ability to work at an occupation of one's choosing and to the "customary and legal acknowledgement of personhood" that flows from it. This means that all who work should be entitled to societally agreed-upon protections. There should be no enclaves of attenuated rights. We should work toward a wage that can support families—no longer paid only to certain groups of men, as in the family wage bargain—but to all workers. Perhaps the best way to do this is to insure that workers have the tools and resource to negotiate their own bargain with employers through unions.

The women in our study had a vision of such changes—not fully formed, in most cases, but in fragments. It structured their responses to those aspects of programs that they found profoundly unfair, such as mandatory placements. It animated their frequently expressed desire for more time at home with infants, their worries about their older children, and their wishes for the future: "I want my kids to have more than what they have." "I need a better job." "If I could just go to school." Touching in their modesty, these goals spoke of an alternative vision of economic justice. Some women, like Darla Tanner, put a sharper point on this critique: "With all the rich people we have in this country, there's no way we should be short on child care or health care." In those few words, Darla pointed to the political decisions that undergird welfare reform policies and her own dilemma. Tacking back and forth between labor markets, policy initiatives, and poor women's lives, this book has traced the implications of our current social contract with the poor. It has argued that policymakers have made poor women raising children a demonstration project for market-led deregulation of work—a move that has figuratively tied their hands as they negotiate the low-wage labor market. In concluding, we ask if the struggles of the women in our study might serve as another kind of demonstration project—as a guide to the supports needed by embodied and encumbered workers and a call for a new vision of economic citizenship.

APPENDIX A

DESCRIPTION OF INTERVIEW PROCESS

Once our sampling plan was in place, we randomly selected names of appropriate interview candidates from the state's administrative database and mailed each a letter explaining the project's goals. We offered to meet at the location of their choice, to provide an inexpensive meal, to provide child care if needed, and to pay $25 for their time. We made follow-up phone calls as necessary to schedule the interviews. Seventy percent of the women we contacted in Milwaukee and Racine counties agreed to be interviewed.

We conducted interviews with participants between April and July 2004. Each interview was taped and lasted from one to three hours. When possible, we arranged for two interviewers to be present, one providing child care or taking notes while the other conducted the interview. We obtained informed consent according to approved human subjects procedures from all participants; we also explained to them that we had obtained a federal certificate of confidentiality from the Department of Health and Human Services that protected us from having to testify if they revealed information about illegal activities. Our interview questions covered many aspects of their family and work lives, as well as social program use. (The complete interview schedule can be found in appendix B). We worked with each woman to reconstruct a detailed work history, paying particular attention to her last five jobs. Because we had access to state data on participation in Wisconsin Works (W-2), food stamp receipt, and Supplemental Security Income (SSI), as well as to unemployment insurance data on jobs, we were able to cross-check each woman's personal account with state records. We found that women's responses to interview questions were consistent with the official data in all instances.

In addition to constructing these multifaceted case histories, we analyzed transcripts of interviews in three different ways. The first was thematic; we coded interviews for preestablished themes (focused coding) and unexpected themes (open coding). Examples of preestablished themes were getting jobs, losing jobs, good jobs, work/family conflicts, temporary work, informal jobs, and crises leading to welfare. Unexpected themes included welfare stigma, homelessness, and domestic violence. Second, we analyzed trajectories, developing timelines of family history, work and livelihood history, and social program use for each woman. Once these trajectories were complete, we explored connections between the realms, as we were particularly interested in how crises in one area of life reverberated in others and how support in one area could mitigate adverse events and prevent them from becoming crises. We also mapped these trajectories onto regional-level changes in policy and labor market conditions. The third type of analysis was comparative. We calculated income and earnings for each woman from 1998 through 2004 and compared the experiences of women in different financial circumstances (see chapter 4, note 10, for a detailed description of how income and earnings were determined). We also made comparisons of the work and family trajectories of long- and short-term welfare participants and comparisons across programs (community service jobs, W-2 Transitions, caretaker-of-newborn). Taken together, these interviews are a primary source of the account produced in this volume.

INTERVIEW PROTOCOL

A. INTRODUCTORY QUESTIONS

Many mothers these days have to try to balance taking care of their kids and bringing in enough income to support themselves and their families. I have some questions for you about how you've managed this.

[Ask for *examples* whenever possible]

FAMILY COMPOSITION

First, I want to learn a little bit about the people you take care of.

1. How many children do you have?
2. Can you tell me their names and how old they are so I can keep track of who you're talking about as we talk?
3. Do all of your kids live with you right now?
4. Are you taking care of any other children or adults right now?
5. Do you and your kids live in your own place or do you share a household with other people?
   ⇒ If share:
   A. Who are you living with right now?
   B. Is it your house?

MOTHERING

6. Are you a single mother?
7. Can you tell me what that is like?
8. Are there any advantages/disadvantages?
9. Everybody has their own ideas about what it means to be a good mother or father. Can you tell me what being a good mother means to you?
10. Where do you think you got these ideas about mothering? Did you have a role model?
11. What kinds of things make it hard for you to take care of your children the way you would like to?

B. WORK AND INCOME

[Ask for *examples* whenever possible]

1. Are you currently employed?
2. Is this a CSJ [community service job]?

⇒ If CSJ:

A. How long have you been enrolled in the W-2 program?
B. What activities do you have to do for your CSJ (W-2T)?
C. How many hours of activities do you have to do a week?
D. Did you have any choice in the hours that you do your activities, or where you do them?
E. Do you feel that you have gotten any job training, or learned any useful skills, in this program?
F. How much income do you get a month for doing these activities?
G. Have you learned about any useful resources from the workers at the W-2 agency?
H. Do you feel that participating in W-2 has had any effect on how you are able to care for your children?
I. Do you feel there have been any drawbacks to being in the program?

⇒ If employed in non-CSJ:

A. What do you do?
B. How long have you been working at this job?
C. How many hours a week do you work?
D. Is there any flexibility in the hours you work?
E. How much do you make an hour?
F. Do you get benefits like sick leave or health insurance?
G. How did you get this job? (i.e., employment agency, temp agency, referral from friend, job ad)
H. Is it a permanent job or temporary position?

⇒ If not employed:

A. Have you held a job in the past?
B. What did you do?
C. How long did you work there?
D. Was it part or full-time?
E. Were the hours flexible?
F. How much did you make an hour?
G. Did you get any benefits?
H. Was it a long-term job or a temporary position?

I. How did you get this job?

J. Why did you leave this job?

3. Go back through past jobs, asking the same questions.
   ⇒ If the narrator has more than five jobs, ask about the last five, and then:
   A. When did you start working?
   B. How many jobs would you guess you have had altogether?
4. What was your favorite job?
5. Why?
6. Why did you have to leave this job?
7. What kinds of skills and education did you need to get this job?
8. What is the highest level of schooling you have completed?
9. Do you have any trouble with reading?
10. Have you completed any job training programs? (CNA, clerical, child care, or factory training?)
11. What was your least favorite job?
12. Why?
13. What would you say is your ideal job?
14. What kinds of education or training do you think you would need to get this job?
15. What has made it hard for you to get the kind of job you would like?
16. Have you ever done work on the side, like braiding hair or babysitting, to bring in a little extra money?
    ⇒ If yes:
    A. What kinds of things?
    B. How important a source of income are they for you?

C. WORK-FAMILY BALANCE

[Ask for *examples* whenever possible]

1. Can you tell me what a typical day is like for you right now, in terms of the things you need to do . . . your schedule? (You might think back to a day last week and describe it.)
2. What kinds of transportation do you use?
3. How long does it take you to get to work? (if applicable)
4. Do you have problems with transportation?
5. Who takes care of your kids when you are not with them? (Ask about each child)
6. Do you feel these arrangements are working out OK?

7. Are there times when you've had to work or do activities and you haven't had someone to care for your kids?
8. What do you do then?
9. What do you do when your kids are sick?
10. Can you think of a time when things were going well for you in terms of having enough income and being able to take care of your kids?
    ⇒ If yes:
    A. How did you arrange things then?
    B. What kinds of income and support did you have then?

    ⇒ If no:
    A. What would you need to have that kind of balance?
    B. What makes it hard for you to have that balance now?

D. SOLVING LIVELIHOOD PROBLEMS

[Ask for *examples* whenever possible]
1. What have been some of the most difficult times you have faced in trying to take care of your family?
2. If you have found yourself short of cash or food or diapers at the end of the month, what have you done?
3. What do you do if someone in your family has a medical emergency?
4. Has your health ever been an obstacle to working or caring for your family?
5. Have you had trouble getting the medical care or medicines that you or one of your kids need?
    ⇒ If yes: ask for details.
6. (If there are school age children) Where do your kids go to school?
7. How do they like school?
8. How are their grades?
   I want to remind you again that I will not pass this information on to anyone, but I want to get an idea of what it takes to support a family in this economy.
9. Do other people in your household bring in income?
   (Ask about each person having job, informal income, or state/federal program income.)
10. Do you have a lot of debt?
11. Are you facing any legal issues right now?

12. Do you have a bank account?

13. How would you say you are doing right now in terms of having enough income?

E. SOCIAL NETWORKS/SOURCES OF SUPPORT

[Ask for *examples* whenever possible]

We've talked about some of the challenges you have faced in caring for your family. Now, I would like to ask you about the different people or organizations that have helped you out when you've needed it. These can be agencies in the community, like a church, or friends or family members. They may be people that you help when *they* need it.

FAMILY AND FRIENDS

1. Who are some of the people who help you out?

2. Over the past year, how has each of these people helped you? (with cash, material goods, time/care)

3. How do you know [name of individual]? Or, What is your relationship to them?

4. Of these people, who are the two or three who give you the most help?

5. Who do you talk to when you are upset about something or need someone to listen?

6. Who do you trust most to help out with your kids?

7. Do you help most of these people in pretty much the same ways they help you?

8. Have you always lived here?

9. Where else have you lived?

FATHERS AND THEIR RELATIVES

I want to ask a couple of questions about the help you are getting from the fathers of your kids. To ask these questions, it would help to know if your kids have the same biological father or not.

(Go through fathers and ask)

9. Does he watch the kids?

10. Does he give you money to get things for the kids or for things like doctor's visits or day care?

11. Does he buy groceries for you and the kids?

12. Does he ever buy the kids clothing, shoes, or diapers?
13. What about toys or games?
14. Does anyone else from his family help you out with any of these things?
15. What other kinds of help, if any, do you think he should provide?
16. I asked before about being a good mother means to you. Can you tell me your ideas about what it means to be a good father?
17. Is there anyone else who has been like a father to your kids?
18. (If no current partner is mentioned) Would you mind if I ask if you are involved with someone right now? Does he help with your kids?

CHILD SUPPORT

19. Have you had to deal with the county child support agency?
20. Can you describe what it's been like to deal with the child support agency staff?
21. Did you have to go through paternity establishment?
22. Do you receive child support for any of your kids?
23. Which ones?
24. Would you mind telling me how much the order is/orders are for?
25. Do you get this as part of your check from the state or from the child's father directly?
26. Do you get about the same amount every month?
27. Have you ever gotten a larger payment all at one time?
28. Do you think it's hard for the child's father to make these payments?
29. Is he employed right now?
30. Do you think having to make these payments affects his relationship to you or the kids?
31. Do your kids get health insurance coverage through their dad?
32. Has [name father] ever been unable to pay child support because he was incarcerated?
33. How important is this money to you in meeting your needs each month?

STATE AND FEDERAL PROGRAMS

34. Do you get cash assistance from the W-2 program now?
35. What about food stamps?
36. Medical assistance?
37. WIC?
38. Does the county or the W-2 agency help you out with child care?

39. Are you living in low-income housing, or do you get rent assistance?
40. Do you get SSI for yourself or any of your children?
41. Do you get bus passes?
42. Have you ever gotten a job access loan, or emergency assistance from a W-2 agency for help with housing, getting a working car, or paying off some bills?
43. Which of these programs have been most important to you?
44. Have you had any problems with the way these programs are run?
45. What other kinds of help do you think the state should provide for people?
46. In your view, what are some of the good or bad things about being in the W-2 program?

COMMUNITY ORGANIZATIONS

47. Are there other organizations that we haven't talked about (churches, community centers, shelters, or advocacy groups) that have helped you out at some point? (Name some local groups if possible.)
    A. Help with shelter or rent?
    B. With food (say at the end of the month)?
    C. With utility payments?
    D. Counseling or treatment?
    E. Legal issues

F. MARRIAGE

[Ask for *examples* whenever possible]
Finally, I want to ask you a couple of questions about marriage.
1. Are you currently married?
   ⇒ If yes:
   A. Are you currently living with your husband or are you separated?
   B. How long have you been married?
   C. Have you ever been married before?
2. The president is currently asking Congress to spend $1.5 billion for promotion of marriage among low-income families. Do you think this is a good idea?
3. What kinds of things do you think would help support marriage?

APPENDIX C

ECONOMIC COMPOSITION OF SAMPLE

TABLE C.1. Comparison of means on key variables for women in the study and all women enrolled in a lower tier of Wisconsin Works, December 2003

Variable	Statewide population	Study participants (Dane, Racine, and Milwaukee counties)*
Unemployment Insurance earnings (dollars)	2,160	2,090
Food stamps (dollars)	2,673	2,719
Child support (dollars)	832	1,040
W-2 grant (dollars)	4,624	3,792
Total personal income (dollars)	10,289	9,692
Mother's age (years)	29	24
% mothers with 1 child	33	25
% mothers with 2 children	28	37
% mothers with 3 children	19	20
% mothers with 4 children	11	15
% mothers with more than 4 children	9	3
Cumulative months of W-2 (Sept 1997 to June 2004)	22.0	15.7
% mothers African American	67	58
% mothers white	23	22
% mothers Latina	8	20
Years of education	11.2	11.3

*Dane County was originally part of the study but is not analyzed in this book because its labor market was so different from that of southeastern Wisconsin (Milwaukee and Racine).

NOTE: Figures cover the third and fourth quarters of 2003 and the first and second quarters of 2004.

INDUSTRIAL COMPOSITION OF MILWAUKEE AND RACINE

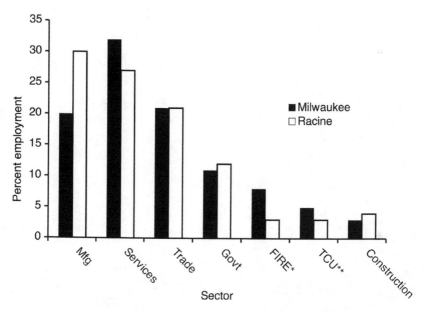

FIGURE D.1. Sectors as percentage of economy, Milwaukee and Racine Counties, 2000.
*Finance, Insurance, and Real Estate; **Transportation, Construction, and Utilities
Source: Wisconsin Department of Commerce, "Milwaukee County Economic Profile" and "Racine County Economic Profile," 2000.

TABLE D.1. Ten largest private sector employers, Milwaukee, 1970

Company	Type of business	Number of local employees
Allis-Chalmers	manufacturing	11,500
A. O. Smith	manufacturing	8,000
Briggs & Stratton	manufacturing	7,400
Allen-Bradley	manufacturing	6,500
Delco	manufacturing	5,000
Harmischfeger	manufacturing	4,450
American Motors	manufacturing	4,000
Jos. Schitz Brewing	brewery	2,800
Pabst Brewing	brewery	2,600
Miller Brewing	brewery	2,400

Source: *Milwaukee Journal Sentinel*, "Ten Largest Employers Then and Now," December 5, 2004.

TABLE D.2. Ten largest private sector employers, Milwaukee, 2004

Company	Type of business	Number of local employees
Aurora Health Care	health care	15,500
Covenant Health	health care	9,250
Roundy's Inc.	retail, grocery	7,400
Marshall & Ilsley	banking	6,800
Wisconsin Energy	utility	6,000
GE HealthCare	health care	5,800
Columbia/St. Mary's	health care	5,600
Kohl's	retail	5,500
Quad Graphics	printing	5,300
Northwestern Mutual	insurance	4,600

Source: *Milwaukee Journal Sentinel*, "Ten Largest Employers Then and Now," December 5, 2004.

APPENDIX E

WISCONSIN WORKS (W-2) DOCUMENTS

STATE OF WISCONSIN
DEPARTMENT OF WORKFORCE DEVELOPMENT
Division of Workforce Solutions

WISCONSIN WORKS (W-2) PARTICIPATION AGREEMENT

Personal information you provide may be used for secondary purposes [Privacy Law, s. 15.04(1)(m)].

I understand and agree that I am responsible for the well-being of myself and my family. Wisconsin Works (W-2) may help me find and keep a job to meet my responsibilities. If I am placed in a W-2 employment position, I agree to the following:

WORK RULES

- My goal is to find and keep a job that is within the limits of my capabilities and family responsibility. If I am placed in a W-2 employment position, I will still look for and accept a job.

- I will meet with a Financial and Employment Planner (FEP). I understand that if I am job-ready, I may receive assistance in finding unsubsidized employment, but I will not receive a cash grant. If I am not job-ready, my FEP may put me into one of the following W-2 employment positions:

    ◊ **Trial Job**--a job with an employer who may hire me permanently. If placed, my employer will pay me at least minimum wage for the hours I work.

    ◊ **Community Service Job (CSJ)**--a work and training activity that helps the community while helping me prepare for a job. I will receive a monthly grant in return for up to 30 hours per week in work and training activities and up to 10 hours per week in education and training activities.

    ◊ **W-2 Transition (W-2 T)**--activities that will help me prepare for a job. I will receive a monthly grant in return for up to 28 hours per week in W-2 T activities and up to 12 hours per week in education and training activities.

- If I am placed in a W-2 employment position, I will do all the activities in my Employability Plan. If I cannot do my required activities, I must report it to my FEP. If I have a medical reason that keeps me from working, I will get a written statement from an approved medical provider.

- I understand that my participation in each of the employment positions (Trial Job, CSJ or W-2 T) is limited to 24 months. Total participation in W-2 employment positions is limited to 60 months.

- CSJ and W-2 T payments will not increase if I have more children.

- I understand that W-2 work assignments will:

    ◊ meet all federal and state labor laws and rules that apply;
    ◊ meet all federal, state and local health and safety standards and be free of discrimination;
    ◊ not require me to give up any labor or union rights; and
    ◊ not replace a worker who is on strike, lockout, or involved in another bona fide labor dispute.

- If I am in a CSJ or W-2 T employment position, my payment will go down by an hourly rate for each hour I fail to do what I was assigned to do without a good reason.

RESPONSIBILITIES

- I will help to legally name and/or locate the other parent(s) of my child(ren). If I fail to cooperate three (3) times, I will not be eligible for W-2 employment positions or child care until I do or for six (6) months, whichever is longer.
- I will give proof of information needed within seven (7) working days of being asked. I will report changes in income, assets, and family structure within 10 days. I will report my child(ren) moving out of my home within five (5) days. If I give false information on purpose, I may be prosecuted.
- I understand that I must have appropriate care for my child during the hours I am participating in W-2. I can contact my local Child Care Resource and Referral agency to help me find child care. If I cannot find appropriate child care I will tell my FEP.
- I will make sure my children go to school. If they do not go to school, my payments may be reduced.
- If I receive a W-2 payment in error, I must pay it back.

DES-10755 (R. 11/2001) **RETAIN COMPLETED FORM IN CASE RECORD**

FIGURE E.1. Wisconsin Works (W-2) participation agreement.

```
                              W-2 EMPLOYABILITY PLAN
                                                                 Printed On: 10/23/2003

       ██████████████

Office: MILW CO REG 3 W-2 EMPLOY/TRNG,                    ███████████████
Worker: ██████████

                        PART 1: EMPLOYMENT AND RELATED GOALS

JOB GOALS DURING PROGRAM PARTICIPATION:

                JOB TITLE                                          · DOT Code

     Primary:    CHILDCARE                                           092
     Secondary:  CNA                                                 079

RELATED GOALS NOT REQUIRED FOR PROGRAM PARTICIPATION:

     Long-Term:  OBTAIN GED
     Short-term: SECURE EMPLOYMENT

                           PART 2: PARTCIPANT PERSONAL GOALS
                           (Not required for program participation)
                                                              Planned Completion Date

Step 1.     BUY OWN HOUSE
Step 2.     WOULD LIKE TO PURSUE A CAREER IN ARCHITECTURE
Step 3.     WOULD LIKE TO OBTAIN DRIVER LICENSE
Step 4.     WOULD LIKE TO OBTAIN GED.
Step 5.     CONTACT JOHN MORAN (FEP) WITH ANY CHANGES 908-3109
Step 6.     PROVIDE EXCUSES FOR MISSED W2 HOURS WITH IN 7 DAYS
*****************************************************************************************

                        PART 3: PARTICIPANT PROGRAM ACTIVITY PLAN
                           (Required for program participation)

The participant program activity plan will begin on 10/23/2003 and will be reviewed by 01/10/2004. During this
time the W-2 placement is FULL COMMUNITY SERVICE JOB    . All W-2 payments may end if a new employability plan
is not completed by the review date.

The participant program activity plan will help you meet your goals to get a job. It lists the activities that
you must do. Your worker will meet with you to talk about your progress and make changes to your plan, if
needed.


---------------------------------------------------------------------------------------
ACTIVITY 1:    WORK EXPERIENCE
Planned Begin and End Dates:  10/23/2003 to 01/10/2004                Hours per week: 25
     Provider of service: KEYS TO LIFE-SULLIVAN CENTER
     Location  : 2947 N MLK DRIVE 10/27/03 @ 9AM
     Supportive Services Provided:       Child Care   YES    Transportation   YES
     Remarks: KEYS TO LIFE
---------------------------------------------------------------------------------------
ACTIVITY 2:    EDUCATION
Planned Begin and End Dates:  10/23/2003 to 01/10/2004                Hours per week: 10
     Provider of service: KEYS TO LIFE-SULLIVAN CENTER
     Location  : 2947 N MLK DRIVE 10/27/03 @ 9AM
     Supportive Services Provided:       Child Care   YES    Transportation   YES
     Remarks: KEYS TO LIFE
---------------------------------------------------------------------------------------
```

FIGURE E.2. Wisconsin Works (W-2) employability plan.

NOTES

PREFACE

1. Catherine Rampell, "As Layoffs Surge, Women May Pass Men in Job Force," *New York Times*, February 6, 2009, http://www.nytimes.com/2009/02/06/business/06women.html.
2. Jason DeParle, "Welfare Aid Isn't Growing as Economy Drops Off," *New York Times*, February 2, 2009, http://www.nytimes.com/2009/02/02/us/02welfare.html.
3. Michael Wines, "Gingrich Comes Out Slugging," *New York Times*, December 7, 1994.
4. Julia Isaacs and Timothy Smeeding, "Wisconsin Poverty Report" (Madison, WI: Institute for Research on Poverty, April 2009), http://www.irp.wisc.edu/research/WisconsinPoverty/pdfs/First_Wisconsin_Poverty_Report_Final-2.pdf.

CHAPTER ONE

1. Lawrence Mead, *Beyond Entitlement: The Social Obligations of Citizenship* (New York: Free Press, 1986), 84.
2. Johnnie Tillmon, "Insights of a Welfare Mother," *Journal of Social Issues*, January/February 1971, 23.
3. The question of what counts as welfare is a complicated one. As Linda Gordon points out, when we talk about welfare today, we are almost always referring exclusively to a few programs of assistance to the very poor, whereas the term could apply to all of a government's contributions to citizens' well-being. Gordon, *Pitied but Not Entitled: Single Mothers and the History of Welfare* (Cambridge, MA: Harvard University Press, 1994), 2. In this volume, we will use the term to refer to means-tested cash assistance programs, including Temporary Assistance to Needy Families (TANF) and its predecessor, Aid to Families with Dependent Children (AFDC). While we will discuss other programs, such as food stamps, Medical Assistance, or public housing, when we use the term welfare, it will refer to cash aid and the case management surrounding it. Workfare refers to labor performed as a condition of cash aid.
4. Mead, *Beyond Entitlement*, 3–4.
5. For example, David K. Shipler, *The Working Poor: Invisible in America* (New York: Vintage, 2005); Beth Shulman, *The Betrayal of Work: How Low-Wage Jobs Fail 30 Million Americans* (New York: New Press, 2005); Katherine S. Newman and Victor Tan Chen, *The Missing Class: Portraits of the Near Poor in America* (New York: Beacon Press, 2007); Katherine S. Newman, *No Shame in My Game: The Working Poor in the Inner City* (New York: Vintage, 2000).
6. Gøsta Esping-Andersen, *The Three Worlds of Welfare Capitalism* (Princeton, NJ: Princeton

University Press, 1990); James O'Connor, *The Fiscal Crisis of the State* (1973; New York: Transaction Publishers, 2001), 150–51; Frances Fox Piven and Richard A. Cloward, *Regulating the Poor: The Functions of Public Welfare* (1971; New York: Vintage, 1993); Karl Polanyi, *The Great Transformation: The Political and Economic Origins of Our Time* (1944; Boston: Beacon, 2001).

7. Wendy Brown, "American Nightmare: Neoliberalism, Neoconservatism, and De-Democratization," *Political Theory* 34 (2006): 694.

8. Jamie Peck, *Workfare States* (New York: Guilford Press, 2001), 52.

9. Frances Fox Piven, "Welfare Reform and the Economic and Cultural Reconstruction of Low Wage Labor Markets," in *The New Poverty Studies: The Ethnography of Power, Politics, and Impoverished People in the United States*, ed. Judith Goode and Jeff Maskovsky (New York: New York University Press, 2001), 142.

10. Peck, *Workfare States*, 52.

11. The phrasing is drawn from John Pilger, "Iraq: The Unthinkable Becomes Normal," *New Statesman*, November 15, 2004.

12. Lawrence Mishel, Jared Bernstein, and Sylvia Allegretto, *The State of Working America, 2004/2005* (Ithaca, NY: Cornell University Press, Economic Policy Institute, 2005), 174.

13. David Elwood, "Winners and Losers in America: Taking the Measure of New Economic Realities," in *A Working Nation: Workers, Work, and Government in the New Economy*, ed. David T. Elwood, Rebecca M. Blank, Joseph Blasi, Douglas Kruse, William A. Niskanen, and Karen Lynn-Dyson (New York: Russell Sage, 2000), 4.

14. Quoted in Mead, *Beyond Entitlement*, 223.

15. American Enterprise Institute, *The New Consensus on Family and Welfare* (Washington, DC: American Enterprise Institute, 1987), 86.

16. Mead, *Beyond Entitlement*, 84.

17. Eileen Appelbaum and Peter Albin, "Shifts in Employment, Occupational Structure and Educational Attainment," in *Skills, Wages, and Productivity in the Service Sector*, ed. Thierry Noyelle (Boulder, CO: Westview Press, 1990).

18. Michael Katz, *The Price of Citizenship: Redefining the American Welfare State* (New York: Henry Holt, 2002), 351.

19. U.S. House of Representatives, Ways and Means Committee, Subcommittee on Human Resources, "A Decade since Welfare Reform: 1996 Welfare Reforms Reduce Welfare Dependence," February 26, 2006, http://waysandmeans.house.gov/media/pdf/welfare/022706welfare.pdf.

20. Lawrence Mead, *Government Matters: Welfare Reform in Wisconsin* (Princeton, NJ: Princeton University Press, 2004), 4.

21. Sharon Parrott and Arloc Sherman, "TANF at Ten: Program Results Are More Mixed Than Often Understood" (press release), Center on Budget and Policy Priorities, Washington, DC, August 17, 2006, http://www.cbpp.org/8-17-06tanf.htm.

22. The most frequent assessment of economists of the impact of such an influx of workers is that "in the long run, as the supply of unskilled workers increases, the wages they earn will tend to fall." Gary Burtless, "Can the Labor Market Absorb Three Million Welfare Recipients?" in *The Low-Wage Labor Market: Challenges and Opportunities for Economic Self-Sufficiency*, ed. Kelleen Kaye and Demetra Smith Nightingale (Washington, DC: U.S. Department of

Health and Human Services, Office of the Assistant Secretary for Planning and Evaluation, 2000), 66. For other accounts, reaching much the same conclusion, see Maria Enchautegui, "Will Welfare Reform Hurt Low-Skilled Workers?," Discussion Paper no. 01-01 (Urban Institute, Washington, DC, February 2001); Timothy Bartik, "Instrumental Variable Estimates of the Labor Market Spillover Effects of Welfare Reform," Staff Working Paper 02-078 (Upjohn Institute, Kalamazoo, MI, April 2002).

23. Peck, *Workfare States*, 52; Mead, *Beyond Entitlement*, 9.

24. Erin Hatton, "The Temp Industry and the Transformation of Work in America" (PhD diss., University of Wisconsin, Madison, 2007), 137.

25. Martha May, "The Historical Problem of the Family Wage: The Ford Motor Company and the Five Dollar Day," *Feminist Studies* 8, no. 2 (1982): 399–424; Jeanne Boydston, *Home and Work: Housework, Wages, and the Ideology of Labor in the Early Republic* (New York: Oxford University Press, 1990).

26. Claudia Von Werlhof, "The Proletarian Is Dead: Long Live the Housewife," in *Households in the World Economy*, ed. Joan Smith, Immanuel Wallerstein, and Hans-Dieter Evers (Beverly Hills, CA: Sage, 1984), 144.

27. Claus Offe, *Disorganized Capitalism: Contemporary Transformations of Work and Politics* (Cambridge: Polity Press, 1985), 26.

28. Joan Tronto, "Who Cares? Public and Private Caring and the Rethinking of Citizenship," in *Women and Welfare: Theory and Practice in the U.S. and Europe*, ed. Nancy J. Hirschmann and Ulrike Liebert (New Brunswick, NJ: Rutgers University Press, 2001), 66–67, 70.

29. Martha Albertson Fineman, *The Autonomy Myth: A Theory of Dependency* (New York: Free Press, 2004).

30. Nancy Fraser and Linda Gordon, "A Genealogy of *Dependency*: Tracing a Keyword of the U.S. Welfare State," *Signs* 19, no. 2 (1994).

31. Daniel Patrick Moynihan, *The Politics of a Guaranteed Income: The Nixon Administration and the Family Assistance Plan* (New York: Random House, 1973), 17.

32. American Enterprise Institute, *New Consensus*, 99.

33. Judith Shklar, *American Citizenship: The Quest for Inclusion* (Cambridge, MA: Harvard University Press, 1991), 4.

34. Suzanne Mettler, *Dividing Citizens: Gender and Federalism in New Deal Public Policy* (Ithaca, NY: Cornell University Press, 1998), 9.

35. Stuart White, *The Civic Minimum: On the Rights and Obligations of Economic Citizenship* (New York: Oxford University Press, 2003), 147.

36. Mead, *Beyond Entitlement*, 7.

37. Ibid., 87–89 (emphasis in original).

38. Patricia J. Williams, *The Alchemy of Race and Rights* (Cambridge, MA: Harvard University Press, 1992), 226.

39. T. H. Marshall, *Citizenship and Social Class* (1950; London: Pluto Press, 1992), 8.

40. White, *Civic Minimum*, 3–6.

41. Ibid., 6.

42. Friedrich Hayek, *The Road to Serfdom* (Chicago: University of Chicago Press, 1994); Milton Friedman, *Capitalism and Freedom* (Chicago: University of Chicago Press, 1963).

43. Victoria Mayer, "Crafting a New Conservative Consensus on Welfare Reform: Redefining Citizenship, Social Provision, and the Public/Private Divide," *Social Politics* 15 (2008); Lucy A. Williams, "Decades of Distortion: The Right's 30-year Assault on Welfare," (Somerville, MA: Political Research Associates, 1997), http://www.publiceye.org/welfare/Decades-of-Distortion .html.

44. George Gilder, *Wealth and Poverty* (New York: Basic Books, 1981). On the rhetoric of moral perversity, see Margaret Somers and Fred Block, "From Poverty to Perversity: Ideas, Markets and Institutions over 200 Years of Welfare Debate," *American Sociological Review* 70 (2005); Albert O. Hirschman, *The Rhetoric of Reaction: Perversity, Futility, Jeopardy* (Cambridge, MA: Harvard University Press, 1991).

45. Charles Murray, *Losing Ground: American Social Policy, 1950-1980* (New York: Basic Books, 1994), 19.

46. Michael Novak, "To Promote the General Welfare: Catholic Principles for Welfare Policy," in *Catholic Social Teaching and the U.S. Economy*, ed. John W. Houck and Oliver F. Williams (Lanham, MD: University Press of America, 1985), 169.

47. Mead, *Beyond Entitlement*, 10–12.

48. Ibid, 11.

49. Ibid., 6.

50. Ibid., 43.

51. Mead, *Government Matters*, 1–2.

52. White, *Civic Minimum*, 15.

53. Chad Alan Goldberg, "Welfare Recipients or Workers? Contesting the Workfare State in New York City," *Sociological Theory*, 19, no. 2 (2001), 202, 204. See also Goldberg, *Citizens and Paupers: Relief, Rights, and Race, from the Freedman's Bureau to Workfare* (Chicago: University of Chicago Press, 2007).

54. Andrea Robles, Fred Doolittle, and Susan Gooden, "Community Service Jobs in Wisconsin Works: The Milwaukee County Experience," *MDRC Report* (Manpower Development Research Corporation, June 2003), 55.

55. Isaac Martin, "Rethinking Welfare Reform," *Contemporary Sociology* 37, no. 2 (2008): 105.

56. Martha Fineman, "The Inevitability of Dependency and the Politics of Subsidy," *Stanford Law and Policy Review* 9, no. 1 (1998): 90.

57. Michael Burawoy, "The Extended Case Method," in *Ethnography Unbound: Power and Resistance in the Modern Metropolis*, ed. Michael Burawoy (Berkeley: University of California Press, 1991), 274.

58. We conducted these interviews as part of a larger project at the Institute for Research on Poverty at the University of Wisconsin: the "W-2 Child Support Demonstration Evaluation, Phase III." Its principal investigators were Maria Cancian and Daniel Meyer, and it was funded by the Wisconsin Department of Workforce Development. The research team was made up of the two authors and two graduate students, Nicole Breazeale and Angela Cunningham. Patricia Brown and Steve Cook of IRP helped draw the sample. For a description of our interview process, and complete list of questions, see appendixes A and B.

59. Latinas are slightly overrepresented in our study, compared to their frequency in the population. Because their proportion of the population was small (8 percent), we deliberately oversampled them in order to collect an adequate array of their perspectives.

60. U.S. House of Representatives, *Green Book: Background Material and Data on Programs within the Jurisdiction of the House Committee on Ways and Means* (Washington, DC: Government Printing Office, 1996), 474.

61. Gwendolyn Mink, *Welfare's End* (Ithaca, NY: Cornell University Press, 1998).

62. Maria Cancian, Robert Haveman, Daniel R. Meyer, and Barbara Wolfe, "Before and after TANF: The Economic Well-Being of Women Leaving Welfare," *Social Service Review* 76, no. 4 (2002): 603–41.

63. U.S. House of Representatives, *Green Book* (1996), 473, 475.

64. For a detailed comparison of our sample to the population of welfare participants in the state, see appendix C.

65. Gregory Acs and Pamela Loprest, "Final Synthesis Report of the Findings from ASPE's 'Leavers' Grants," (Washington, DC: U.S. Department of Health and Human Services, Office of the Assistant Secretary for Policy and Evaluation, 2001); Rebecca M. Blank and Lucie Schmidt, "Work, Wages, and Welfare," in *The New World of Welfare*, ed. Rebecca Blank and Ron Haskins (Washington, DC: Brookings Institution, 2001); Maria Cancian, Robert Haveman, Daniel R. Meyer, and Barbara Wolfe, "The Employment, Earnings and Income of Single Mothers in Wisconsin Who Left Cash Assistance: Comparisons among Three Cohorts," Special Report no. 85 (Institute for Research on Poverty, University of Wisconsin, Madison, 2003); Sheldon Danziger, Colleen M. Heflin, Mary E. Corcoran, Elizabeth Otlmans, and Hui-Chen Wang, "Does It Pay to Move from Welfare to Work?" *Journal of the Association for Policy Analysis and Management* 21 (2002); Pamela Loprest and Sheila Zedlewski, "The Changing Role of Welfare in the Lives of Low-Income Families with Children" (Washington, DC: Urban Institute, 2006); Robert Moffit, "From Welfare to Work: What the Evidence Shows" (Washington, DC: Brookings Institution, 2001).

66. Richard P. Nathan and Thomas L. Gais, "Implementing the Personal Responsibility Act of 1996: A First Look" (Albany: State University of New York, Rockefeller Institute of Government, 1999).

67. Cancian et al., "Before and after TANF," 2.

68. Jason DeParle, *American Dream: Three Women, Ten Kids, and a Nation's Drive to End Welfare.* (New York: Viking, 2004), 125.

69. "For those who can work, only work should pay," Wisconsin governor Tommy Thompson said in a November 1994 speech introducing his plans for welfare reform. The line became a "guiding principle" of the state's welfare-to-work program.

CHAPTER TWO

1. Evelyn Glenn, "From Servitude to Service Work: Historical Continuities in the Racial Division of Paid Reproductive Labor," *Signs* 18, no. 1 (1992), 3.

2. Jamie Peck, *Work-Place: The Social Regulation of Labor Markets* (New York: Guilford, 1996), 5, 15.

3. Private Industry Council of Milwaukee County/University of Milwaukee Employment and Training Institute, "Survey of Job Openings in the Milwaukee Metropolitan Area," weeks of October 20, 2003, and May 23, 2005, http://www.uwm.edu/Dept/ETI/jobs.htm.

4. Jamie Peck and Nikolas Theodore, "'Work First': Workfare and the Regulation of Contingent Labour Markets," *Cambridge Journal of Economics*, 24, no. 1 (2000), 123.

5. Averaging ranks across the five indexes that the Census Bureau uses to measure urban inequality, Milwaukee ranked number one. John Iceland, Daniel H. Weinberg, and Erika Steinmetz, "U.S. Census Bureau, Series CENSR-3. Racial and Ethnic Residential Segregation in the U.S.: 1980–2000" (Washington, DC: Government Printing Office, 2002), 68–69.

6. Marc V. Levine, "The Two Milwaukees: Separate and Unequal," paper presented to Milwaukee County Task Force on Segregation and Race Relations, April 30, 2003, http://www.ced.uwm.edu.

7. Anthony M. Orum, *City-Building in America* (Boulder, CO: Westview Press, 1995), 25–35; William Cronon, *Nature's Metropolis: Chicago and the Great West* (New York: W. W. Norton, 1996), 27.

8. Isabel Wilkerson, "How Milwaukee Has Thrived While Leaving Blacks Behind," *New York Times*, March 19, 1991.

9. Greg Ip, "Degrees of Separation: As Economy Shifts, a New Generation Fights to Keep Up," *Wall Street Journal*, June 22, 2005, A1.

10. James J. Lorence, "Mining 'Salt of the Earth,'" *Wisconsin Magazine of History*, Winter 2001–2, 33.

11. *Milwaukee Journal Sentinel*, "Labor Newspaper in Racine, Wisconsin Is Latest Victim of Layoffs, Plant Closings," December 25, 2001.

12. Orum, *City-Building in America*, 104–5; Jack Norman, "Congenial Milwaukee: A Segregated City," in *Unequal Partnerships: The Political Economy of Urban Redevelopment in Postwar America*, ed. Gregory D. Squires (New Brunswick, NJ: Rutgers University Press, 1989), 183.

13. John Schmid, "Still Separate and Unequal: A Dream Derailed," *Milwaukee Journal Sentinel*, December 5, 2004, A1.

14. Joe William Trotter Jr., *Black Milwaukee: The Making of an Industrial Proletariat, 1914–45* (Chicago: University of Illinois Press, 2007), 147. While the Milwaukee AFL rejected black membership, even during World War II, when demand for labor was high, the city's CIO unions accepted blacks as members from their inception in 1936 and sought to increase both employment and job quality for African American workers. Ibid., 149, 173.

15. Paul Geib, "From Mississippi to Milwaukee: A Case Study of the Southern Black Migration to Milwaukee, 1940–1970," *Journal of Negro History* 83, no. 4 (1998).

16. Trotter, *Black Milwaukee*, 149; Geib, "From Mississippi to Milwaukee"; Alan J. Borsuk and Leonard Sykes Jr., "City Population Lowest since 1940: Minorities Outnumber Whites in City for First Time," *Milwaukee Journal Sentinel*, March 8, 2001, http://www2.jsonline.com/news/census2000/mar01/race09030801.asp.

17. Matthew Zeidenberg, "Moving Outward: The Shifting Landscape of Poverty in Milwaukee" (Center on Wisconsin Strategy, University of Wisconsin, Madison, August 2004); Marc V. Levine, "The Crisis of Black Male Joblessness in Milwaukee: Trends, Explanations and Policy Options" (University of Wisconsin–Milwaukee Center for Economic Development, March 2007), http://www.ced.uwm.edu.

18. Bisbing Business Research, "Attitude Study among Negro and White Residents in the Milwaukee Negro Residential Areas" (Milwaukee, WI: Bisbing Business Research, 1965), http://www.wisconsinhistory.org/turningpoints/search.asp?id=1199.

19. Trotter, *Black Milwaukee*, 231.

20. Joseph Rodriguez and Walter Sava, *Images of America: Latinos in Milwaukee* (Charleston, SC: Arcadia Publishing, 2006) 9, 21; "Wisconsin's Hispanic or Latino Population, Census 2000 Population Trends" (Extension and Applied Population Laboratory, University of Wisconsin, Madison, n.d.).

21. Inter-collegiate Council on Intergroup Relations, "The Housing of Negroes in Milwaukee" (Milwaukee, WI.: Inter-collegiate Council on Intergroup Relations, 1955), http://www.wisconsinhistory.org/turningpoints/search.asp?id=1098.

22. Norman, "Congenial Milwaukee," 185, John Gurda, *The Making of Milwaukee* (Brookfield, WI: Milwaukee County Historical Society, 1999), 363.

23. Ibid., 179.

24. Alexander Shashko, "Blues, Bebop and Bulldozers: Why Milwaukee Never Became a Motown," *Wisconsin Academy Review* 46, no. 3 (Summer 2000).

25. Ibid.

26. Norman, "Congenial Milwaukee," 191.

27. William Albert Vick, "From Walnut Street to No Street: Milwaukee's African American Businesses, 1945–67" (MA thesis, University of Wisconsin, Milwaukee, 1993).

28. Trotter, *Black Milwaukee*, 171.

29. Ibid., 174.

30. Wisconsin Historical Society, "Desegregation and Civil Rights, Turning Points in Wisconsin History," http://www.wisconsinhistory.org/turningpoints/tp-049/?action=more_essay; Jack Dougherty, *More Than One Struggle: The Evolution of Black School Reform in Milwaukee* (Chapel Hill: University of North Carolina Press, 2004).

31. Gurda, *Making of Milwaukee*, 365–76; Patrick D. Jones, *The Selma of the North: Civil Rights Insurgency in Milwaukee* (Cambridge, MA: Harvard University Press, 2009).

32. Gregory D. Squires and William Vélez, "Insurance Redlining and the Transformation of an Urban Metropolis," *Urban Affairs Quarterly* 23, no. 1 (1987).

33. Gurda, *Making of Milwaukee*, 346.

34. Levine, "Crisis of Black Male Joblessness," 24; Gregory D. Squires and William Vélez, "Mortgage Lending and Race: Is Discrimination Still a Factor?" *Environment and Planning A* 28 (1996).

35. Levine, "Crisis of Black Male Joblessness," 30.

36. David Harvey, *The Limits to Capital* (1982; New York: Verso, 1999).

37. Annette Bernhardt, Laura Dresser, and Joel Rogers, "Taking the High Road in Milwaukee: The Wisconsin Regional Training Partnership," in *Partnering for Change: Unions and Community Groups Build Coalitions for Economic Justice*, ed. David Reynolds (New York: M. E. Sharpe, 2004).

38. Marc V. Levine, "'Stealth Depression': Joblessness in the City of Milwaukee since 1990" (University of Wisconsin–Milwaukee Center for Economic Development, August 25, 2003), http://www.ced.uwm.edu.

39. Schmid, "Still Separate and Unequal."

40. Ip, "Degrees of Separation"; Rich Rovito, "Racine County Struggles to Revive Manufacturing after Long Economic Slide," *Business Journal of Milwaukee*, February 4, 2005.

41. Schmid, "Still Separate and Unequal."

42. David Elwood, "Winners and Losers in America: Taking the Measure of New Economic Realities," in *A Working Nation: Workers, Work, and Government*, ed. David Elwood, Rebecca M. Blank, Joseph Blasi, Douglas Kruse, William A. Niskanen, and Karen Lynn-Dyson (New York: Russell Sage, 2000), 16.

43. Ip, "Degrees of Separation."

44. Marc V. Levine, "The Crisis of Low Wages in Milwaukee: Wage Polarization in the Labor Market: 1970–1990," Policy Research Report (University of Wisconsin–Milwaukee Center for Economic Development, November 1994), http://www.ced.uwm.edu; Norman, "Congenial Milwaukee," 192. See also appendix D, figure D.1, "Sectors as Percentage of Economy."

45. Saskia Sassen, Globalization and Its Discontents: Essays on the New Mobility of People and Money (New York: New Press, 1998), 143.

46. Ibid., 145–46.

47. Beth Shulman, The Betrayal of Work: How Low-Wage Jobs Fail 30 Million Americans (New York: New Press, 2005), 32–33.

48. Evelyn Nakano Glenn, Unequal Freedom: How Race and Gender Shaped American Citizenship and Labor (Cambridge, MA: Harvard University Press, 2002).

49. Susan Thistle, *From Marriage to the Market: The Transformation of Women's Lives and Work* (Berkeley: University of California Press, 2006), 111.

50. Jason DeParle, American Dream: Three Women, Ten Kids, and a Nation's Drive to End Welfare (New York: Viking, 2004), 175.

51. Philip Moss and Chris Tilly, *Stories Employers Tell: Race, Skill, and Hiring in America* (New York: Russell Sage, 2001); Joleen Kirschenman and Katherine Neckerman, "'We'd Love to Hire Them But . . .': The Meaning of Race for Employers," in *The Urban Underclass*, ed. Christopher Jencks and Paul Peterson (Washington, DC: Brookings Institution, 1991).

52. Devah Pager, Bruce Western, and Bart Bonikowsky, "Discrimination in a Low Wage Labor Market," *American Sociological Review* 74, no. 5(2009): 777–99.

53. Schmid, "Still Separate and Unequal."

54. Erin Hatton, "The Temp Industry and the Transformation of Work in America" (PhD diss., University of Wisconsin, Madison, 2007).

55. Shulman, *Betrayal of Work*; Lance Compa, *Unfair Advantage: Workers' Freedom of Association in the United State under International Human Rights Standards* (Ithaca, NY: Cornell University, Institute for Labor Relations Press, 2004).

56. Ken Germanson, "Milestones in Wisconsin Labor History," Wisconsin Labor History Society, http://www.wisconsinlaborhistory.org/milestones.html.

57. Ibid.; Joe Chambers and Scott Godshaw, "History of Local 2-232," (Milwaukee, WI: United Steelworkers Local 2-232, n.d.), http://www.wisconsinlaborhistory.org/milestones.html.

58. National Union of Hospital and Health Care Employees Local 1199W (Milwaukee, WI), *1199 Frontline*, January 1979, March 1979, June 1979, March 1980, April 1980.

59. "St. Luke's Workers Beat Back Concessions Push," *Racine Labor*, May 17, 1985, 5; "St. Luke's Workers Seek to Catch Up on Wages," *Racine Labor*, April 12, 1985, 3.

60. "SEIU Local 150 Joins in Ethiopia Fund Drive," *Racine Labor*, March 1, 1985, 5.

61. "St. Luke's Slams Door on Aides," *Racine Labor*, June 28, 1985, 1.

62. Levine, "Crisis of Low Wages," 9.

63. Richard Florida, *The Rise of the Creative Class* (New York: Perseus, 2002).

64. Sassen, *Globalization and Its Discontents*, 138.

65. Wilkerson, "How Milwaukee Has Thrived."

66. Bernhardt, Dresser, and Rogers, "Taking the High Road."

67. Levine, "Stealth Depression," 3, 12.

68. Levine, "Two Milwaukees."

69. Nancy A. Denton and Douglas Massey, *American Apartheid: Segregation and the Making of the Underclass* (Cambridge, MA: Harvard University Press, 1998).

70. See note 5.

71. Charles Jaret, Lesley Williams Reid, and Robert M. Adelman, "Black-White Income Inequality and Metropolitan Socio-Economic Structure," *Journal of Urban Affairs* 25, no. 3 (2003).

72. David Rusk, "Sprawl, Race, and Concentrated Poverty in Greater Kenosha and Racine," paper presented to "Housing First: Kenosha and Racine Conference on Homelessness and Affordable Housing," University of Wisconsin, Parkside, November 14, 2003.

73. Lawrence Mishel, Jared Bernstein, and Sylvia Allegretto, *The State of Working America, 2004/2005* (Ithaca, NY: Cornell University Press, Economic Policy Institute, 2005), 8–9, 21–24.

74. Benjamin Bernanke, remarks at the Global Economic and Investment Outlook Conference, Carnegie Mellon University, Pittsburgh, PA, November 6, 2003, http://www.federalreserve.gov/BoardDocs/Speeches/2003/200311062/default.htm.

75. Levine, "Stealth Depression."

76. The specific figure was 58.8 percent. Marc V. Levine, "After the Boom: Joblessness in Milwaukee since 2000" (University of Wisconsin–Milwaukee Center for Economic Development, April 5, 2004), http://www.ced.uwm.edu.

77. Ibid.

78. Levine, "Stealth Depression," 16–20.

79. Pamela Oliver, "Summary of Findings on Racial Disparities in Criminal Justice in Wisconsin," paper presented to Community Justice Action Coalition Conference, November 2, 2001; Pamela Oliver and James Yocum, "Racial Disparities in Criminal Justice: Madison and Dane County in Context" (Institute for Research on Poverty, University of Wisconsin, Madison, 2002).

80. Devah Pager, "The Mark of a Criminal Record," *American Journal of Sociology* 108, no. 5 (2003): 955–58.

81. Lois Quinn, "New Indicators of Neighborhood Need in Zip Code 53206" (Employment and Training Institute, University of Wisconsin–Milwaukee 2007), http://www.eti.uwm.edu.

82. Lois Quinn and John Pawasarat, "Tracking the Progress of Welfare Reform: A Model for Measuring Neighborhood Health and Change" (Employment and Training Institute, University of Wisconsin–Milwaukee, October 2001).

83. Quinn, "New Indicators," 4, 21.

84. Daniel R. Meyer, "The Effects of Child Support on the Economic Status of Non-resident Fathers," in *Fathers under Fire: The Revolution in Child Support Enforcement*, ed. Irwin Garfinkel, Sara MacLanahan, Daniel R. Meyer, and Judith Seltzer (New York: Russell Sage, 1998).

85. Jamie Peck and Nikolas Theodore, "Labor-Market Lockdown: A Paper on the Urban Labor Market Consequences of Large-Scale Incarceration" (Brennan Center for Justice, New York University, 2005).

86. Quinn, "New Indicators," 16.

87. Ibid., 33, 36.

88. Ibid., 45.

89. Maria Cancian, Robert Haveman, Daniel R. Meyer, and Barbara Wolfe, "The Employment, Earnings and Income of Single Mothers in Wisconsin Who Left Cash Assistance: Comparisons among Three Cohorts," Special Report no. 85 (Institute for Research on Poverty, University of Wisconsin, Madison, 2003), 17–19.

90. Wisconsin Legislative Audit Bureau, "An Evaluation: Wisconsin Works (W-2) Program," Report 05-6 (2005), 5.

91. Following Cancian and her coauthors, we calculated after-federal-tax earnings as the sum of unemployment insurance (UI) earnings and federal Earned Income Tax Credit (EITC), less federal income tax paid and payroll tax, and calculated the EITC under the assumptions that the case head claims all eligible children for tax purposes and that the earnings reported to the UI system are the only earnings reported for tax purposes. Our source for the EITC parameters was the 2004 Green Book, table 13-12 (U.S. House of Representatives, Green Book: Background Material and Data on Programs within the Jurisdiction of the House Committee on Ways and Means (Washington, DC: Government Printing Office, 2004). We calculated the federal income tax under the assumptions that the case head files as head of household, takes the standard deduction, and has exemptions equal to the number of children plus 1. Taxable income = UI earnings – standard deduction – exemptions. We used the appropriate year's tax schedules to calculate the tax due. We calculated payroll tax based on the earnings reported to the UI system. The sources for the rates were the 2000 and 2004 Green Book, table 1-1. (See Cancian et al., "Employment, Earnings and Income, 10, 47.) The mean earnings reported include women with negligible or no earnings for that year.

92. Wisconsin Legislative Audit Bureau, "Evaluation," 50–52.

93. Metropolitan Milwaukee Association of Commerce, Economic Research Division, "Metro Milwaukee Economic Trends," December 2005, http://www.mmac.org.

94. Center on Wisconsin Strategy, "Economic Picture Darkens: Study Shows Declining Wages and Benefits" (press release), September 4, 2005.

95. Mishel, Bernstein, and Allegretto, State of Working America, 111.

CHAPTER THREE

1. Lawrence Mead, Beyond Entitlement: The Social Obligations of Citizenship (New York: Free Press, 1986), 21; Michael Wiseman, "State Strategies for Welfare Reform: The Wisconsin Story," Journal of Policy Analysis and Management 15, no. 4 (1996), 518.

2. Thomas Corbett, "The Wisconsin 'Welfare Magnet' Debate," Focus 13, no. 3 (1991).

3. Wiseman, "State Strategies," 522.

4. Thomas Corbett, "Welfare Reform in Wisconsin: The Rhetoric and the Reality," in The Politics of Welfare Reform, ed. Donald F. Norris and Lyke Thompson (Thousand Oaks, CA: Sage, 1995).

5. Cited in Wiseman, "State Strategies," 520.

6. Cited in Nancy A. Naples, "The 'New Consensus' on the Gendered 'Social Contract': The 1987–1988 U.S. Congressional Hearings on Welfare Reform," Signs 22, no. 4 (1997), 926.

7. Ibid., 926.

8. Amy Rinard, "State Audit Blasts Learnfare Errors," *Milwaukee Journal Sentinel*, July 3, 1990.

9. Corbett, "Welfare Reform in Wisconsin," 22.

10. Lawrence Mead, *Government Matters: Welfare Reform in Wisconsin* (Princeton, NJ: Princeton University Press, 2004), 133.

11. Ibid., 27–29; Corbett, "Welfare Reform in Wisconsin," 23–6.

12. Thomas Kaplan, "Wisconsin's W-2 Program: Welfare as We Might Come to Know It" (Institute for Research on Poverty, University of Wisconsin, Madison, September 1998).

13. Mead, *Government Matters*, 1.

14. Wiseman, "State Strategies," 522; Mead, *Government Matters*, 32–34.

15. Wiseman, "State Strategies."

16. Bradley Foundation, Annual Report, 1995; see also http://www.bradleyfdn.org.

17. Victoria Mayer, "Crafting a New Conservative Consensus on Welfare Reform: Redefining Citizenship, Social Provision, and the Public/Private Divide," *Social Politics* 15 (2008).

18. Kaplan, "Wisconsin's W-2 Program," 13.

19. Corbett, "Welfare Reform in Wisconsin," 23–26; Mead, *Government Matters*, 29–31.

20. Mead, *Government Matters*, 133.

21. Wiseman, "State Strategies," 530; Mead, *Government Matters*, 69.

22. Kathleen Mulligan-Hansel and Pamela Fendt, "TANF Reauthorization: The Bush Administration Proposal and Wisconsin's W-2 Program" (Institute for Wisconsin's Future, Milwaukee, 2002), http://www.wisconsinsfuture.org/publications/workingfamilies/BushTANFAnalysis.pdf. "Worklike activities" included medical appointments for the participant or her family, therapies, rehabilitation, preparation for the high school equivalency exam, courses and training, and job searches.

23. The "light touch" policy was dropped during the 2002–2003 contract period by the administration of Scott McCallum, who succeeded Thompson as governor, in response to pressure from antipoverty advocates.

24. Kaplan, "Wisconsin's W-2 Program," 9.

25. Chad Alan Goldberg, *Citizens and Paupers: Relief, Rights, and Race, from the Freedmen's Bureau to Workfare* (Chicago: University of Chicago Press, 2007); John Krinsky, *Free Labor: Workfare and the Contested Language of Neoliberalism* (Chicago: University of Chicago Press, 2008); John Krinsky and Ellen Reese, "Forging and Sustaining Labor-Community Coalitions: The Workfare Justice Movement in Three Cities," *Sociological Forum* 21, no. 4 (2006).

26. Kaplan, "Wisconsin's W-2 Program," 15–16.

27. Wisconsin Department of Workforce Development, "Request for Proposals to Administer W-2 and Related Programs, 1997–1999, Addendum No. 3," September 13, 1996, 2.

28. Wendy Brown, "American Nightmare: Neoliberalism, Neoconservatism, and De-Democratization," *Political Theory* 34 (2006), 694.

29. Ultimately 63 of 72 counties did so. Mead, *Government Matters*, 138.

30. The Kaiser Group and CRN, a mental health services provider, dropped out after the first contract period, leaving the YWCA to manage its for-profit subsidiary alone.

31. Answers.com, Business & Finance, "Company History, Maximus, Inc.," http://www.answers.com/topic/maximus-inc?cat=biz-fin.

32. Mead, *Government Matters*, 141.

33. Steve Schulze, "W-2 Denials Ruled Invalid: State's 'Job-Ready' Category at Odds with 1996 Law, Court Says," *Milwaukee Journal Sentinel*, June 19, 2007; Pat De Lessio, "Court Nixes W-2 'Job Ready' Policy," *WisKids Journal* [Wisconsin Council on Children and Families] (July/August 2007), http://www.wccf.org/wkj/807/story3.htm, http://www.jsonline.com/story/indes.aspx?id=622140.

34. Wisconsin Department of Workforce Development, "Unduplicated W-2 Participants by Placement Type" (2007), http://www.dwd.state.wi.us/dws/w2/wisworks.htm; Kaplan, "Wisconsin's W-2 Program," 25.

35. Initially, agencies considered high school equivalency programs the only allowable educational activity. They later relaxed these rules, and for a brief period in 2002 and 2003 allowed some parents to count up to fifteen hours a week of short-term vocational training toward their forty hours of assigned activities (Wisconsin Legislative Fiscal Bureau, "Wisconsin Works [W-2] and Other Economic Support Programs," Informational Paper no. 45 [January 2005]).

36. National Employment Law Project, "Limiting State Workfare Programs under the New TANF Rules" (press release), New York, September 15, 2006.

37. There seemed to be some flexibility in the number of hours that parents placed in the W-2 Transitions tier were required to participate. Milwaukee agencies assigned a total of forty hours of activities per week, whereas some counties required only thirty-five.

38. Wiseman, "State Strategies," 536.

39. Mead, *Government Matters*, 133.

40. Daniel R. Meyer and Maria Cancian, "W-2 Child Support Demonstration Evaluation Phase 1: Final Report" (Institute for Research on Poverty, University of Wisconsin, Madison, 2001), vol. 1, chap. 3.

41. Thomas Kaplan and Thomas Corbett, with Victoria Mayer, "W-2 Child Support Demonstration Evaluation Phase 1: Final Report," vol. 2, chap. 1.

42. Maria Cancian and Robert Haveman, "W-2 Child Support Demonstration Evaluation Phase 1: Final Report," vol. 2, table II.5.3.

43. John Pawarasat, "The Employer Perspective: Jobs Held by the Milwaukee County Single Parent Population" (Employment and Training Institute, University of Wisconsin–Milwaukee, March 1997), http://www.uwm.edu/Dept/ETI/employer.htm.

44. Melissa Monroe, "Temp Agencies Targeting Welfare Recipients," *San Antonio Business Journal*, September 19, 1997.

45. Robert Mullins, "W-2 Workforce Lures Serigraph South," *Business Journal of Milwaukee*, August 25, 1997, http://milwaukee.bizjournals.com/milwaukee/stories/1997/08/25/story8.html.

46. Mark Fitzgerald, "From Welfare to Payroll," *AllBusiness.com*, January 24, 1998, http://www.allbusiness.com/services/business-services-miscellaneous-business/4699462-1.html.

47. Pete Millard, "Warts and All, Welfare Reform Worked," *Business Journal of Milwaukee*, September 29, 2000.

48. A Job Is a Right Campaign, "Why We Are Marching Today," *A Job is a Right Newsletter*, April 4, 1998.

49. Pete Millard, "Profit Ventures Intrigue Non-profits," *Business Journal of Milwaukee*, August 9, 2002.

50. Millard, "Profit Ventures"; Julia Taylor, "Testimony before the Subcommittee on Human Resources of the House Committee on Ways and Means," April 3, 2001, http://waysandmeans .house.gov/Legacy/humres/107cong/4-3-01/4-3jtay.htm.

51. Pete Millard, "For-profit Ventures Sour for YWCA," *Business Journal of Milwaukee*, February 14, 2003; Bruce Murphy, "Missions Collide When Non-profits Try Business," *Milwaukee Journal Sentinel,* May 30, 2004.

52. Kaplan, Corbett, and Mayer, "W-2 Child Support Demonstration," 3.

53. Once in the program, employed women could receive the subsidies until they earned 200 percent of the poverty line.

54. This was $4,476 more than the annual cost to the state for cash assistance. If a woman had two children in day care, it was $16,488 more. If three, the cost of child care subsidies exceeded cash assistance payments by $28,500 annually. John Pawarasat and Lois M. Quinn, "The Child Care Costs of Engaging the Welfare Population at Work: The Milwaukee Experience" (Employment and Training Institute, University of Wisconsin–Milwaukee, 2002), 1–2, http://www.uwm.edu/Dept/ETI/reprints/MilwaukeeChildCareExperience.pdf.

55. Ibid.

56. Wisconsin Department of Workforce Development, "Families and Children Served by the CARES Child Care Payment System (2008), http://www.dwd.wisc.gov/childcare/wishares/ pdf/served.pdf.

57. Ibid.

58. Wisconsin Legislative Fiscal Bureau, "Comparative Summary of Budget Provisions Enacted as 2003 Act 33" (September 2003), http://www.legis.state.wi.us/lfb/2003-05budget/Act33.

59. Pawasarat and Quinn, "Child Care Costs," 3.

60. Wisconsin Legislative Audit Bureau, "A Review of Wisconsin Works (W-2) Expenditures," Report 99-3 (1999), 7.

61. Victoria Mayer, "Contracting Citizenship: Shifting Public/Private Boundaries in the Context of Welfare Reform" (PhD diss., University of Wisconsin, Madison, 2007).

62. Mark Kessenich, "Job Training Is the Solution to Labor Shortage," *Business Journal of Milwaukee*, April 9, 1999.

63. See Jason DeParle, *American Dream: Three Women, Ten Kids, and a Nation's Drive to End Welfare* (New York: Viking, 2004).

64. Wisconsin Legislative Audit Bureau, "Administration of the Wisconsin Works Program by Maximus, Inc." (letter report, July 2000); Wisconsin Legislative Audit Bureau, "Administration of the Wisconsin Works Program by Employment Solutions, Inc., and Other Selected Agencies" (letter report, February 2001); "An Evaluation: Wisconsin Works (W-2) Program," Report 01-7 (2001).

65. Child care for infants cost between $1,000 and $1,200 per month during this period, while the caretaker-of-newborn benefit check was $673.

66. As part of its contract agreement with OIC-GM, the Department of Workforce Development required the agency to subcontract with Wisconsin Works for case management services. This requirement proved extremely valuable when the state was later forced to find an alternative provider to assume responsibility for cases removed from the troubled OIC-GM. Mayer, "Contracting Citizenship."

67. Ibid.

68. Wisconsin Department of Workforce Development, "Wisconsin Works (W-2) Manual," version 1-31-04, sect. 6.1.0, "Employability Plan" (2004); Wisconsin Department of Workforce Development, "Food Share Employment and Training Manual," version 10-02, sect. 4.10.0, "Employability Plan" (2002).

69. See Jamie Peck, *Workfare States* (New York: Guilford Press, 2001), chap. 5, for a description of the pioneering of such motivational sessions in work-first programs in Riverside, California.

CHAPTER FOUR

1. Lisa Duggan, *The Twilight of Equality? Neoliberalism, Cultural Politics and the Attack on Democracy* (New York: Beacon Press, 2003), 64.

2. Lawrence Mead, *Beyond Entitlement: The Social Obligations of Citizenship* (New York: Free Press, 1986), 3.

3. At the time of our study (December 2003), one-third of women were receiving caretaker-of-newborn benefits, and another 7 percent were receiving W-2 Transitions funding for pregnancy-related health problems or the health problems of a newborn. Altogether, a third of the study's participants were receiving W-2 Transitions funding to deal with a health crisis (theirs or their child's). The remaining third were returning to work through the community service job program; most of these women had also entered welfare through the W-2 Transitions or caretaker-of-newborn programs and then been placed in community service jobs as a way to reenter the workforce. Overall, the women in our sample received cash assistance for an average of sixteen months between 1998 and 2004.

4. Wisconsin Legislative Audit Bureau, "An Evaluation: Wisconsin Works (W-2) Program," Report 05-6 (2005).

5. Marcia Meyers, Henry Brady, and Eva Seto, *Expensive Children in Poor Families: The Intersection of Childhood Disabilities and Welfare* (San Francisco: Public Policy Institute of California, 2000); W. J. Jameson and N. Halfon, "Health Status and Income: The Impact of Poverty on Child Health," *Journal of School Health* 64, no. 6 (1994); Karen Seccombe and Kim A. Hoffman, *Just Don't Get Sick: Access to Health Care in the Aftermath of Welfare Reform* (New Brunswick, NJ: Rutgers University Press, 2007).

6. Casualized work includes jobs without long-term contracts, jobs with part-time schedules or fluctuating hours, and temporary agency placements.

7. Erik Eckholm, "Disability Cases Last Far Longer as Backlogs Rise," *New York Times*, December 10, 2007, A1.

8. Rebecca Smith, Rick McHugh, Andrew Stettner, and Nancy Segal, "Between a Rock and a Hard Place: Confronting the Failure of State Unemployment Insurance Systems to Serve Women and Working Families" (National Employment Law Project, New York, July 2003), http://www.nelp.org.

9. Beth Shulman, *The Betrayal of Work: How Low-Wage Jobs Fail 30 Million Americans* (New York: New Press, 2005), 34.

10. Lisa Dodson, "Wage-Poor Mothers and Moral Economy," *Social Politics* 14, no. 2 (2007), 269.

11. Lisa Dodson, Tiffany Manuel, and Ellen Bravo, "Keeping Jobs and Raising Families in Low-Income America: It Just Doesn't Work" (Radcliffe Institute for Advanced Study, Harvard University, 2002), http://www.9to5.org/sites/default/files/no boundaries.pdf, 16.

12. Gwendolyn Mink, *Welfare's End* (Ithaca, NY: Cornell University Press, 1998), 25.

13. Joel Dresang, "Boy's Death Spurs W-2 Criticism," *Milwaukee Journal Sentinel,* June 19, 1998, 3; *Milwaukee Journal Sentinel,* "Money, Services Are Needed to Make Sure Kids Stay Safe" (editorial), June 29, 1998, 9.

14. In November 2008, Milwaukee residents overwhelming approved a binding referendum calling for private employers in the city to provide paid sick leave for all their workers. On June 12, 2009, Milwaukee County Circuit judge Thomas Cooper struck down the ordinance. Georgia Pabst, "Paid Sick Leave Referendum Wins Big," *Milwaukee Journal Sentinel,* November 4, 2008, http://www.jsonline.com/news/statepolitics/33874059.html; Georgia Pabst, "Judge Finds City's Sick Leave Mandate Unconstitutional," *Milwaukee Journal Sentinel,* June 12, 2009, http://www.jsonline.com/news/milwaukee/47930647.html.

15. David Elwood, "Introduction," in *A Working Nation: Workers, Work, and Government in the New Economy,* ed. David T. Elwood, Rebecca M. Blank, Joseph Blasi, Douglas Kruse, William A. Niskanen, and Karen Lynn-Dyson, (New York: Russell Sage, 2000), xi.

16. David Elwood, "Winners and Losers in America: Taking the Measure of New Economic Realities," in Elwood et al., *Working Nation,* 16.

17. Susan Thistle, *From Marriage to the Market: The Transformation of Women's Lives and Work* (Berkeley: University of California Press, 2006), 5, 112.

18. Ibid., 113.

19. Ibid., 106.

20. Ibid., 134.

21. Ibid., 65.

22. Ibid., 134.

23. Ibid., 110.

24. American Enterprise Institute, *The New Consensus on Family and Welfare* (Washington, DC: American Enterprise Institute, 1987), 72, 43.

25. Mead, *Beyond Entitlement,* 74.

26. For a pre-reform critique of these assumptions see Stacey J. Oliker, "Proximate Contexts of Welfare and Work," *Sociological Quarterly* 36, no. 2 (1995).

27. *Economist,* "Open Up: A Special Report on Migration," January 5, 2008.

28. Michael Burawoy, "The Functions and Reproduction of Migrant Labor: Comparative Material from Southern Africa and the United States," *American Journal of Sociology* 81(1978).

29. See Jacob Hacker, *The Great Risk Shift: The Assault on American Jobs, Families, Health Care, and Retirement, and How You Can Fight Back* (New York: Oxford University Press, 2006).

30. For an account of Child Welfare Services caseloads among TANF recipients, see Mark Courtney and Amy Dworsky, "Child Welfare Services' Involvement: Findings from the Milwaukee TANF Applicant Study" (Chapin Hall Center for Children, University of Chicago, 2006).

31. American Enterprise Institute, *New Consensus,* 52.

32. Ann Shola Orloff, "Explaining U.S. Welfare Reform: Power, Gender, Race and the U.S. Policy Legacy," *Critical Social Policy* 22, no. 1 (2002), 110.

33. Kathryn Edin and Laura Lein, *Making Ends Meet: How Single Mothers Survive Welfare and Low-Wage Work* (New York: Russell Sage, 1997).

34. Melvin L. Oliver and Thomas M. Shapiro, "Black Wealth/White Wealth," in *Great Divides: Readings in Social Inequality in the United States,* 2nd ed., ed. Thomas M. Shapiro (Toronto: Mayfield Publishing, 2004); Brett Williams, *Debt for Sale: A Social History of the Credit Trap* (Philadelphia: University of Pennsylvania Press, 2004). For data on such lending practices

in central-city Milwaukee, see Lois Quinn, "New Indicators of Neighborhood Need in Zip Code 53206" (Employment and Training Institute, University of Wisconsin–Milwaukee 2007), http://www.eti.uwm.edu.

35. This disparity was evident in the fact that the very same week Congress passed PRWORA, it also passed a law granting middle-class homemakers the right to establish independent retirement accounts (IRAs), affirming their right to stay at home and offering them tax breaks while doing so. Mink, *Welfare's End*, 29.

36. American Enterprise Institute, *New Consensus*, 11.

CHAPTER FIVE

1. Judith Shklar, *American Citizenship: The Quest for Inclusion* (Cambridge, MA: Harvard University Press, 1991), 97.

2. Lawrence Mead, *Beyond Entitlement: The Social Obligations of Citizenship* (New York: Free Press, 1986), 87.

3. American Enterprise Institute, *New Consensus*, 86.

4. Mead, *Beyond Entitlement*, 223.

5. Wisconsin Department of Workforce Development, "Wisconsin Works (W-2) Overview" (1999), http://www.dwd.state.wi.us/dws/w2/wisworks.htm.

6. Wisconsin Legislative Fiscal Bureau, "Wisconsin Works (W-2) and Other Economic Support Programs," Informational Paper no. 45 (January 2005).

7. Andrea Robles, Fred Doolittle, and Susan Gooden, "Community Service Jobs in Wisconsin Works: The Milwaukee County Experience," *MDRC Report* (Manpower Development Research Corporation, June 2003), 21, 50–55.

8. Ibid., 49.

9. Mark Ragan, "Service Integration in Wisconsin: Racine and Kenosha Counties" (Rockefeller Institute of Government, Albany, NY, August 12, 2002).

10. Robles, Doolittle, and Gooden, "Community Service Jobs," 33, 51.

11. Several of the women we interviewed suggested that the private agencies preferred that participants enroll in their GED programs because they could charge the state for their participation.

12. Steve Schulze, "Pay Is Low, Progress Is Slow," *Milwaukee Journal Sentinel*, August 8, 2005.

13. Robles, Doolittle, and Gooden, "Community Service Jobs."

14. Jamie Peck, *Workfare States* (New York: Guilford Press, 2001), 14, 6, 188.

15. Chad Alan Goldberg, "Welfare Recipients or Workers? Contesting the Workfare State in New York City." *Sociological Theory* 19, no. 2 (2001), 204.

16. Vee Burke, "Welfare Recipients and Workforce Laws. Federal Publications: Key Workplace Documents" (Washington, DC: Congressional Research Service, 2004), http://www.digitalcommons.ilr.cornell.edu/key_workplace/228.

17. Ibid. The federal Balanced Budget Act of 1997 appeared to contradict evolving interpretations of the law when it stated that if a state imposed a penalty on a participant for failure to comply with a requirement, this could "not be construed to be a reduction in any wage paid to the individual." This allowed states to reduce the benefit level of participants for failure to complete an activity, even if this penalty resulted in a subminimum wage (Sharon Dietrich, Maurice Emsellem, and Catherine Ruckelshaus, "Work Reform: The Other Side of Welfare Reform," *Stanford Law and Policy Review* 9, no. 1 [1998]).

18. CNN.com, "States Must Pay Minimum Wage for Workfare, Administration Rules," http:// www.cnn.com/ALLPOLITICS/1997/05/16/welfare.minwage.

19. Craig L. Briskin and Kimberly A. Thomas, "The Waging of Welfare: All Work and No Pay?" *Harvard Civil Rights-Civil Liberties Law Review* 33 (1998), 567–68; Vadim Mahmoudov, "Are Workfare Participants 'Employees'? Legal Issues Presented by a Two-Tiered Labor Force," *New York University Annual Survey of American Law* 55 (1998), 367–68.

20. Wisconsin Department of Workforce Development, "Request for Proposals to Administer W-2 and Related Programs, 1997–1999, Addendum No. 3" (September 13, 1996), 2. State claims that women's work assignments were "training" were somewhat jarring given that the women had no say in these placements and that most training programs to date had allowed participants to choose the kinds of jobs for which they would be trained.

21. The case was *Archie v. Grant Central Partnership*. See Dietrich, Emsellem, and Ruckelshaus, "Work Reform."

22. John Krinsky, *Free Labor: Workfare and the Contested Language of Neoliberalism* (Chicago: University of Chicago Press, 2008); Chad Alan Goldberg, *Citizens and Paupers: Relief, Rights, and Race, from the Freedman's Bureau to Workfare* (Chicago: University of Chicago Press, 2007).

23. U.S. Department of Health and Human Services, Code of Federal Regulations, Title 45 (Public Welfare), Part 260 (TANF Provisions) (1999).

24. Robin Toner, "Bush Promises Minimum Wage in Welfare Jobs," *New York Times*, March 7, 2002.

25. Matthew Diller, "Working without a Job: The Social Messages of the New Workfare," *Stanford Law and Policy Review* 9, no. 1 (1998).

26. Tom Held, "Another Complaint Calls W-2 Unfair to Disabled," *Milwaukee Journal Sentinel*, February 20, 2000, 9B.

27. American Civil Liberties Union, letter from Karyn Rotker, staff attorney, ACLU of Wisconsin, to the Office of Civil Rights, U.S. Department of Health and Human Services, February 19, 2002, http://www.aclu-wi.org/wisconsin/rights_of_poor/ocrada.html.

28. Wisconsin Department of Workforce Development, "Wisconsin Works (W-2) Sanctions Study" (December 2004), http://www.aclu-wi.org/wisconsin/rights_of_minorities/ SanctionsStudyExecutiveSummary.pdf. See also Kathleen Mulligan-Hansel and Pamela Fendt, "Unfair Sanctions: Does W-2 Punish People of Color?" (Institute for Wisconsin's Future and University of Milwaukee Center for Economic Development, 2003). http://www4.uwm .edu/ced/publications/race_execsum.pdf.

29. Katia Hetter, "Workfare Workers' Rights in Question," *Newsday* July 27, 2001; James Barron, "City Settles Workfare Harassment Lawsuit," *New York Times*, May 13, 2006.

30. Pete Millard, "Bias Claims Filed against W-2 Agency," *Business Journal of Milwaukee*, January 7, 2000, http://sanfrancisco.bizjournals.com/milwaukee/stories/2000/01/10/story2.html.

31. Nina Bernstein, "Federal Agency Finds Workfare Contractor Violated Wage Law," *New York Times*, September 1, 2000.

32. Wisconsin Legislative Audit Bureau, "Administration of the Wisconsin Works Program by Maximus, Inc." (letter report, July 2000).

33. Tamika Capers, Mery Mejia, Omar Torres, and Sylvia Ruff, "Welfare as They Know It," *Harper's Magazine* 295, no. 1770 (November 1997); Joe Sexton, "Woman's Death Prompts Concerns over Workfare," *New York Times,* June 24, 1997; Neil MacFarquhar, "Worker's Death Prompts

Call of Workfare Review," *New York Times*, July 13, 1999, B3; Thomas Lueck, "Workfare Critics Cite the Case of a Woman Who Died on the Job," *New York Times*, August 31, 2000.

34. Dietrich, Emsellem, and Ruckelshaus, "Work Reform," 5.

35. Burke, "Welfare Recipients."

36. Dietrich, Emsellem, and Ruckelshaus, "Work Reform," 50.

37. Diller, *Working without a Job*, 28 and n128; Dietrich, Emsellem, and Ruckelshaus, "Work Reform," 40.

38. Wisconsin Department of Workforce Development, "Request for Proposals," 1.

39. Ibid., 40.

40. The case was AFSCME Council 66, NY Public Employment Relations Board, No. U-18133, August 11, 1998 (Sharon Dietrich, Maurice Emsellem, and Jennifer Paradise, "Employment Rights of Workfare Participants and Displaced Workers," National Employment Law Project Report, March 2000).

41. Steven Greenhouse, "Compromise with Unions on Workfare," *New York Times*, August 8, 1997, B2. See also Goldberg, *Citizens and Paupers*; Krinsky, *Free Labor*; Vanessa Tait, *Poor Workers' Unions: Rebuilding Labor from Below* (Boston: South End Press, 2005), chap. 5.

42. Kevin Miller, "Welfare and the Minimum Wage: Are Workfare Participants 'Employees' under the Fair Labor Standards Act?" *University of Chicago Law Review* 66, no. 1 (Winter 1999): 188.

43. Briskin and Thomas, "Waging of Welfare," 568.

44. U.S. Department of Labor. "Guidance: How Workplace Laws Apply to Welfare Recipients," *Daily Labor Report* (Bureau of News Analysis), no. 103, May 29, 2007.

45. Mahmoudov, "Are Workfare Participants 'Employees'?," 372.

46. *Coppage v. Kansas*, 236 U.S. 1 (1915), 14.

47. Alice Kessler-Harris, *In Pursuit of Equity: Women, Men, and the Quest for Economic Citizenship in 20th Century America* (New York: Oxford University Press, 2001); Arthur McEvoy, "Freedom of Contract, Labor, and the Administrative State," in *The State and Freedom of Contract*, ed. Harry N. Scheiber (Stanford, CA: Stanford University Press, 1998).

48. T. H. Marshall, *Citizenship and Social Class* (1950; London: Pluto Press, 1992), 10.

49. Mahmoudov, "Are Workfare Participants 'Employees'?," 377–78.

50. Ibid., 378–81.

51. Charles R. Bogle, " 'Unconscionable' Conditions: A Contractual Analysis of Conditions on Public Assistance Benefits," *Columbia Law Review* 94 (1994): 223.

52. Ibid., 229.

53. Ibid., 195, 223n144.

54. Shklar, *American Citizenship*, 67.

55. Ibid., 64.

56. Nancy Fraser and Linda Gordon, "A Genealogy of *Dependency*: Tracing a Keyword of the U.S. Welfare State," *Signs* 19, no. 2 (1994).

57. Shklar, *American Citizenship*, 67.

58. Kessler-Harris, *In Pursuit of Equity*, 4.

59. Marshall, *Citizenship and Social Class*, 15.

60. Kessler-Harris, *In Pursuit of Equity*, 4.

61. Barbara Nelson, "The Origins of the Two-Channel Welfare State: Workmen's Compensation and Mother's Aid," *Women, the State, and Welfare*, ed. Linda Gordon (Madison: University of Wisconsin Press, 1990).

62. Gwendolyn Mink, "The Lady and the Tramp: Gender, Race, and the Origins of the American Welfare State," in *Women, the State, and Welfare,* ed. Linda Gordon (Madison: University of Wisconsin Press, 1990), 106–8, 111.

63. Ruth Lister, *Citizenship: Feminist Perspectives* (New York: New York University Press, 1997).

64. Michael Katz, *The Price of Citizenship: Redefining the American Welfare State* (New York: Henry Holt, 2002), 258–59.

65. Ibid., 259–60.

66. Erik Eckholm, "Disability Cases Last Far Longer as Backlogs Rise," *New York Times* December 10, 2007, A1.

67. Douglas J. Besharov, "End Welfare Lite as We Know It," *New York Times*, August 15, 2006.

68. The WIC program provides supplemental foods, health care referrals, and nutrition education for low-income pregnant, breastfeeding, and non-breastfeeding postpartum women and to infants and children up to age five who are found to be at nutritional risk.

69. Liza Featherstone, *Selling Women Short: The Landmark Battle for Workers' Rights at Wal-Mart* (New York: Basic Books, 2004), 239–40.

70. Beth Shulman, *The Betrayal of Work: How Low-Wage Jobs Fail 30 Million Americans* (New York: New Press, 2005); Eileen Appelbaum, Annette D. Bernhardt, and Richard Murnane, eds., *Low-Wage America: How Employers are Reshaping Opportunity in the Workplace* (New York: Russell Sage, 2003); David K. Shipler, *The Working Poor: Invisible in America* (New York: Vintage, 2005).

71. The State Legislative Audit Bureau reports 10,115 persons receiving cash assistance in Milwaukee County in June 2004 (Wisconsin Legislative Audit Bureau, "An Evaluation: Wisconsin Works [W-2] Program," Report 05-6 [2005], 59). Not all those who receive cash assistance also receive food stamps.

72. The University of Wisconsin Extension Program's Wisconsin Food Security Project reports 202,667 food stamp recipients in Milwaukee County in 2004 (http://www.uwex.edu/ces/flp.cfs/completedata.cfm).

CHAPTER SIX

1. Vadim Mahmoudov, "Are Workfare Participants 'Employees'? Legal Issues Presented by a Two-Tiered Labor Force," *New York University Annual Survey of American Law* 55 (1998), 349.

2. Wisconsin, Office of the Governor, "Governor Doyle to Establish New Department of Children and Families" (press release), November 27, 2007. Welfare had been housed in social service agencies prior to the 1996 reforms, but in that period its policies did not require labor force participation in the same way.

3. Wisconsin, Office of the Governor, "Governor Doyle Announces New Effort for Children and Families" (press release), January 29, 2007.

4. Joan Williams, *Unbending Gender: Why Family and Work Conflict and What to Do about It* (New York: Oxford University Press, 2001).

5. Rebecca Smith, Rick McHugh, Andrew Stettner, and Nancy Segal, "Between a Rock and a Hard Place: Confronting the Failure of State Unemployment Insurance Systems to Serve Women and Working Families" (National Employment Law Project, New York, July 2003), http://www.nelp.org.

6. Steven Wisensale, "The Family and Medical Leave Act in Court," *Working USA* 3, no. 4 (2004).

7. Beth Shulman, *The Betrayal of Work: How Low-Wage Jobs Fail 30 Million Americans* (New York: New Press, 2005), 34.

8. Robert Thomas, *Citizenship, Gender, and Work: Social Organization of Industrial Agriculture* (Berkeley: University of California Press, 1992), 215.

9. International Labor Organization, "Labor Practices in the Footwear, Leather, Textiles and Clothing Industries" (Geneva, October 16–20, 2000), 6.

10. David Harvey, *The Limits to Capital* (New York: Verso, 1999).

11. Torben Iverson and Anne Wren, "Equality, Employment, and Budgetary Restraint: The Trilemma of the Service Economy," *World Politics* 50, no. 4 (1998): 511.

12. Iverson and Wren, "Equality, Employment, and Budgetary Restraint," 511. See also Robert J. Gordon, "Productivity, Wages, and Prices Inside and Outside of Manufacturing in the U.S., Japan, and Europe," *European Economic Review* 31 (1987).

13. Noah Zatz, "Beyond the Reach or Grasp of Employment Law," in *The Gloves-Off Economy: Problems and Possibilities at the Bottom of America's Labor Market*, ed. Annette Bernhardt, Heather Boushey, Laura Dresser, and Chris Tilley (Ithaca, NY: Cornell University Press, 2008).

14. Gordon Lafer, "Split to Win? Assessing the State of the Labor Movement," *Dissent*, Winter 2006.

15. Thomas B. Edsall, "Insurrection Is a Big Gamble for Labor," *Washington Post*, July 30, 2005, A11.

16. Paula England and Nancy Folbre, "The Cost of Caring," *Annals of the American Academy of Political and Social Sciences* 561 (1999).

17. Frances Fox Piven, "The New Reserve Army of Labor," in *Audacious Democracy: Labor, Intellectuals, and the Social Reconstruction of America*, ed. Steven Fraser and Joshua B. Freeman (Boston: Houghton Mifflin, 1997), 114.

18. Bill Fletcher Jr., "Seizing the Time Because the Time Is Now: Welfare Repeal and Labor Reconstruction," in *Audacious Democracy: Labor, Intellectuals, and the Social Reconstruction of America*, ed. Steven Fraser and Joshua B. Freeman (Boston: Houghton Mifflin, 1997), 125.

19. Michael Reisch, "Welfare Reform and the Transformation of the U.S. Welfare State," in *The Promise of Welfare Reform: Political Rhetoric and the Reality of Poverty in the Twenty-First Century*, ed. Keith M. Kilty and Elizabeth Segal (New York: Haworth Press, 2006), 75–76.

20. Fletcher, "Seizing the Time," 125.

21. AFL-CIO, "Democratizing the Global Economy." June 27, 2005, http://www.afl-cio.org/aboutus/thisistheaflcio/ecouncil/ec06272005c.cfm.

22. Noah Zatz, "Working at the Boundaries of Markets: Prison Labor and the Economic Dimension of Employment Relationships," *Vanderbilt Law Review* 61(2008); Fletcher, "Seizing the Time," 125.

23. Zatz, "Beyond the Reach."

24. Erin Hatton, "The Temp Industry and the Transformation of Work in America" (PhD diss., University of Wisconsin, Madison, 2007).

25. Harvey, *Limits to Capital*.

26. Lauren Berlant, *The Queen of America Goes to Washington City: Essays on Sex and Citizenship* (Durham, NC: Duke University Press, 1997), 20.

27. Ange-Marie Hancock, *The Politics of Disgust: The Public Identity of the Welfare Queen* (New York: New York University Press, 2004).

28. David M. Gordon, Richard Edwards, and Michael Reich, *Segmented Work, Divided Workers: The Historical Transformation of Labor in the United States* (New York: Cambridge University Press, 1982).

29. Wisconsin Department of Workforce Development, "Wisconsin Works (W-2) Manual," version 10-01-02 (2002).

CHAPTER SEVEN

1. Karl Polanyi, *The Great Transformation: The Political and Economic Origins of Our Time* (1944; Boston: Beacon, 2001), 76.

2. Torben Iverson and Anne Wren, "Equality, Employment, and Budgetary Restraint: The Trilemma of the Service Economy," *World Politics* 50, no. 4 (1998): 511.

3. Elizabeth Lower-Basch and Mark H. Greenberg, "Single Mothers in the Era of Welfare Reform," in *The Gloves-Off Economy: Problems and Possibilities at the Bottom of America's Labor Market*, ed. Annette Bernhardt, Heather Boushey, Laura Dresser, and Chris Tilley (Ithaca, NY: Cornell University Press, 2008), 175–78; Pablo Mitnik and Matt Zeidenburg, "From Bad to Good Jobs? An Analysis of the Prospects for Career Ladders in the Service Industries" (Center on Wisconsin Strategy, Madison, WI, 2007), http://www.cows.org/pdf/rp-bad-good.pdf; Beth Shulman, *The Betrayal of Work: How Low-Wage Jobs Fail 30 Million Americans* (New York: New Press, 2005), 48–50.

4. Jacob Hacker, *The Great Risk Shift: The Assault on American Jobs, Families, Health Care, and Retirement, and How You Can Fight Back* (New York: Oxford University Press, 2006).

5. Chad Alan Goldberg, *Citizens and Paupers: Relief, Rights, and Race, from the Freedman's Bureau to Workfare* (Chicago: University of Chicago Press, 2007).

6. John Edwards, Marion Crain and Arne L. Kalleberg, eds., *Ending Poverty in America: How to Restore the American Dream* (New York: New Press, 2007); Richard Kazis and Marc S. Miller, eds., *Low-Wage Workers in the New Economy* (Washington, DC: Urban Institute, 2001); Stuart White, *The Civic Minimum: On the Rights and Obligations of Economic Citizenship* (New York: Oxford University Press, 2003); Hacker, *Great Risk Shift*, 65–95.

7. Eve Feder Kittay, "A Feminist Public Ethic of Care Meets the New Communitarian Family Policy," *Ethics* 111, no. 3 (2001), 527, 546.

8. Alice Kessler-Harris, *In Pursuit of Equity: Women, Men, and the Quest for Economic Citizenship in 20th Century America* (New York: Oxford University Press, 2001), 13.

REFERENCES

BOOKS AND ARTICLES

Appelbaum, Eileen, and Peter Albin. "Shifts in Employment, Occupational Structure and Educational Attainment." In *Skills, Wages, and Productivity in the Service Sector*, ed. Thierry Noyelle, 31–66. Boulder, CO: Westview Press, 1990.

Appelbaum, Eileen, Annette D. Bernhardt, and Richard Murnane, eds. *Low-Wage America: How Employers Are Reshaping Opportunity in the Workplace*. New York: Russell Sage, 2003.

Bartik, Timothy. "Instrumental Variable Estimates of the Labor Market Spillover Effects of Welfare Reform." Upjohn Institute Staff Working Paper 02-78, Kalamazoo, MI, April 2002.

Berlant, Lauren. *The Queen of America Goes to Washington City: Essays on Sex and Citizenship*. Durham, NC: Duke University Press, 1997.

Bernhardt, Annette, Laura Dresser, and Joel Rogers. "Taking the High Road in Milwaukee: The Wisconsin Regional Training Partnership." In *Partnering for Change: Unions and Community Groups Build Coalitions for Economic Justice*, ed. David Reynolds, 230–48. New York: M. E. Sharpe, 2004.

Bisbing Business Research. "Attitude Study among Negro and White Residents in the Milwaukee Negro Residential Areas." Milwaukee, WI: Bisbing Business Research, 1965. http://www.wisconsinhistory.org/turningpoints/search.asp?id=1189.

Blank, Rebecca M., and Lucie Schmidt. "Work, Wages, and Welfare." In *The New World of Welfare*, ed. Rebecca Blank and Ron Haskins, 70–96. Washington, DC: Brookings Institution, 2001.

Bogle, Charles R. "'Unconscionable' Conditions: A Contractual Analysis of Conditions on Public Assistance Benefits." *Columbia Law Review* 94 (1994): 193–241.

Boydston, Jeanne. *Home and Work: Housework, Wages, and the Ideology of Labor in the Early Republic*. New York: Oxford University Press, 1990.

Briskin, Craig L., and Kimberly A. Thomas. "The Waging of Welfare: All Work and No Pay?" *Harvard Civil Rights–Civil Liberties Law Review* 33 (1998): 559–91.

Brown, Wendy. "American Nightmare: Neoliberalism, Neoconservatism, and De-Democratization." *Political Theory* 34 (2006): 690–714.

Burawoy, Michael. "The Functions and Reproduction of Migrant Labor: Comparative Material from Southern Africa and the United States." *American Journal of Sociology* 81 (1978): 1050–86.

———. "The Extended Case Method." In *Ethnography Unbound: Power and Resistance in the Modern Metropolis*, ed. Michael Burawoy, 271–90. Berkeley: University of California Press, 1991.

Burtless, Gary. "Can the Labor Market Absorb Three Million Welfare Recipients?" In *The Low-Wage Labor Market: Challenges and Opportunities for Economic Self-Sufficiency*, ed. Kelleen Kaye and Demetra Smith Nightingale, 65–84. Washington, DC: U.S. Department of Health and Human Services, Office of the Assistant Secretary for Planning and Evaluation, 2000.

Cancian, Maria, Robert Haveman, Daniel R. Meyer, and Barbara Wolfe. "Before and after TANF: The Economic Well-Being of Women Leaving Welfare." *Social Service Review* 76, no. 4 (2002): 603–41.

Compa, Lance. *Unfair Advantage: Workers' Freedom of Association in the United State under International Human Rights Standards*. Ithaca, NY: Cornell University, Institute for Labor Relations Press, 2004.

Corbett, Thomas. "Welfare Reform in Wisconsin: The Rhetoric and the Reality." In *The Politics of Welfare Reform*, ed. Donald F. Norris and Lyke Thompson, 19–54. Thousand Oaks, CA: Sage, 1995.

———. "The Wisconsin 'Welfare Magnet' Debate." *Focus* 13, no. 3 (1991): 19–28.

Cronon, William. *Nature's Metropolis: Chicago and the Great West*. New York: W. W. Norton, 1996.

Danziger, Sheldon, Colleen M. Heflin, Mary E. Corcoran, Elizabeth Otlmans, and Hui-Chen Wang. "Does It Pay to Move from Welfare to Work?" *Journal of the Association for Policy Analysis and Management* 21 (2002): 671–92.

Denton, Nancy A., and Douglas Massey. *American Apartheid: Segregation and the Making of the Underclass*. Cambridge, MA: Harvard University Press, 1998.

DeParle, Jason. *American Dream: Three Women, Ten Kids, and a Nation's Drive to End Welfare*. New York: Viking, 2004.

Dietrich, Sharon, Maurice Emsellem, and Catherine Ruckelshaus. "Work Reform: The Other Side of Welfare Reform." *Stanford Law and Policy Review* 9, no. 1 (1998): 53–76.

Diller, Matthew. "Working without a Job: The Social Messages of the New Workfare." *Stanford Law and Policy Review* 9, no. 1 (1998): 19–43.

Dodson, Lisa. "Wage-Poor Mothers and Moral Economy." *Social Politics* 14, no. 2 (2007): 258–80.

Dodson, Lisa, Tiffany Manuel, and Ellen Bravo. "Keeping Jobs and Raising Families in Low-Income America: It Just Doesn't Work." Radcliffe Institute for Advanced Study, Harvard University, 2002. http://www.9to5.org/sites/default/files/no boundaries.pdf.

Dougherty, Jack. *More Than One Struggle: The Evolution of Black School Reform in Milwaukee*. Chapel Hill: University of North Carolina Press, 2004.

Duggan, Lisa. *The Twilight of Equality? Neoliberalism, Cultural Politics, and the Attack on Democracy*. New York: Beacon Press, 2003.

Edin, Kathryn, and Laura Lein. *Making Ends Meet: How Single Mothers Survive Welfare and Low-Wage Work*. New York: Russell Sage, 1997.

Edwards, John, Marion Crain, and Arne L. Kalleberg, eds. *Ending Poverty in America: How to Restore the American Dream*. New York: New Press, 2007.

Elwood, David. "Introduction." In *A Working Nation: Workers, Work, and Government in the New Economy*, ed. David T. Elwood, Rebecca M. Blank, Joseph Blasi, Douglas Kruse, William A. Niskanen, and Karen Lynn-Dyson, ix–xvi. New York: Russell Sage, 2000.

———. "Winners and Losers in America: Taking the Measure of New Economic Realities." In *A Working Nation: Workers, Work, and Government in the New Economy*, ed. David T. Elwood,

Rebecca M. Blank, Joseph Blasi, Douglas Kruse, William A. Niskanen, and Karen Lynn-Dyson, 1–41. New York: Russell Sage, 2000.

Enchautegui, Maria. "Will Welfare Reform Hurt Low-Skilled Workers?" Urban Institute Discussion Paper no. 01-01. Urban Institute, Washington, DC, February 2001.

England, Paula, and Nancy Folbre. "The Cost of Caring." *Annals of the American Academy of Political and Social Sciences* 561 (1999): 39–51.

Esping-Andersen, Gøsta. *The Three Worlds of Welfare Capitalism*. Princeton, NJ: Princeton University Press, 1990.

Featherstone, Liza. *Selling Women Short: The Landmark Battle for Workers' Rights at Wal-Mart*. New York: Basic Books, 2004.

Fineman, Martha Albertson. *The Autonomy Myth: A Theory of Dependency*. New York: Free Press, 2004.

———. "The Inevitability of Dependency and the Politics of Subsidy." *Stanford Law and Policy Review* 9, no. 1 (1998): 89–99.

Fletcher, Bill, Jr. "Seizing the Time Because the Time Is Now: Welfare Repeal and Labor Reconstruction." In *Audacious Democracy: Labor, Intellectuals, and the Social Reconstruction of America*, ed. Steven Fraser and Joshua B. Freeman, 119–31. Boston: Houghton Mifflin, 1997.

Florida, Richard. *The Rise of the Creative Class*. New York: Perseus, 2002.

Fraser, Nancy, and Linda Gordon. "A Genealogy of *Dependency*: Tracing a Keyword of the U.S. Welfare State." *Signs* 19, no. 2 (1994): 309–36.

Friedman, Milton. *Capitalism and Freedom*. Chicago: University of Chicago Press, 1963.

Geib, Paul. "From Mississippi to Milwaukee: A Case Study of the Southern Black Migration to Milwaukee, 1940–1970." *Journal of Negro History* 83, no. 4 (1998): 229–48.

Gilder, George. *Wealth and Poverty*. New York: Basic Books, 1981.

Glenn, Evelyn. "From Servitude to Service Work: Historical Continuities in the Racial Division of Paid Reproductive Labor." *Signs* 18, no. 1 (1992): 1–43.

———. *Unequal Freedom: How Race and Gender Shaped American Citizenship and Labor*. Cambridge, MA: Harvard University Press, 2002.

Goldberg, Chad Alan. *Citizens and Paupers: Relief, Rights, and Race, from the Freedman's Bureau to Workfare*. Chicago: University of Chicago Press, 2007.

———. "Welfare Recipients or Workers? Contesting the Workfare State in New York City." *Sociological Theory* 19, no. 2 (2001): 187–218.

Gordon, David M., Richard Edwards, and Michael Reich. *Segmented Work, Divided Workers: The Historical Transformation of Labor in the United States*. New York: Cambridge University Press, 1982.

Gordon, Linda. *Pitied but Not Entitled: Single Mothers and the History of Welfare*. Cambridge, MA: Harvard University Press, 1994.

Gordon, Robert J. "Productivity, Wages, and Prices Inside and Outside of Manufacturing in the U.S., Japan, and Europe." *European Economic Review* 31 (1987): 733–36.

Gurda, John. *The Making of Milwaukee*. Brookfield, WI: Milwaukee County Historical Society, 1999.

Hacker, Jacob. *The Great Risk Shift: The Assault on American Jobs, Families, Health Care, and Retirement, and How You Can Fight Back*. New York: Oxford University Press, 2006.

Hancock, Ange-Marie. *The Politics of Disgust: The Public Identity of the Welfare Queen*. New York: New York University Press, 2004.

Harvey, David. *The Limits to Capital*. New York: Verso, 1999.

Hatton, Erin. "The Temp Industry and the Transformation of Work in America." PhD diss., University of Wisconsin, Madison, 2007.

Hayek, Friedrich. *The Road to Serfdom*. Chicago: University of Chicago Press, 1994.

Hirschman, Albert O. *The Rhetoric of Reaction: Perversity, Futility, Jeopardy*. Cambridge, MA: Harvard University Press, 1991.

Iverson, Torben, and Anne Wren. "Equality, Employment, and Budgetary Restraint: The Trilemma of the Service Economy." *World Politics* 50, no. 4 (1998): 507–46.

Jameson, W. J., and N. Halfon. "Health Status and Income: The Impact of Poverty on Child Health." *Journal of School Health* 64, no. 6 (1994): 229–33.

Jaret, Charles, Lesley Williams Reid, and Robert M. Adelman. "Black-White Income Inequality and Metropolitan Socio-Economic Structure." *Journal of Urban Affairs* 25, no. 3 (2003): 305–33.

Jones, Patrick D. *The Selma of the North: Civil Rights Insurgency in Milwaukee*. Cambridge, MA: Harvard University Press, 2009.

Katz, Michael. *The Price of Citizenship: Redefining the American Welfare State*. New York: Henry Holt, 2002.

Kazis, Richard, and Marc S. Miller, eds. *Low-Wage Workers in the New Economy*. Washington, DC: Urban Institute, 2001.

Kessler-Harris, Alice. *In Pursuit of Equity: Women, Men, and the Quest for Economic Citizenship in 20th Century America*. New York: Oxford University Press, 2001.

Kirschenman, Joleen, and Katherine Neckerman. "'We'd Love to Hire Them But . . .': The Meaning of Race for Employers." In *The Urban Underclass*, ed. Christopher Jencks and Paul Peterson, 203–34. Washington, DC: Brookings Institution, 1991.

Kittay, Eve Feder. "A Feminist Public Ethic of Care Meets the New Communitarian Family Policy." *Ethics* 111, no. 3 (2001): 523–47.

Krinsky, John. *Free Labor: Workfare and the Contested Language of Neoliberalism*. Chicago: University of Chicago Press, 2008.

Krinsky, John, and Ellen Reese. "Forging and Sustaining Labor-Community Coalitions: The Workfare Justice Movement in Three Cities." *Sociological Forum* 21, no. 4 (2006): 623–58.

Lafer, Gordon. "Split to Win? Assessing the State of the Labor Movement." *Dissent*, Winter 2006.

Lister, Ruth, *Citizenship: Feminist Perspectives*. New York: New York University Press, 1997.

Lorence, James J. "Mining 'Salt of the Earth.'" *Wisconsin Magazine of History*, Winter 2001–2.

Lower-Basch, Elizabeth, and Mark H. Greenberg. "Single Mothers in the Era of Welfare Reform." In *The Gloves-Off Economy: Problems and Possibilities at the Bottom of America's Labor Market*, ed. Annette Bernhardt, Heather Boushey, Laura Dresser, and Chris Tilley, 163–89. Ithaca, NY: Cornell University Press, 2008.

Mahmoudov, Vadim. "Are Workfare Participants 'Employees'? Legal Issues Presented by a Two-Tiered Labor Force." *New York University Annual Survey of American Law* 55 (1998), 349–387.

Marshall, T. H. *Citizenship and Social Class*. 1950; London: Pluto Press, 1992.

Martin, Isaac. "Rethinking Welfare Reform." *Contemporary Sociology* 37, no. 2 (2008): 105–8.

May, Martha. "The Historical Problem of the Family Wage: The Ford Motor Company and the Five Dollar Day." *Feminist Studies* 8, no. 2 (1982): 399–424.

Mayer, Victoria. "Contracting Citizenship: Shifting Public/Private Boundaries in the Context of Welfare Reform." PhD diss., University of Wisconsin, Madison, 2007.

———. "Crafting a New Conservative Consensus on Welfare Reform: Redefining Citizenship, Social Provision, and the Public/Private Divide." *Social Politics* 15 (2008): 154–81.

McEvoy, Arthur. "Freedom of Contract, Labor, and the Administrative State." In *The State and Freedom of Contract*, ed. Harry N. Scheiber, 198–235. Stanford, CA: Stanford University Press, 1998.

Mead, Lawrence. *Beyond Entitlement: The Social Obligations of Citizenship*. New York: Free Press, 1986.

———. *Government Matters: Welfare Reform in Wisconsin*. Princeton, NJ: Princeton University Press, 2004.

Mettler, Suzanne. *Dividing Citizens: Gender and Federalism in New Deal Public Policy*. Ithaca, NY: Cornell University Press, 1998.

Meyer, Daniel R. "The Effects of Child Support on the Economic Status of Non-resident Fathers." In *Fathers under Fire: The Revolution in Child Support Enforcement*, ed. Irwin Garfinkel, Sara MacLanahan, Daniel R. Meyer, and Judith Seltzer, 67–93. New York: Russell Sage, 1998.

Meyers, Marcia, Henry Brady, and Eva Seto. *Expensive Children in Poor Families: The Intersection of Childhood Disabilities and Welfare*. San Francisco: Public Policy Institute of California, 2000.

Miller, Kevin. "Welfare and the Minimum Wage: Are Workfare Participants 'Employees' under the Fair Labor Standards Act?" *University of Chicago Law Review* 66, no. 1 (Winter 1999): 183–212.

Mink, Gwendolyn. "The Lady and the Tramp: Gender, Race, and the Origins of the American Welfare State." In *Women, the State, and Welfare*, ed. Linda Gordon, 92–122. Madison: University of Wisconsin Press, 1990.

———. *Welfare's End*. Ithaca, NY: Cornell University Press, 1998.

Mishel, Lawrence, Jared Bernstein, and Sylvia Allegretto, *The State of Working America, 2004/2005*. Ithaca, NY: Cornell University Press, Economic Policy Institute, 2005.

Moss, Philip, and Chris Tilly. *Stories Employers Tell: Race, Skill, and Hiring in America*. New York: Russell Sage, 2001.

Moynihan, Daniel Patrick. *The Politics of a Guaranteed Income: The Nixon Administration and the Family Assistance Plan*. New York: Random House, 1973.

Murray, Charles. *Losing Ground: American Social Policy, 1950–1980*. New York: Basic Books, 1994.

Naples, Nancy A. "The 'New Consensus' on the Gendered 'Social Contract': The 1987–1988 U.S. Congressional Hearings on Welfare Reform." *Signs* 22, no. 4 (1997): 907–45.

Nelson, Barbara. "The Origins of the Two-Channel Welfare State: Workmen's Compensation and Mother's Aid." In *Women, the State, and Welfare*, ed. Linda Gordon, 123–50. Madison: University of Wisconsin Press, 1990.

Newman, Katherine S. *No Shame in My Game: The Working Poor in the Inner City*. New York: Vintage, 2000.

Newman, Katherine S., and Victor Tan Chen. *The Missing Class: Portraits of the Near Poor in America*. New York: Beacon Press, 2007.

Norman, Jack. "Congenial Milwaukee: A Segregated City." In *Unequal Partnerships: The Political Economy of Urban Redevelopment in Postwar America*, ed. Gregory D. Squires, 178–201. New Brunswick, NJ: Rutgers University Press, 1989.

Novak, Michael. "To Promote the General Welfare: Catholic Principles for Welfare Policy." In *Catholic Social Teaching and the U.S. Economy*, ed. John W. Houck and Oliver F. Williams, 165–86. Lanham, MD: University Press of America, 1985.

O'Connor, James. *The Fiscal Crisis of the State*. 1973; New York: Transaction Publishers, 2001.

Offe, Claus. *Disorganized Capitalism: Contemporary Transformations of Work and Politics*. Cambridge: Polity Press, 1985.

Oliker, Stacey J. "Proximate Contexts of Welfare and Work." *Sociological Quarterly* 36, no. 2 (1995): 251–72.

Oliver, Melvin L., and Thomas M. Shapiro. "Black Wealth/ White Wealth." In *Great Divides: Readings in Social Inequality in the United States*, 2nd ed., ed Thomas M. Shapiro. Toronto: Mayfield Publishing, 2004.

Orloff, Ann Shola. "Explaining U.S. Welfare Reform: Power, Gender, Race and the U.S. Policy Legacy." *Critical Social Policy* 22, no. 1 (2002): 96–118.

Orum, Anthony M. *City-Building in America*. Boulder, CO: Westview Press, 1995.

Pager, Devah. "The Mark of a Criminal Record." *American Journal of Sociology* 108, no. 5 (2003): 937–75.

Pager, Devah, Bruce Western, and Bart Bonikowsky. "Discrimination in a Low Wage Labor Market." *American Sociological Review* 74, no. 5 (2009): 777–99.

Peck, Jamie. *Workfare States*. New York: Guilford Press, 2001.

———. *Work-Place: The Social Regulation of Labor Markets*. New York: Guilford Press, 1996.

Peck, Jamie, and Nikolas Theodore. "Labor-Market Lockdown: A Paper on the Urban Labor Market Consequences of Large-Scale Incarceration." Brennan Center for Justice, New York University, 2005.

———. "'Work First': Workfare and the Regulation of Contingent Labour Markets." *Cambridge Journal of Economics*, 24, no. 1 (2000): 119–38.

Pilger, John. "Iraq: The Unthinkable Becomes Normal." *New Statesman*, November 15, 2004.

Piven, Frances Fox. "The New Reserve Army of Labor." In *Audacious Democracy: Labor, Intellectuals, and the Social Reconstruction of America*, ed. Steven Fraser and Joshua B. Freeman, 106–18. Boston: Houghton Mifflin, 1997.

———. "Welfare Reform and the Economic and Cultural Reconstruction of Low Wage Labor Markets." In *The New Poverty Studies: The Ethnography of Power, Politics, and Impoverished People in the United States*, ed. Judith Goode and Jeff Maskovsky, 135–51. New York: New York University Press, 2001.

Piven, Frances Fox, and Richard A. Cloward. *Regulating the Poor: The Functions of Public Welfare*. 1971; New York: Vintage, 1993.

Polanyi, Karl, *The Great Transformation: The Political and Economic Origins of Our Time*. 1944; Boston: Beacon Press, 2001.

Reisch, Michael. "Welfare Reform and the Transformation of the U.S. Welfare State." In *The Promise of Welfare Reform: Political Rhetoric and the Reality of Poverty in the Twenty-First Century*, ed. Keith M. Kilty and Elizabeth Segal, 69–81. New York: Haworth Press, 2006.

Rodriguez, Joseph, and Walter Sava. *Images of America: Latinos in Milwaukee*. Charleston, SC: Arcadia Publishing, 2006.

Rusk, David. "Sprawl, Race, and Concentrated Poverty in Greater Kenosha and Racine." Paper presented to "Housing First: Kenosha and Racine Conference on Homelessness and Affordable Housing," University of Wisconsin, Parkside, November 14, 2003.

Sassen, Saskia. *Globalization and Its Discontents: Essays on the New Mobility of People and Money.* New York: New Press, 1998.

Seccombe, Karen, and Kim A. Hoffman. *Just Don't Get Sick: Access to Health Care in the Aftermath of Welfare Reform.* New Brunswick, NJ: Rutgers University Press, 2007.

Shashko, Alexander. "Blues, Bebop and Bulldozers: Why Milwaukee Never Became a Motown." *Wisconsin Academy Review* 46, no. 3 (Summer 2000): n.p.

Shipler, David K. *The Working Poor: Invisible in America.* New York: Vintage, 2005.

Shklar, Judith. *American Citizenship: The Quest for Inclusion.* Cambridge, MA: Harvard University Press, 1991.

Shulman, Beth. *The Betrayal of Work: How Low-Wage Jobs Fail 30 Million Americans.* New York: New Press, 2005.

Somers, Margaret, and Fred Block. "From Poverty to Perversity: Ideas, Markets and Institutions over 200 Years of Welfare Debate." *American Sociological Review* 70 (2005): 260–87.

Squires, Gregory D., and William Vélez. "Insurance Redlining and the Transformation of an Urban Metropolis." *Urban Affairs Quarterly* 23, no. 1 (1987): 63–83.

———. "Mortgage Lending and Race: Is Discrimination Still a Factor?" *Environment and Planning A* 28 (1996): 1199–1208.

Tait, Vanessa. *Poor Workers' Unions: Rebuilding Labor from Below.* Boston: South End Press, 2005.

Thistle, Susan. *From Marriage to the Market: The Transformation of Women's Lives and Work.* Berkeley: University of California Press, 2006.

Thomas, Robert J. *Citizenship, Gender, and Work: Social Organization of Industrial Agriculture.* Berkeley: University of California Press, 1992.

Tillmon, Johnnie. "Insights of a Welfare Mother." *Journal of Social Issues,* January/February 1971, 13–23.

Tronto, Joan. "Who Cares? Public and Private Caring and the Rethinking of Citizenship." In *Women and Welfare: Theory and Practice in the U.S. and Europe,* ed. Nancy J. Hirschmann and Ulrike Liebert, 65–83. New Brunswick, NJ: Rutgers University Press, 2001.

Trotter, Joe William, Jr. *Black Milwaukee: The Making of an Industrial Proletariat, 1914–45.* Chicago: University of Illinois Press, 2007.

Vick, William Albert. "From Walnut Street to No Street: Milwaukee's African American Businesses, 1945–67." MA thesis, University of Wisconsin, Milwaukee, 1993.

Von Werlhof, Claudia. "The Proletarian Is Dead: Long Live the Housewife." In *Households in the World Economy,* ed. Joan Smith, Immanuel Wallerstein, and Hans-Dieter Evers, 131–50. Beverly Hills, CA: Sage, 1984.

White, Sammis B., and Lori A. Geddes. "Economic Lessons for Welfare Mothers." *Wisconsin Policy Research Institute Report* 14, no. 1 (February 2001): 1–32.

White, Stuart. *The Civic Minimum: On the Rights and Obligations of Economic Citizenship.* New York: Oxford University Press, 2003.

Williams, Brett. *Debt for Sale: A Social History of the Credit Trap.* Philadelphia: University of Pennsylvania Press, 2004.

Williams, Joan. *Unbending Gender: Why Family and Work Conflict and What to Do about It.* New York: Oxford University Press, 2000.

Williams, Patricia J. *The Alchemy of Race and Rights*. Cambridge, MA: Harvard University Press, 1992.

Wiseman, Michael. "State Strategies for Welfare Reform: The Wisconsin Story." *Journal of Policy Analysis and Management* 15, no. 4 (1996): 515–46.

Wisensale, Steven. "The Family and Medical Leave Act in Court." *Working USA* 3, no. 4 (2004): 96–119.

Zatz, Noah. "Beyond the Reach or Grasp of Employment Law." In *The Gloves-Off Economy: Problems and Possibilities at the Bottom of America's Labor Market*, ed. Annette Bernhardt, Heather Boushey, Laura Dresser, and Chris Tilley, 31–64. Ithaca, NY: Cornell University Press, 2008.

———. "Working at the Boundaries of Markets: Prison Labor and the Economic Dimension of Employment Relationships." *Vanderbilt Law Review* 61 (2008): 857–958.

REPORTS, WORKING PAPERS, DOCUMENTS, NEWSPAPER AND MAGAZINE ARTICLES

American Civil Liberties Union. Letter from Karyn Rotker, staff attorney, ACLU of Wisconsin, to the Office of Civil Rights, U.S. Department of Health and Human Services. February 19, 2002. http://www.nclej.org/pdf/ocrada1.pdf.

Acs, Gregory, and Pamela Loprest. "Final Synthesis Report of the Findings from ASPE's 'Leavers' Grants." Washington, DC: U.S. Department of Health and Human Services, Office of the Assistant Secretary for Policy and Evaluation, 2001.

AFL-CIO. "Democratizing the Global Economy." June 27, 2005. http://www.afl-cio.org/aboutus/thisistheaflcio/ecouncil/eco6272005c.cfm.

American Enterprise Institute. *The New Consensus on Family and Welfare*. Washington, DC: American Enterprise Institute, 1987.

Answers.com, Business & Finance. "Company History, Maximus, Inc." http://www.answers.com/topic/maximus-inc?cat=biz-fin.

Barron, James. "City Settles Workfare Harassment Lawsuit." *New York Times*, May 13, 2006.

Bernanke, Ben. Remarks at the Global Economic and Investment Outlook Conference, Carnegie Mellon University, Pittsburgh, PA, November 6, 2003. http://www.federalreserve.gov/BoardDocs/Speeches/2003/200311062/default.htm.

Bernstein, Nina. "Federal Agency Finds Workfare Contractor Violated Wage Law." *New York Times*, September 1, 2000.

Besharov, Douglas J. "End Welfare Lite as We Know It." *New York Times*, August 15, 2006.

Borsuk, Alan J., and Leonard Sykes Jr. "City Population Lowest since 1940: Minorities Outnumber Whites in City for First Time." *Milwaukee Journal Sentinel*, March 8, 2001.

Bradley Foundation. Annual Report, 1995.

Burke, Vee. "Welfare Recipients and Workforce Laws. Federal Publications: Key Workplace Documents." Washington, DC: Congressional Research Service, 2004. http://www.digitalcommons.ilr.cornell.edu/key_workplace/228.

Cancian, Maria, and Robert Haveman. "W-2 Child Support Demonstration Evaluation Phase 1: Final Report." Vol. 2. Institute for Research on Poverty, University of Wisconsin, Madison, 2001.

Cancian, Maria, Robert Haveman, Daniel R. Meyer, and Barbara Wolfe. "The Employment, Earnings and Income of Single Mothers in Wisconsin Who Left Cash Assistance: Comparisons among Three Cohorts." Special Report no. 85, Institute for Research on Poverty, University of Wisconsin, Madison, 2003.

Capers, Tamika, Mery Mejia, Omar Torres, and Sylvia Ruff. "Welfare as They Know It." *Harper's Magazine* 295, no. 1770 (November 1997).

Center on Wisconsin Strategy. "Economic Picture Darkens: Study Shows Declining Wages and Benefits" (press release). University of Wisconsin, Madison, September 4, 2005.

Chambers, Joe, and Scott Godshaw. "History of Local 2-232." Milwaukee, WI: United Steelworkers Local 2-232, n.d. http://www.wisconsinlaborhistory.org/milestones.html.

Courtney, Mark, and Amy Dworsky. "Child Welfare Services' Involvement: Findings from the Milwaukee TANF Applicant Study." Chapin Hall Center for Children, University of Chicago, 2006.

CNN.com. "States Must Pay Minimum Wage for Workfare, Administration Rules." May 16, 1997. http://www.cnn.com/ALLPOLITICS/1997/05/16/welfare.minwage.

De Lessio, Pat. "Court Nixes W-2 'Job Ready' Policy." *WisKids Journal* [Wisconsin Council on Children and Families], July/August 2007. http://www.wccf.org/wkj/807/story3.htm.

Dietrich, Sharon, Maurice Emsellem, and Jennifer Paradise. "Employment Rights of Workfare Participants and Displaced Workers." National Employment Law Project Report, March 2000.

Dresang, Joel. "Boy's Death Spurs W-2 Criticism." *Milwaukee Journal Sentinel*, June 19, 1998.

Eckholm, Erik. "Disability Cases Last Far Longer as Backlogs Rise." *New York Times*, December 10, 2007, A1.

Economist. "Open Up: A Special Report on Migration." January 5, 2008.

Edsall, Thomas B. "Insurrection Is a Big Gamble for Labor." *Washington Post*, July 30, 2005, A11.

Fitzgerald, Mark. "From Welfare to Payroll." *AllBusiness.com*, January 24, 1998. http://www.allbusiness.com/services/business-services-miscellaneous-business/4699462-1.html.

Germanson, Ken. "Milestones in Wisconsin Labor History." Wisconsin Labor History Society. http://www.wisconsinlaborhistory.org/milestones.html.

Greenhouse, Steven. "Compromise with Unions on Workfare." *New York Times*, August 8, 1997.

Held, Tom. "Another Complaint Calls W-2 Unfair to Disabled." *Milwaukee Journal Sentinel*, February 20, 2000, 9B.

Hetter, Katia. "Workfare Workers' Rights in Question." *Newsday*, July 27, 2001.

Iceland, John, Daniel H. Weinberg, and Erika Steinmetz. "U.S. Census Bureau, Series CENSR-3. Racial and Ethnic Residential Segregation in the U.S.: 1980–2000." Washington, DC: Government Printing Office, 2002.

Inter-collegiate Council on Intergroup Relations. "The Housing of Negroes in Milwaukee." Milwaukee, WI: Inter-collegiate Council on Intergroup Relations, 1955. http://www.wisconsinhistory.org/turningpoints/search.asp?id=1098.

International Labor Organization. "Labor Practices in the Footwear, Leather, Textiles and Clothing Industries." Geneva, October 16–20, 2000.

Ip, Greg. "Degrees of Separation: As Economy Shifts, a New Generation Fights to Keep Up." *Wall Street Journal*, June 22, 2005, A1.

A Job Is a Right Campaign. "Why We Are Marching Today." *A Job Is a Right Newsletter*, April 4, 1998.

Kaplan, Thomas. "Wisconsin's W-2 Program: Welfare as We Might Come to Know It." Institute for Research on Poverty, University of Wisconsin, Madison, September 1998.

Kaplan, Thomas, and Thomas Corbett, with Victoria Mayer. "W-2 Child Support Demonstration Evaluation Phase 1: Final Report." Vol. 2. Institute for Research on Poverty, University of Wisconsin, Madison, 2001.

Kessenich, Mark. "Job Training Is the Solution to Labor Shortage." *Business Journal of Milwaukee,* April 9, 1999.

Levine, Marc V. "After the Boom: Joblessness in Milwaukee since 2000." Policy Research Report, University of Wisconsin–Milwaukee Center for Economic Development, April 5, 2004. http://www.ced.uwm.edu.

———. "The Crisis of Black Male Joblessness in Milwaukee: Trends, Explanations and Policy Options." University of Wisconsin–Milwaukee Center for Economic Development, March 2007. http://www.ced.uwm.edu.

———. "The Crisis of Low Wages in Milwaukee: Wage Polarization in the Labor Market: 1970–1990." Policy Research Report, University of Wisconsin–Milwaukee Center for Economic Development, November 1994. http://www.ced.uwm.edu.

———. "Rolled Over by Unemployment." *Milwaukee Journal-Sentinel,* August 31, 2003. http://www.jsonline.com/story/index.aspx?id=166013.

———. " 'Stealth Depression': Joblessness in the City of Milwaukee since 1990." University of Wisconsin–Milwaukee Center for Economic Development, August 25, 2003. http://www.ced.uwm.edu.

———. "The Two Milwaukees: Separate and Unequal." Paper presented to Milwaukee County Task Force on Segregation and Race Relations, April 30, 2003. http://www.ced.uwm.edu.

Loprest, Pamela, and Sheila Zedlewski. "The Changing Role of Welfare in the Lives of Low-Income Families with Children." Washington, DC: Urban Institute, 2006.

Lueck, Thomas. "Workfare Critics Cite the Case of a Woman Who Died on the Job." *New York Times,* August 31, 2000.

MacFarquhar, Neil. "Worker's Death Prompts Call of Workfare Review." *New York Times,* July 13, 1999, B3.

Metropolitan Milwaukee Association of Commerce, Economic Research Division. "Metro Milwaukee Economic Trends." December 2005. http://www.mmac.org.

Meyer, Daniel, and Maria Cancian. "W-2 Child Support Demonstration Evaluation Phase 1: Final Report." Vol. 1. Institute for Research on Poverty, University of Wisconsin, Madison, 2001.

Millard, Pete. "Bias Claims Filed against W-2 Agency." *Business Journal of Milwaukee,* January 7, 2000.

———. "For-profit Ventures Sour for YWCA." *Business Journal of Milwaukee,* February 14, 2003.

———. "Profit Ventures Intrigue Non-profits." *Business Journal of Milwaukee,* August 9, 2002.

———. "Warts and All, Welfare Reform Worked." *Business Journal of Milwaukee,* September 29, 2000.

Milwaukee Journal Sentinel. "Labor Newspaper in Racine, Wisconsin Is Latest Victim of Layoffs, Plant Closings." December 25, 2001.

———. "Money, Services Are Needed to Make Sure Kids Stay Safe" (editorial). June 29, 1998.

Mitnik, Pablo, and Matt Zeidenburg. "From Bad to Good Jobs? An Analysis of the Prospects for Career Ladders in the Service Industries." Center on Wisconsin Strategy, Madison, WI, 2007. http://www.cows.org/pdf/rp-bad-good.pdf.

Moffit, Robert. "From Welfare to Work: What the Evidence Shows." Washington, DC: Brookings Institution, 2001.

Monroe, Melissa. "Temp Agencies Targeting Welfare Recipients." *San Antonio Business Journal*, September 19, 1997.

Mulligan-Hansel, Kathleen, and Pamela Fendt. "TANF Reauthorization: The Bush Administration Proposal and Wisconsin's W-2 Program." Institute for Wisconsin's Future, Milwaukee, 2002. http://www.wisconsinsfuture.org/publications/_pdfs/past_projects_pdfs/Bushtanfanalysis.pdf.

———. "Unfair Sanctions: Does W-2 Punish People of Color?" Institute for Wisconsin's Future and University of Wisconsin–Milwaukee Center for Economic Development, 2003. http://www4.uwm.edu/ced/publications/race_execsum.pdf.

Mullins, Robert. "W-2 Workforce Lures Serigraph South." *Business Journal of Milwaukee*, August 25, 1997. http://milwaukee.bizjournals.com/milwaukee/stories/1997/08/25/story8.html.

Murphy, Bruce. "Missions Collide When Non-profits Try Business." *Milwaukee Journal Sentinel*, May 30, 2004.

National Employment Law Project. "Limiting State Workfare Programs under the New TANF Rules" (press release). New York, September 15, 2006.

National Union of Hospital and Health Care Employees Local 1199W (Milwaukee, WI). *1199 Frontline*. January 1979, March 1979, June 1979, March 1980, April 1980. Wisconsin Historical Society archives, Madison.

Nathan, Richard P., and Thomas L. Gais. "Implementing the Personal Responsibility Act of 1996: A First Look." Albany: State University of New York, Rockefeller Institute of Government, 1999.

Oliver, Pamela. "Summary of Findings on Racial Disparities in Criminal Justice in Wisconsin." Paper presented to Community Justice Action Coalition Conference, November 2, 2001.

Oliver, Pamela, and James Yocum. "Racial Disparities in Criminal Justice: Madison and Dane County in Context." Institute for Research on Poverty, University of Wisconsin, Madison, 2002.

Pabst, Georgia. "Paid Sick Leave Referendum Wins Big." *Milwaukee Journal Sentinel Online*, November 4, 2008. http://www.jsonline.com/news/statepolitics/33874059.html.

Parrott, Sharon, and Arloc Sherman. "TANF at Ten: Program Results Are More Mixed Than Often Understood" (press release). Center on Budget and Policy Priorities, Washington, DC, August 17, 2006. http://www.cbpp.org/8-17-06tanf.htm.

Pawarasat, John. "The Employer Perspective: Jobs Held by the Milwaukee County Single Parent Population." Employment and Training Institute, University of Wisconsin–Milwaukee, March 1997. http://www.uwm.edu/Dept/ETI/employer.htm.

Pawarasat, John, and Lois M. Quinn. "The Child Care Costs of Engaging the Welfare Population at Work: The Milwaukee Experience." Employment and Training Institute, University of Wisconsin–Milwaukee, 2002.

Private Industry Council of Milwaukee County/University of Milwaukee Employment and Training Institute. "Survey of Job Openings in the Milwaukee Metropolitan Area." Weeks of October 20, 2003, and May 23, 2005. http://www.uwm.edu/Dept/ETI/jobs.htm.

Quinn, Lois. "New Indicators of Neighborhood Need in Zip Code 53206." Employment and Training Institute, University of Wisconsin–Milwaukee, 2007. http://www4.uwm.eti/2007/53206N.pdf.

Quinn, Lois, and John Pawasarat. "Tracking the Progress of Welfare Reform: A Model for Measuring Neighborhood Health and Change." Employment and Training Institute, University of Wisconsin–Milwaukee, October 2001.

Racine Labor. "SEIU Local 150 Joins in Ethiopia Fund Drive." March 1, 1985, 5.

———. "St. Luke's Slams Door on Aides." June 28, 1985, 1.

———. "St. Luke's Workers Beat Back Concessions Push." May 17, 1985, 5.

———. "St. Luke's Workers Seek to Catch Up on Wages." April 12, 1985, 3.

Ragan, Mark. "Service Integration in Wisconsin: Racine and Kenosha Counties." Rockefeller Institute of Government, Albany, NY, August 12, 2002.

Rinard, Amy. "State Audit Blasts Learnfare Errors." *Milwaukee Journal Sentinel*, July 3, 1990.

Robles, Andrea, Fred Doolittle, and Susan Gooden. "Community Service Jobs in Wisconsin Works: The Milwaukee County Experience." *MDRC Report*. Manpower Development Research Corporation, June 2003.

Rovito, Rich. "Racine County Struggles to Revive Manufacturing after Long Economic Slide." *Business Journal of Milwaukee*, February 4, 2005.

Schmid, John. "Still Separate and Unequal: A Dream Derailed." *Milwaukee Journal Sentinel*, December 5, 2004.

Schulze, Steve. "Pay Is Low, Progress Is Slow." *Milwaukee Journal Sentinel*, August 8, 2005.

———. "W-2 Denials Ruled Invalid: State's 'Job-Ready' Category at Odds with 1996 Law, Court Says." *Milwaukee Journal Sentinel*, June 19, 2007. http://www.jsonline.com/story/index.aspx?id=622140.

Sexton, Joe. "Woman's Death Prompts Concerns over Workfare." *New York Times*, June 24, 1997.

Smith, Rebecca, Rick McHugh, Andrew Stettner, and Nancy Segal. "Between a Rock and a Hard Place: Confronting the Failure of State Unemployment Insurance Systems to Serve Women and Working Families." National Employment Law Project, New York, July 2003. http://www.nelp.org/page/-/UI/between.pdf.

Taylor, Julia. "Testimony before the Subcommittee on Human Resources of the Committee on Ways and Means, U.S. House of Representatives." April 3, 2001. http://waysandmeans.house.gov/Legacy/humres/107cong/4-3-01/4-3jtay.htm.

Toner, Robin. "Bush Promises Minimum Wage in Welfare Jobs." *New York Times*, March 7, 2002.

U.S. Department of Health and Human Services. Code of Federal Regulations, Title 45 (Public Welfare), Part 260 (TANF Provisions). 1999.

U.S. Department of Labor. "Guidance: How Workplace Laws Apply to Welfare Recipients." *Daily Labor Report* (Bureau of News Analysis), no. 103, May 29, 2007.

U.S. House of Representatives, Ways and Means Committee, Subcommittee on Human Resources. "A Decade since Welfare Reform: 1996 Welfare Reforms Reduce Welfare

Dependence." February 26, 2006. http://waysandmeans.house.gov/media/pdf/welfare/022706welfare.pdf.

Wilkerson, Isabel. "How Milwaukee Has Thrived While Leaving Blacks Behind." *New York Times*, March 19, 1991.

Williams, Lucy A. "Decades of Distortion: The Right's 30-year Assault on Welfare." Somerville, MA: Political Research Associates, 1997. http://www.publiceye.org/welfare/Decades-of-Distortion.html.

Wisconsin, Office of the Governor. "Governor Doyle Announces New Effort for Children and Families" (press release). January 29, 2007.

———. "Governor Doyle to Establish New Department of Children and Families" (press release). November 27, 2007.

Wisconsin Department of Workforce Development. "Families and Children Served by the CARES Child Care Payment System." 2008. http://www.dwd.wisc.gov/childcare/wishares/pdf/served.pdf (accessed June 18, 2008).

———. "Food Share Employment and Training Manual." 2002.

———. "Request for Proposals to Administer W-2 and Related Programs, 1997–1999, Addendum No.3." September 13, 1996.

———. "Unduplicated W-2 Participants by Placement Type." 2007. http://www.dwd.state.wi.us/dws/w2/wisworks.htm.

———. "Wisconsin Works (W-2) Overview." 1999. http://www.dwd.state.wi.us/dws/w2/wisworks.htm.

———. "Wisconsin Works (W-2) Manual." 2002.

———. "Wisconsin Works (W-2) Manual." 2004.

———. "Wisconsin Works (W-2) Sanctions Study." December 2004.

Wisconsin Historical Society. "Desegregation and Civil Rights, Turning Points in Wisconsin History." http://www.wisconsinhistory.org/turningpoints/tp-049/?action=more_essay.

Wisconsin Legislative Audit Bureau. "Administration of the Wisconsin Works Program by Employment Solutions, Inc., and Other Selected Agencies" (letter report), February 2001.

———. "Administration of the Wisconsin Works Program by Maximus, Inc." (letter report), July 2000.

———. "An Evaluation: Wisconsin Works (W-2) Program." Report 01-7. 001.

———. "An Evaluation: Wisconsin Works (W-2) Program." Report 05-6. 2005.

———. "A Review of Wisconsin Works (W-2) Expenditures." Report 99-3. 1999.

Wisconsin Legislative Fiscal Bureau. "Comparative Summary of Budget Provisions Enacted as Act 33." September 2003. http://www.legis.state.wi.us/lfb/2003-05budget/Act33.

———. "Wisconsin Works (W-2) and Other Economic Support Programs." Informational Paper no. 45. January 2005.

Zeidenberg, Matthew. "Moving Outward: The Shifting Landscape of Poverty in Milwaukee." Center on Wisconsin Strategy, University of Wisconsin, Madison, August 2004.

INDEX